The Discipline of Taste and Feeling

The Discipline of Taste and Feeling

CHARLES WEGENER

THE UNIVERSITY OF CHICAGO PRESS
Chicago & London

CHARLES WEGENER is the Howard L. Willett Professor emeritus in
the College and professor emeritus, Committee on the Analysis of Ideas
and Study of Methods, at the University of Chicago.

The University of Chicago Press, Chicago 60637
The University of Chicago Press, Ltd., London
© 1992 by The University of Chicago
All rights reserved. Published 1992
Printed in the United States of America
01 00 99 98 97 96 95 94 93 92   5 4 3 2 1

ISBN (cloth): 0–226–87893–7

Library of Congress Cataloging-in-Publication Data

Wegener, Charles.
    The discipline of taste and feeling / Charles Wegener.
        p.   cm.
    Includes bibliographical references and index.
    1. Aesthetics.   I. Title.
    BH39.W375   1992
    111'.85—dc20   91–44410
                                                            CIP

♾ The paper used in this publication meets the minimum requirements of the
American National Standard for Information Sciences—Permanence of Paper for
Printed Library Materials, ANSI Z39.48–1984.

In Memoriam

G.W.C.   J.C.T.

Denn so, wie wir dem, der in der Beurtei-
lung eines Gegenstandes der Natur, welchen
wir schön finden, gleichgültig ist, Mangel
des *Geschmacks* vorwerfen, so sagen wir von
dem, der bei dem, was wir erhaben zu sein
urteilen, unbewegt bleibt, er habe kein
Gefühl. Beides aber fordern wir von jedem
Menschen, und setzen es auch, wenn er
einige Kultur hat, an ihm voraus. . . .

For just as we charge with want of taste *a man*
who is indifferent when passing judgment on a
natural object which we find beautiful, so we say of
a man who remains unmoved in the presence of
what we judge sublime, that he has no feeling.
But we demand both of every man, and presuppose
them in anyone who has any culture at all. . . .

Immanuel Kant, *Critique of Judgment*

CONTENTS

ix

PREFACE

Those who find this book a somewhat bizarre commentary on certain parts of Kant's third critique are to be congratulated on their perspicacity. I can only hope that most readers will find that insight and connection wholly uninteresting and unnecessary, yet I would not have it thought that I am unconscious of my debt to Kant (above all) and to many others who have thought about these problems. Colleagues, friends, students, members of my family have, of course, contributed more than I can ever know or acknowledge. I hope the result is not unworthy of these authors of my aesthetic and intellectual being—all of whom have been my teachers. I can only repeat the lapidary words of Emerson which the reader will, if perseverant, meet with later in this book: "how indispensable has been the ministry of our friends to us, our teachers,—the living and the dead."

Florence

Et est mirabile in oculis nostris.
It is marvelous in our eyes.
Psalm 117

T o seek the ultimate source of the wonder which issues in an inquiry of this sort is probably hopeless, but some account of how it seemed to take shape in the author's mind may be useful to the reader. In that simple sense it began in the summer of 1978 in the Brancacci Chapel of the church of Santa Maria del Carmine in Florence. There I had come to see, of course, Masaccio's frescoes of the expulsion from Paradise and the life of St. Peter. For all who love the art of Italy—or, for that matter, the tradition of Western art since the Renaissance—this spot is holy ground. The frescoes are now variously attributed; only two or three are the 'undoubted' work of Masaccio (the others being currently parceled out between Masolino and Filippino Lippi), but from the beginning these works have exerted an unusual authority. Henry Moore, who as a young student living in Florence in 1925 each day "paid an early morning visit to the Carmine Chapel before going anywhere else,"[1] was merely following in the footsteps of Botticelli, Leonardo, Michelangelo, Raphael, and Perugino—to

1. "I have loved Florence since my first visit in 1925, as a young student spending a five-months' travelling scholarship to Italy. It was the most impressionable stage of my development. Out of the full five months I stayed three months in Florence. At first it was the early Florentines I studied most, especially Giotto, because of his evident sculptural qualities. Later Masaccio became an obsession, and each day I paid an early morning visit to the Carmine Chapel before going anywhere else. . . . Towards the end of my three months it was Michelangelo who engaged me most, and he has remained an ideal ever since. . . ." Quoted from a letter written by

1

name only a few from Vasari's long list.[2] (Indeed, if we can believe
Cellini, it seems that it was here that the otherwise obscure Torri-
giano permanently damaged, in a student scuffle, Michelangelo's
nose.)[3]

The church of the Carmine was then—before the work of restoration begun in the middle eighties and now completed[4]—somewhat off the beaten track of Florentine cultural tourism; the crowds
which pour through the Accademia, the Uffizi, the Medici Chapels
or the Pitti Palace were there reduced to a thin but steady trickle.
For that reason, perhaps, the pilgrims were more easily observable.
And pilgrims they were, with all the puzzling ambiguities of that
persistent vocation: multinational and multilingual (discriminable
by the titles of the guidebooks most of them carry, if by no other
sign), solitary, paired, in silent little herds or chattering groups, all
ages and sexes, lay and clerical, silent immobile starers, pointers
and whisperers, agile jockeyers for promising vantage points, information consumers (consulting guidebooks and patronizing the
taped message machines judiciously spotted at the entrance to the
chapel), and above all, nowadays, photographers—many having
their cameras in an operative position almost simultaneously with
their arrival at the object of their quest. That object, at least, would
seem to be unambiguous. Like pigeons or jetliners, with or without
guidebook, they moved more or less unhesitatingly down the nave
and, turning to the right at the crossing, homed unerringly on the
terminus of the transept, the Brancacci Chapel, where, with almost
equal efficiency they singled out the naked figures of Adam and
Eve at the entrance and, on the left wall, that astonishing panel of

Moore to the Mayor of Florence in connection with an exhibit of his work there in
1972 (*Catalogo della Mostra, Firenze, Forte di Belvedere, 1972*) in Olive Hamilton, *Paradise of Exiles, Tuscany and the British* (London, 1974), p. 182.

2. Vasari, *Vite*, "Masaccio." (There are so many editions of Vasari's *Lives* that it
seems pointless to cite any one of them.)

3. Cellini, *Vita*, I, xiii. (Again, many editions, translations.)

4. Everything that is said about the physical condition of the Brancacci Chapel
and the rest of the Carmine is now (happily) dated by this massive work of restoration, which has produced, in the case of the chapel, a revelation similar in effect to
that of the cleaning of the Sistine ceiling. Initially, the reopening of the chapel in
1990 to public view (under special conditions of access) with a considerable fanfare
of publicity produced a considerable change in number and quality of visitors. What
the effect in the long run may be remains to be seen, but future visitors will certainly
have golden opportunities.

the *Tribute Money*. Some, after more fully exploring the chapel's frescoes, might move less purposefully into other parts of the church—perhaps even penetrating into the sacristy or the cloister (if it happened to be open)—but many departed as directly as they had come.

My own behavior in the church did not, initially, differ substantially from that of my fellow pilgrims. But as it happened, I visited the church many times and came, eventually, to see it rather differently—partly because I was reading during my stay Eric Cochrane's *Florence in the Forgotten Centuries*.[5] Present-day guidebooks (which are largely guidebooks to Renaissance Florence and even more particularly to the Florence of the *early* Renaissance) usually mention (somewhat brusquely) the Corsini Chapel in the left transept and possibly the sacristy, where there are frescoes of the early quattrocento, variously attributed. But they barely notice the existence of the main fabric of the church. Reading Cochrane's book suggested further exploration and reflection, raising puzzling questions about my behavior, my perception, and my purposefulness: questions neither original nor profound and certainly not uniquely dependent upon encountering this building in this city with its contents and its history. Whether they are of more than personal interest is for you, brutal reader, to determine.

II

Given the focus of interest of most present guidebooks, it is not surprising that they should mention a fire which destroyed most of the church in 1771 primarily in order to say that it "spared" the Brancacci Chapel (1423–28?). Sometimes it also spared the Corsini Chapel, completed in 1683 in the opposite transept. And thereby hangs a tale: a tale which emerges from Cochrane's account of those centuries of Florentine history (1527–1800) which do seem largely 'forgotten' in the guidebooks.

The fire, as we have noted, occurred in 1771. A century earlier, the Corsini family had made its mark in the world of Florentine art by a fashionable move. Cochrane's account tries to convey something of its contemporary significance. Nowadays we are inclined

5. Eric Cochrane, *Florence in the Forgotten Centuries 1527–1800* (Chicago, 1973).

to find the 'baroque' style something of an intrusion in the Florence we know and love; in the closing decades of the seventeenth century perceptions were different.

> It never occurred to the artists and patrons of the late seventeenth century that they would one day be charged with the responsibility of saving Florence from Roman baroque. No one objected when Giovan Battista Foggini . . . transformed the Feroni chapel at the Annunziata into a minor masterpiece of baroque decoration, with scores of stucco bodies wiggling up past twisted columns and windblown branches into a spiraled infinity. . . . Neither did anyone object when a whole team of painters and architects created an entirely baroque interior for the new convent of Santa Maria Maddelena de' Pazzi in Borgo Pinti. And everyone applauded when the Corsini family brought in the least Florentine of all contemporary baroque artists to do their chapel at the Carmine— Luca Giordano of Naples. Giordano was immediately commissioned to decorate the great hall of the Palazzo Medici, which the Riccardi had recently bought from the grand duke. When he there succeeded beyond all expectations in making the current members of the ruling family float upwards from the clutters of allegorical landscape around the four sides, he was forthwith elevated to the rank of [Pietro da] Cortona himself, not as an example for Florentines to shun, but as a model for them to imitate.[6]

Nowadays the Regional Council of Tuscany meets in the great hall of the Palazzo Medici-Riccardi, rechristened for tourists Luca Giordano Hall (Sala Luca Giordano), but most of them seem rather amused or bemused by the "Apotheosis of the Medici" Cochrane so pitilessly describes, just as most of them (I among them) seem initially to find the Corsini Chapel in the Carmine rather more amazing and fantastic than exciting or moving. In any case, it was this masterpiece of Florentine baroque which was 'spared' along with the austere (and what must have appeared to Luca Giordano hopelessly old-fashioned) frescoes of the Brancacci Chapel in the fire of 1771.

This fire, as it turned out, required the attention of one of the more engaging of the long list of remarkable personages who figure in Cochrane's narrative. Pietro Leopoldo, Grand Duke of Tuscany from 1765 to 1790, is perhaps better known to 'history' as the

6. Ibid., pp. 282–83.

Austrian emperor (for a reign of two years), Leopold II. Pietro Leopoldo was a man of many ideas—economic, political, cultural. In a
period when everyone was busily repudiating the baroque traditions represented by the Corsini Chapel, he tried to create a new
Florentine renaissance by placing Florentine art in the artistic
avant-garde, then occupied by what has since become known as
'neoclassicism.'

> He filled the classrooms of the Accademia delle Belle Arti with plaster
> casts shipped up from Civitavecchia. . . . He gave annual prizes to those
> students who best reproduced the casts in paint. . . . He commissioned
> his chief architect, Gaspare Paoletti, to redecorate the interior of the
> Poggio Imperiale and to construct a new ballroom . . . in the Pitti. He
> added a whole new wing to the Boboli, little caring, apparently, about
> the obvious disharmony between its delicate lines and Buontalenti's
> heavy masonry nearby. . . . [H]e had one of the most celebrated mon-
> uments of Hellenistic sculpture, the Niobe, brought up from the Villa
> Medici in Rome and installed under Paoletti's impeccably neoclassical
> ceiling in the Uffizi. But his real chance came on the night of January
> 28–29, 1771, when the Church of the Carmine—all of it, that is, except
> the Corsini and Brancacci chapels, which are all most tourists look at
> today—was completely destroyed by fire. When, after twelve years of
> hard work by the royal architect, Zanobi dal Rosso, and after enormous
> expenditures by the grand duke and the Corsini family, the simple, mo-
> tionless, monochrome interior was at last exposed to the admiration of
> the public, even the official orator could do nothing more than quote
> from Psalm 117: *A Domino factum est illud. Et est mirabile in oculis nostris.*
> [This is the work of the Lord; it is marvelous in our eyes.][7]

And, turning the page of Cochrane's book, I find confronting me
a photograph of that nave which, like my fellow pilgrims, I had so
often walked through and never seen.

III

It is true, as I found when I came to look at it, that there were
obvious difficulties about seeing it.[8] It has not been well pre-

---

7. Ibid., pp. 474–75.
8. The restoration noted above (note 4) has changed all this, but it may be
doubted that it has made either the 'neoclassic' nave or the 'baroque' Corsini Chapel
any easier for most of us to see appreciatively. In the Brancacci Chapel, however,

served—the painted ceiling, with its elaborate false architecture, is dimmed and spotted, the walls are variously dirtied and here and there disfigured by vulgar images and clumsily installed electrical fittings, just as the work of Giordano and his collaborator Foggini in the Corsini Chapel is dusty and badly illuminated, conveying the impression of a stage-set long inefficiently warehoused and dimly seen by the unfriendly light of common day. But the Masaccio frescoes are, if anything, in worse case, and them one had no difficulty seeing—except, of course, that they are awkwardly high on the wall, the light usually bad, the colors faded, and the plaster uneven and occasionally patched. Nevertheless, they are "marvelous in our eyes."

No, clearly the problem is not one of the biological, the physical, the literally optical conditions of 'seeing,' but rather of an educated perception, a trained eye, a receptive and disciplined imagination. In this sense, of course, what we see and admire is not literally "marvelous in our *eyes*": as to 'seeing' what seventeenth- and eighteenth-century eyes found marvelous we may number ourselves among those "which have eyes and see not." The question, then, which formed itself vaguely in my mind as, watching my fellow visitors, I stood where Michelangelo, Ruskin, Burckhardt, Henry Moore, and thousands of simpler pilgrims like myself had stood, was initially something like, "How did we get here? From what does this organized, purposeful, intent behavior arise?" It might have been "what brought us here?" but not in the form in which that question could be answered by pointing to the walls, rather in the sense in which an intelligent answer might be "our ability to see this marvelous thing," this thing, which, in another sense, brought us here. Cochrane and Giordano and Pietro Leopoldo's architects (not to mention the public orator) enabled me eventually to grasp another dimension of the problem, for they reminded me forcefully how discriminating, how sensitive (and insensitive), and therefore how functionally and powerfully determinate "what brought us here"—that educated, organized, trained sensibility, perception, imagination—must be. It may be that, like

the immediate impression is that now we can 'see' much more clearly what we always 'saw' was there to be appreciated.

all good things, what is marvelous in our eyes is of the Lord's making, but proximately this is another case in which the Lord's work must be our own, a purposeful, discriminating, immensely satisfying activity of our perception and imagination in which what is marvelous becomes present for *us*.

Moments of radical reflection on ourselves and our experience are as often (perhaps *more* often) disconcerting as they are reassuring or self-congratulatory. To realize that one has a certain kind of functional purposefulness—that is, an organized ability to carry on an activity which issues in deep satisfaction—may be, as in this case, a recognition not only of powers but of limits, for here, in the Church of the Carmelites, one may wonder as much about what might be seen and is not as rejoice in one's ability to be delighted and moved by what is seen. Naturally enough we are likely to prefer those reflective moments in which we are—or think ourselves to be—rather conscious of some expansion, some refinement, some consolidation of our powers—moments in which we seem to be able to recognize what we think of as positive development or even 'progress.' Young John Ruskin (he was twenty-six), after visiting the Carmine to see Masaccio on a morning in early June 1845,

> walked up to Fiesole. As I was coming down again, I found myself, unexpectedly, standing on the *very* spot, at the end of the cypress avenue, where five years ago—— I stood, refusing to look at the Giottos in the little chapel, and running up to this point to see the mountains. What a wonderful change in me since then. . . . Then, I had hardly heard Giotto's name, & cared for him no more than for so many signposts. Now, I had spent half the remains of my forenoon (after Masaccio) before three saints of Giotto's in a chapel of Santo Spirito, and look for him everywhere, the first thing and the last.[9]

Moments of this sort might be thought to be the special privilege of the young—that is, characteristic of a rapidly developing, 'un-

9. Harold I. Shapiro, ed., *Ruskin in Italy. Letters to His Parents, 1845* (Oxford, 1972), p. 95 (letter of June 2, 1845). Ruskin's editor identifies the "Giotto" in Santo Spirito as a polyptych in the Vettori Chapel now generally attributed to Maso di Banco. This is plausible for various reasons except that Ruskin says "three saints" and the "polyptych" suggested is a Madonna and Child with four saints. Cf. Walter and Elisabeth Paatz, *Die Kirchen von Florenz*, band V, p. 142 and note 165, p. 189.

formed,' impressionable sensibility. In later years, when we can no longer remember what we made of the *Eroica* at first hearing (when, indeed, it comes to seem inconceivable that we should ever have lived in a world of which it was not a part), we may yet have some sense of the feeling of enormous expansion of possibilities, of whole unrealized reaches of experience which such encounters bring with them. Though gifted with less power of expression, we may remember—or seem to remember—that, like Keats encountering Homer, we

> felt . . . like some watcher of the skies
> When a new planet swims into his ken;
> Or like stout Cortez when with eagle eyes
> He sta'rd at the Pacific . . .

IV

But, in fact, age may have little to do with the matter. Hawthorne was fifty-three when he first came to Italy and was able for the first time to see "pictures": "able" not only in the simple sense that there were pictures to see on a scale and of a variety which did not exist in his homeland but also in the sense in which *becoming* able to see is a problem of reflective development of sensibility. After a brief stop in Genoa, he arrived in Rome in January 1858 and went on to Florence in early June. A notebook entry of June 15 preserves for us one of many moments of rumination on what he had been "seeing" and the process that was putting him "in a state to see pictures" in the six months he had been in Italy. The day before he had revisited the Uffizi, partly to see whether his new Florentine friend Hiram Powers, the American sculptor, was justified in his "attack" upon the Medici Venus. What follows is worth extended quotation.

> We looked pretty thoroughly through the gallery, and I saw many pictures that impressed me; but, among such a multitude, with only one poor mind to take note of them, the stamp of each new impression helps to obliterate a former one. I am sensible, however, that a process is going on—and has been, ever since I came to Italy—that puts me in a state to see pictures with less toil, and more pleasure, and makes me more fastidious, yet more sensible of beauty where I saw none before.

It is a sign, I presume of a taste still very defective, that I take singular pleasure in the elaborate imitations of Van Mieris, Gerard Douw, and the other old Dutch wizards who painted such brass pots that you can see your face in them, and such earthen jugs that they will surely hold water; and who spent weeks and months in turning a foot or two of canvass into a perfect, microscopic illusion of some homely scene. For my part, I wish Raphael had painted the Transfiguration in this style, at the same time preserving his breadth and grandeur of design; nor do I believe that there is any real impediment to the combination of the two styles, except that no possible span of human life would suffice to cover a quarter part of the canvas of the Transfiguration with such touches as Gerard Douw's. But one feels the vast scope of this wonderful art, when we think of two excellences so far apart as that of this last painter and Raphael. I pause a good while, too, before the Dutch paintings of fruit and flowers, where tulips and roses acquire an immortal bloom; and grapes have kept the freshest juice in them for two or three hundred years. Often in these pictures, there is a bird's nest, every straw perfectly represented, and the stray feather, or the down that the mother has plucked from her bosom, with the three or four small, speckled eggs, that seem as if they be yet warm. These petty miracles have their use in assuring us that painters really can do something that takes hold of us in our most matter of fact moods; whereas the merits of the grander style of art may be beyond our ordinary appreciation, and leave us in doubt (nine times out of ten that we look at them) whether we have not befooled ourselves with a false admiration. Until we learn to appreciate the cherubs and angels that Raphael scatters through the blessed air, in a picture of the Nativity, it is not amiss to look at a Dutch fly settling on a peach, or a humble-bee burying himself in a flower.

It is another token of imperfect taste, no doubt, that queer pictures, and absurd pictures, remain in my memory, when better ones pass away by the score. There is a picture of Venus combing her son Cupid's head with a small-tooth comb, and looking with maternal care among his curls; this I shall not forget. Likewise, a picture of a broad rubicund Judith, by Bordone—a widow of fifty, of an easy, lymphatic cheerful temperament, who has just killed Holofernes, and is as self-complaisant as if she had been carving a goose. What could possibly have stirred up this pudding of a woman (unless it were a pudding-stick) to do such a deed! I looked with much pleasure at an ugly, old, fat, jolly Bacchus, astride on a barrel, by Rubens; the most natural and lifelike representation of a tipsy rotundity of flesh, that it is possible to imagine. And sometimes, amid these sensual images, I caught the divine pensiveness of a Madonna's face, or the glory and majesty of the babe Jesus in her lap, with his Father shining through him. This is a sort of revelation, whenever it comes.[10]

V

Of course, the forms which such adventures of taste may take are many and their concomitant moods equally various—revelatory, ruminative, problematic, sometimes disillusioning. The more dramatic incidents (Schumann introducing his friends to Chopin's Opus 2: "Hats off, gentlemen, a genius!") are, like Hawthorne's "queer" and "absurd" pictures, more likely to be remembered, but the sober satisfactions of a matured sensibility are no less interesting and perhaps more fruitful. In 1815 Walter Scott, then in his middle forties, was a versatile, accomplished literary professional. Not only was he an enormously successful poet and (secretly) novelist, but he was also editor, translator, literary historian, and critic. (Nowadays those of us not literary historians may vaguely recollect the *Minstrelsy of the Scottish Border*, but we are not likely ever to have known that Scott had translated Goethe, edited Dryden, and was a regular contributor to the august critical pages of the *Quarterly Review*, of which he was one of the founders.) His was an erudite, sophisticated, cosmopolitan (he read voraciously in six languages—seven if one counts Scottish), appreciatively discriminating literary mind. But he was by no means blasé. Even the stately language of public criticism cannot wholly conceal his satisfaction in encountering the imaginative possibilities realized by "Miss Austen." Reviewing *Emma* in the *Quarterly Review* he remarked that

> in the novel, as in every style of composition which appeals to the public taste, the more rich and easily worked mines being exhausted, the adventurous author must . . . have recourse to those which were disdained by his predecessors as unproductive. . . . Accordingly a style of novel has arisen . . . differing from the former in the points upon which the interest hinges; neither alarming our credulity nor amusing our imagination by wild variety of incident, or by those pictures of romantic

10. Nathaniel Hawthorne, *French and Italian Notebooks*, entry for June 15, 1858. Several editions with no significant textual differences for our purposes. See, for example, in the Centenary Edition of Hawthorne's works, volume 14, *The French and Italian Notebooks*, edited by Thomas Woodson (Columbus, Ohio, 1980), pp. 316–18.

affection and sensibility, which were formerly as certain attributes of fictitious characters as they are of rare occurrence among those who actually live and die. The substitute for these excitements . . . was the art of copying from nature as she really exists in the common walks of life. . . . We bestow no mean compliment upon the author of *Emma*, when we say that, keeping close to common incidents, and to such characters as occupy the ordinary walks of life, she has produced sketches of such spirit and originality, that we never miss the excitation which depends upon the narrative of uncommon events, arising from the consideration of minds, manners, and sentiments, greatly above our own. In this class she stands almost alone.[11]

It might be tempting to read this account as a merely intellectual—though graciously friendly—recognition of the ingenuity of a fellow professional solving a difficult technical problem. However, it was also a recognition of a new source of continuing enjoyment. Some ten years later, in the more intimate language of his *Journal*, Sir Walter privately celebrated one of his many journeys into the world of Miss Austen's imagination.

Also read again and for the third time at least Miss Austen's very finely written novel of *Pride and Prejudice*. That young lady had a talent for describing the involvements and feelings and characters of ordinary life which is to me the most wonderful I have ever met with. The Big Bow wow strain I can do myself like any other now going but the exquisite touch which renders ordinary common-place things and characters interesting from the truth of the description and the sentiment is denied to me. What a pity such a gifted creature died so early.[12]

From one author—and novelist—to another a review such as Scott's bears an aspect of professional generosity; for those of us who are not in the business, such discoveries might be free from the suspicion of the alloy of rivalry or envy, though they are subject to other complications. Beyond price, such wonders and marvels

11. *Quarterly Review* 14, no. 27 (October, 1815): 192–93. Later Scott published a review of *Northanger Abbey* and *Persuasion*, completing his account of Jane Austen's work (Ibid., 24, no. 48: 352 et seq.). Both these articles are well worth reading as criticism . They are reprinted in various editions of Scott's prose works. The first (on *Emma*) is to be found in B. C. Southam, *Jane Austen, The Critical Heritage* (London, 1968).

12. Sir Walter Scott, *Journal* (several editions indistinguishable for our purposes), March 14, 1826.

seem, in moments of unalloyed satisfaction to be free gifts from and to the spirit.

But of course we know that is not so. Just as we know that the process of artistic creation is often laborious and always (however great the talent with which one may be endowed) the fruit of discipline and practice, so also we know that the complex adjustment of sensibility required for satisfactory seeing, reading, and listening is not easily achievable on a given occasion and that the ability to accomplish it with any consistency is the fruit of a process of learning and practice marked by many failures, frustrations, and incompletions. 'What brought us here' is that process; the more difficult question raised by my experience in the church of the Carmine is whether it can be thought of as a purposeful development over which we can exercise some control or rather is to be understood as a random conditioning radically controlled by circumstances—including, of course, our cultural environment. In the latter case, it would be a development in which reflective purpose and its inherent standards play at best a subordinate role. Were that the case we might still be grateful (though the object of our gratitude would be somewhat difficult to locate) for the satisfactions—the marvels—to which some succession of influences had enfranchised us, but we would be at a loss to take hold of the process in any effective way, to undertake, that is, to develop ourselves, to further our own disciplined capacity to share in what is marvelous. We might, perhaps, be capable of noting that our past had as effectively closed as opened our eyes—if only by noting that others have found things which fail to move us marvelous in *their* eyes—but we would be unable to address ourselves to that fact as a problem to be raised and solved in our own activity. However, were we able to take even an insecure command of our own development, we might secure for these wonders a more secure, a more stable place in our individual worlds and become more fully the sort of person to whom they reliably disclose themselves.

The Eighteenth Century

*By this means his sentiments are perverted; nor have the same
beauties and blemishes the same influence upon him, as if he had
imposed a proper violence upon his imagination.*
David Hume, "Of the Standard of Taste," 1757

T he gentle reader will have noted with indulgence and the
captious with sardonic condescension how this deceptively
guileless account of personal experiences has in fact
placed the problem which it attempts to raise in an increasingly
determinate intellectual setting. Indeed, that process might be said
to have begun with the title and the quotation from Kant which
precede all else. Terms such as 'enjoyment,' 'satisfaction,' or even
'marvelous' and 'wonderful' might seem harmless enough , if only
because of their vagueness, but when they begin to be modified
contextually by others such as 'perception,' 'imagination,' and constant reference to 'seeing' and 'hearing' the plot which is thickening
is apparent, only to be finally revealed by the unashamed use of
such a phrase as 'adventures of *taste*' and the prominent place as-
signed above to a quotation from an eighteenth century essay entitled "Of the Standard of Taste."

And, if readers will allow me slightly more personal reminis-
cence, I will confess that one of the 'thoughts' which passed
through my mind as I stood in the presence of Masaccio and the
pilgrims to his shrine, was the notion of an inquiry which for some
years I had vaguely formulated for myself by a title also derived
from Hume—from his essay "The Natural History of Religion."
Frequently I had thought of something to be called "The Natural
History of Taste" and as frequently rejected it as somehow inap-

13

propriate to what, very vaguely, I had in mind. For the *natural* history of taste would be an account of those causes or influences which, in the case of cultures, nations, or other human groupings similarly endowed and similarly circumstanced, had produced certain preferences, discriminations, and capacities for perceptual and imaginative enjoyment. What I had more in mind was the personal, individual history which would in this respect differentiate, within any given similarity of situation, one individual from another. But individuality was not for me the problem with the notion of a *natural* history of taste. Presumably one could attempt a biographical or autobiographical account in the same mode. The real difficulty I felt with such a project had only recently become clearer to me. Relative clarity had emerged, as it happened, in teaching Hume's essay "Of the Standard of Taste." I had once indulged an impulse by attempting to translate most of what Hume has to say about the requirements which the "critic" as "the standard of taste" must satisfy into what I called a kind of 'organon' or methodology of taste—that is, an array of disciplinings to which one might consciously subject oneself in the selection and ordering of perceiving and imagining in order to *become* that sort of critical sensibility which, according to Hume, *is* the standard. In this effort—which, incidentally (and perhaps ominously) my students seemed to find uninteresting and unintelligible—I had been struck by a phrase of Hume's in the passage quoted above: "as if he had imposed *a proper violence* upon his imagination."[1]

"A proper violence"—it seemed (and still seems) a richly provocative phrase. With some adjustment to the circumstances in which Hume constructed his essay (an adjustment not in principle different from what might be "a proper violence"), what Hume says might be read almost as a commentary on the situation in which I found myself in the church of the Carmelites.

> We may observe, that every work of art, in order to produce its due effect upon the mind, must be surveyed in a certain point of view, and cannot be relished by persons whose situation, real or imaginary, is not conformable to that which is required by the performance. . . . A per-

---

1. David Hume, "Of the Standard of Taste," in *Essays Moral, Political and Literary*. Many editions, many printings, frequently printed by itself or anthologized. The emphasis is mine.

son influenced by prejudice complies not with this condition, but obstinately maintains his natural position, without placing himself in that point of view which the performance supposes. If [an oration, for example] be addressed to persons of a different age and nation, he makes no allowance for their peculiar views and prejudices; but, full of the manners of his own age and country, rashly condemns what seemed admirable in the eyes of those for whom alone the discourse was calculated. If the work be executed for the public, he never sufficiently enlarges his comprehension, or forgets his interest as a friend or enemy, as a rival or a commentator. By this means his sentiments are perverted; nor have the same beauties and blemishes the same influence upon him, as if he had imposed a proper violence upon his imagination, and had forgotten himself for a moment. So far his taste evidently departs from the true standard, and of consequence loses all credit and authority.[2]

In other words, the fact that every work of art demands "a certain point of view" requires an adjustment of the process of perception and imagination itself. Such adjustment is "violent" because it is opposed to and thus requires direction of energy to change the "natural" position in which we find ourselves in relation to the work, and it is "proper" since it is justified and appropriate if the function of the perceptive imagination is to be performed— that function being the accurate sensing ("relish") of "beauties and blemishes" alike as disclosed in the process of constituting an object from the required "point of view."

Of course, by lifting this phrase out of the context of Hume's argument I have run the risk of an intellectual distortion analogous to the error he warns us against. Moved not by "prejudice"—at least not by prejudice in the sense of a too precipitate exclusion from consideration or a *negative* misapprehension—but by the attraction of a brilliantly provocative expression, I have plunged the reader into a situation of thought—an intellectual "point of view"—without due consideration of the consequences. It is tempting to repair that error by turning to a more careful analysis of Hume's argument, but in fact the context in which I hope to locate this inquiry is broader than Hume—it may fairly be called a generic attitude common in the eighteenth century, if one recognizes

2. Ibid.

that 'modes of thought' do not align themselves obediently with calendars.

II

From the point of view of the problems we have been trying to formulate so far—informally, of course—the essential feature of this attitude is that it approaches, as we have, the relevant matters as problems of perception and the constructive imagination of the perceiver. That was what was originally meant by aesthetics, a discipline or even science concerned with the status of perception in that mode in which it is distinguishable as sensation and imaging. Again, of course, all the words we have recourse to here are confusingly ambiguous, and the Greek *aisthesis* is no exception. However, 'aesthetics' was 'invented' when Alexander Gottlieb Baumgarten, in 1735, attempted to develop a discipline which would bear the same relation to objects of perception (*aistheta*) that logic might bear to objects of thought or 'intellection' (*noeta*).[3] The intellectual history out of which this invention came and to which it contributed is complex, but it contains no more interesting feature than the processes by which aesthetics, having been born to meet the demands of an inquiry into the conditions of satisfactory perception has come to be a somewhat awkward name for the philosophy of art in traditions centering their attention on processes of expression, creativity, and action. It is true that the connection was there from the beginning: Baumgarten projected the problems of aesthetics in a treatise designed to relocate and resolve the ancient problem of the relation of philosophy and poetry. At something like the other end of this development, a philosopher like John Dewey, who writes about art and for whom "esthetic" is almost a synonym for 'artistic,' finds the proper problem of criticism to be the "reeducation of perception."[4] But these are but the crudest

3. See Alexander Gottlieb Baumgarten, *Metaphysica* (7th edition, Halle, 1779; photographic reprint, Hildesheim, 1963), sec. 533.
4. John Dewey, *Art as Experience* (New York, 1934), p. 324 (or John Dewey, *The Later Works, 1925–1953*, vol. 10: 1934 [Carbondale and Edwardsville, Illinois, 1987], p. 328). "The function of criticism is the reeducation of perception of works of art; it is an auxiliary in the process, a difficult process, of learning to see and hear."

(and unconvincing) signs of changes (and continuities) in intellectual stance and location.

Fortunately, I am not writing intellectual history, nor is it essential to my purpose to construe at length the records of their thought which Baumgarten and his successors have left us. Nevertheless, at its beginning (if we count Baumgarten as its beginning) there appears another of those phrases (like Hume's "a proper violence") which may be helpful to us in attempting to clarify just what it is that we *are* trying to do.

Baumgarten offers a number of *phrases* apparently synonymous with "aesthetics" (*aesthetica*), such as "the logic of the lower cognitive faculty" (*logica facultatis cognitivae inferioris*).[5] Among them appears a somewhat startling one: "the art of thinking beautifully" (*ars pulchre cogitandi*). This is likely to sound to us as if there should be a technique for having 'beautiful thoughts,' a suggestion mildly ridiculous both in its pretentiousness and its triviality, since a 'beautiful thought' is for us a sentimental moralism, a moralistic piety, or an effete and affected 'aestheticism.' Somewhat more sensibly, but not much more successfully, it might suggest the 'art of thinking what is beautiful,' which we might hear as a clumsy and inadequate attempt to characterize the activity of an artistic imagination. However, if we subject *our* thinking to that kind of "proper violence" which requires us to approach matters from the position of the percipient subject searching for an organized way to direct functions of apprehension so that one rather than another kind of object may emerge from the welter of what we grossly call our 'experience,' the phrase reorients itself accordingly. In fact, is it not an attempt to point to that directing of ourselves Hawthorne thought of as putting him "in a state to see pictures with less toil, and more pleasure," making him "more fastidious, yet more sensible of beauty where I saw none before"? It would not be stretching our language to say that he would have been trying to think more logically, rationally, intelligibly, or truthfully if he had been trying to put himself into a state in which he would be able to "discern reasons with less toil, and more satisfaction," making him "more intellectually critical, yet more understanding of intelligibility and truth where I saw none before." Such a sense of 'thinking beautifully'

5. Baumgarten, *Metaphysica*, sec. 533.

may require some 'violence' in relocating the problem in our universe of things to investigate and think about, but the problem itself, as experienced, is a familiar one. And perhaps we can even intelligibly extend this so as to give a new meaning to the phrase 'to think the beautiful.' For we might recognize this as a way of referring to a coherent activity in which we adjust ourselves so as to maximize the probability that *what* we perceive, imagine, or encounter in perception and imagination meets the conditions of an identifiable satisfaction, is an object of a certain quality. For the moment, at least, we may waive the question of whether this activity is simply a matter of adjusting ourselves so as to perceive what is already there or a process in which something of a certain sort is generated by our activity, since *in either case* some purposive direction of ourselves, of our activity, is required, just as it is required if we are to 'think the true' and maximize the probability that something cogently intelligible will be produced or discovered.

The object of this inquiry is to investigate what might be said about directing ourselves so as to realize (make actual) more consistently and more effectively in our worlds what is beautiful: in that sense it is an attempt to formulate the "art of thinking beautifully."

III

The ambiguity of such a formula is, of course, enormous. What follows will largely serve to remove these ambiguities so far as is possible (and desirable). And we might begin by warning readers with respect to the scope *and* the limits of what we are about and to offer some reason for holding that it has some pertinence to *their* activity.

We might begin, perversely, by suggesting that such a project is redundant: after all, is not the world already replete with works—learned, inspiring, enthusiastic, critical—designed to enable us to read, to see, to hear more critically, more sensitively, more imaginatively, more appreciatively? And is not this the case at almost any level of application? If, that is, the beauties of the neoclassical nave of the church of the Carmine are not apparent to me, there are not lacking those who might undertake to point them out. If my guidebooks (and Eric Cochrane) are rather condescending about

Foggini, Luca Giordano and their wriggling cherubs, soaring Medici princes and Corsini saints, there are other, more sympathetic guides, not only for these artists and their works but for 'the baroque' in general, willing (and often eager) to articulate intentions, disclose the power of styles and techniques, and generally explain how these things came to be expressively marvelous in contemporary eyes and may become so in mine. Have I hitherto found Beethoven's *Overture for the Consecration of the House* a case of Homer contrapuntally nodding? Sir Donald Tovey may enable me to hear it for what it "is" (or I shall find it to be) "one of Beethoven's grandest and least understood works," a "sublime combination of energy and immobility." [6] Have I found *Paradise Lost* drearily pompous-pious; Browning unintelligible; abstract expressionism, twelve-tone music, post-Joycean novels or pop art outrageous; opera boring or chamber music and art songs precious and trivial—there are those who can enlighten me, discriminate possibilities, remove prejudices, and in not a few cases open up for me a new region for hitherto unappreciated successes and failures. 'Failures' because, of course, a developing taste issues in reevaluations both positive and negative, and both changes are mediated by contexts of criticism, analysis, and comparison.

It will be necessary in due course to concern ourselves with the functioning of these aids to the "reeducation" of perception and imagination, but for the present we should simply note that the literature (and other forms of communication) available to perform this function is much broader than guidebooks, handbooks of appreciation, or other forms of explicitly 'critical' commentary. In fact, they are part of a cultural *milieu* in which all of us to some extent live and by which we are, frequently insensibly, influenced.

One of the most powerfully pervasive of these cultural 'attitudes' might also be said to have been born (or perhaps come of age) in the eighteenth century. Goethe, traveling to Italy in 1786, picked up a copy of Winckelmann's *History of Art in Antiquity* (1764) in a

6. D. F. Tovey, *Essays in Musical Analysis* (London, 1935), vol. 2, p. 157. (These essays have been much reprinted in various formats.) Incidentally, I have never understood why the German title of this work (*Die Weihe des Hauses* or *Zur Weihe des Hauses*) is translated as "*consecration* of the house," since the "house" in question was a theater. Would not "dedication" be sufficiently dignified?

new Italian translation.[7] Its effect on his practice in "thinking the beautiful" was profound. Writing in his journal on January 28, 1787, in Rome he finds that he "must not fail to record," now that it has become clear to him, a consideration which "affects everything," namely,

> with respect to every object of art one is required to ask to what age it owes its existence. Winckelmann urgently requires us to distinguish periods, to understand the different styles which peoples have employed and which in the course of time they have developed and, eventually, corrupted. Every true friend of art is persuaded of the rightness of this. We all grant the rightness and the importance of such an inquiry.
>
> But, now, how is one to achieve this insight? For the unpracticed the concept may be correctly and clearly grasped but the individual object remains in an uncertain vagueness. Many years of discriminating use of the eye is necessary, and one must first learn in order to be able to inquire. In this matter shilly-shallying is useless, attention nowadays is vigorously addressed to this important point, and everyone who is serious about it perceives that it is true in this field as well that no judgment is possible unless one can develop it historically.[8]

The placement of works of all the arts by styles and periods which "peoples" and "ages" invent, develop, and corrupt has become for us so automatic an activity that we may find it hard to believe not only that apparently there was a time when "attention" was *not* given to this important point but even that there is, in fact, any alternative to it. Indeed, it "affects everything," but the point to be noted here is that there is a vast historical literature which is effectively transformed into ways of adjusting 'ourselves'—our perceptions, our imagination, our concrete expectations—in the presence of works of all the arts, just as Goethe, grappling with the riches offered him in eighteenth century Rome, adapted Winckelmann to the discriminating use of his eyes. While it is the case that there persistently surfaces a certain tension between scholars who

7. According to the entry for December 3, 1786, in Goethe's journals (*Italienische Reise*—numerous editions), the version he seems to have been reading is that of Carlo Fea, that is, *Storia delle arti del disegno presso gli antichi tradotta dal Tedesco e in questo edizione correta e aumentata dall'Abate Carlo Fea. In Roma, 1783–84.*

8. Goethe, *Italienische Reise*, January 28, 1787. Numerous editions, translations. (I am responsible for this version.)

think of themselves as historically oriented and those who think in terms of 'criticism,' it seems fair to say that so far as they actually function in our efforts to understand what we have before us, both 'history' and 'criticism' are powerfully present and more often than not indiscriminable in operation. It is indeed difficult to imagine anyone "nowadays" who is willing to contend that one makes judgments which cannot be "developed historically." What we tend to dispute about is rather what sort of history or the history of what?

So massive is this historical-critical-analytical preoccupation and so multifarious the forms it has developed (and sometimes corrupted) that escape from it—were that thought desirable—seems almost impossible. At the moment, for instance, it is a nice question whether, in those circles, restricted as they are, in which they are read, the novels of Virginia Woolf are not perceived primarily as episodes in a larger literature constituted by her diaries and letters, in which they appear largely as moments of crisis in the career of a tormented psyche. Alternatively, they are episodes in the feminist consciousness of European-American culture in all the available senses of 'feminism,' 'consciousness,' and 'culture.' Somewhere there may be someone who stumbles upon *Mrs. Dalloway* or *To the Lighthouse* innocent of knowledge of those circumstances to which these works "owe their existence," but should such an innocent become sufficiently intrigued by Mrs. Woolf's "exquisite touch which renders ordinary common-place things and characters interesting" and seek enlightenment from those who know about such matters, his or her perceptions will be profoundly affected when informed by insights into her works as moments in the development of Mrs. Woolf, feminism, novelistic technique, or the changing functions of literature and literati in one or another context in which these judgments can be 'historically developed.'

On the surface, it is somewhat astonishing that objects which, as perceived, seem to be distinguished by a qualitative unity, a lucid integrity, a commanding self-containedness, should so easily be resolvable into episodes and fragments of something larger, but perhaps it is better to see these efforts at understanding and appreciation as at least in part a tribute to the fascination which the works themselves have for us: after all, we tend to seek out the origins and grounds of what we find most interesting. Such a concentra-

tion on what is wonderful may be, in a way, 'unscientific,' but it is
certainly intelligible, the underlying question not being whether we
should inquire but rather what the appropriate kind of inquiry may
be and what light it may shed on what.

IV

Goethe translated a history and a set of hypotheses about the development of styles and artistic ideals into an array of questions he
could address to himself in the presence of a work of art. Such a
practice, if persistent, would develop into a continuing personal
inquiry training the senses and the imagination in discriminations
issuing in an appreciative understanding. This process has something to tell us without any reference to the form it took in his case
or in any other instance. It is difficult to think of a body of information, knowledge, or theory which does not, in its way, admit of
such a translation, and to this rule of thumb aesthetics itself is no
exception. At first glance it might be thought that "aesthetics" differs from other theories or knowledges only in that, first, it explicitly takes as its subject matter aesthetic experience or art and therefore does not require any applicative transformation to be made
relevant to that experience, as do, for example, psychoanalytical or
anthropological ideas. Second, it is couched, in relation to its subject matter, at an extreme level of generality—that is, aesthetics is
presumably relevant to all art or all aesthetic experience, not only
to Renaissance art, to literature, to Masaccio's frescoes. It is in this
sense, of course, that aesthetics is both distinguishable from and
may at the same time serve as the basis of a mode of criticism. The
question raised in this inquiry, however, is whether there might not
be an aesthetics which would claim for itself a function not reducible to a consequence of these relationships, separately or con-
jointly.

An inquiry into the ways in which we direct ourselves so as to
realize more consistently and effectively in our worlds what is beautiful would not be so much an account of aesthetic experience as it
would be an inquiry into criteria for making ourselves capable (and
ever more capable) of experiencing the world aesthetically, a capability of which aesthetic experience would be the *consequence*.
Nor would such an aesthetics be an account of art, unless we make

the assumption (so often a feature of recent aesthetics) that *the* mode of constituting such experience is to be found in the creative process of the artist which, then, the rest of us reenact. Such an inquiry would not be alien to the tradition of aesthetics, but it would differ radically in starting point, in emphasis, and in consequence from much of that tradition. One of its consequences would be that it would seek criteria of relevance for the translation of all that we know and can do into ways of orienting ourselves toward the world in order to realize the beautiful. It would in this respect be a critical reflection upon those moments of self-orientation in which are comprehended as directing elements history, criticism, and all the other available candidates for guidance. It would be in the tradition of aesthetics in a strong sense, for it would be—as aesthetics was in its origin—an attempt to deal with a series of problems in terms of taste—the relevant characteristics of the percipient subject—but it would differ from most of even that tradition because it would take as its starting point problems of the formation and development of taste—the organizing of our capabilities in constituting that sort of satisfaction we call beauty. It is in this sense that our inquiry is aesthetic and may be said to begin in the eighteenth century.

The rest of our inquiry will be concerned with exploring this possibility and developing this hypothesis—not historically in a 'natural history of taste' but functionally in a *discipline* of taste and feeling. We presume that the development of an aesthetic capability takes place in a sequence of concrete events of perceiving, imagining and feeling, however these may be mediated by reflective intelligence. That is, this discipline is developed in and by practice and emerges in an ever more secure, refined, and internally articulated practice. Some of the features of 'practice' in both senses have been represented already in the records of their experience left us by Hawthorne, Ruskin, Goethe, and others who had some gift for self-analysis and self-reflection. But we assume that the problems with which they found themselves confronted and the enterprise in which they were engaged (the pursuit which created these problems for them) are shareable and more than likely actually shared by all of us. On that point, you, gentle reader, are better informed in your own case than anyone else is likely to be.

V

Just because an individual discipline of taste and feeling must be forged in practice, the course of its development will necessarily be circumstantially determined or, more accurately, will become determinate circumstantially. Each career will have its own starting points, its own turning points, its profoundly different content and ordering. Whatever 'genetic' differences may constitute part of our particular endowments, our 'cultural' circumstances differ so significantly and so profoundly influence the ways in which we encounter our problems, define them reflectively (or unreflectively), and grapple with them more or less successfully that it takes a considerable effort of the imagination to place ourselves in something like the situation of another person at even a short remove in cultural space and time.

In these matters all 'normalities' are suspect. They are probably provincialisms. Winckelmann, Goethe's mentor, wrote a history of "the art of antiquity." Yet apparently he never saw an original piece of Greek sculpture. How could he, never having visited Greece, have known works which for us loom so large and have been so influential—the sculptures of the Parthenon (all still reposing on the Acropolis, not yet 'stolen' by Lord Elgin for, as it turned out, the British Museum)—nor could even a trip to Greece have enabled him to see the Hermes of Praxiteles, the charioteer of Delphi, or the Victory of Samothrace, all of which were discovered (by being *un*covered) only in the nineteenth century. The point here, of course, is not the questions which might be raised about the worth of Winckelmann's history, but simply that the world of art, of taste, of available artifacts was so strikingly different from our own. Nor are the 'touchstones' of taste and tradition exempt from this mutability. Goethe, in later life, read and enjoyed the novels of Walter Scott, but by neither of them could that monumental force exerted on novels, novelists, and readers by "the Russian School" have been felt, since it did not yet exist. Anthony Powell, discussing a contemporary, the novelist Henry Green (Henry Yorke), remarks that he "was accustomed to take the line that he did not like Shakespeare (not a good sign as a rule)."[9] "As a rule" it may not be a good

---

9. Anthony Powell, *Infants of the Spring* (New York, 1977), p. 68.

sign, but only in a tradition in which 'everybody' knows Shake-speare as a living imaginative presence. What sort of a sign is it in an aspiring German novelist who knows Shakespeare only in trans-lation or 'by reputation'?

And, of course, one can extend the argument indefinitely, for even within traditions the canon of masterworks which partially outline a cultural world undergoes striking changes rather more rapidly and confusingly than is comfortably normal. Much is made (frequently inaccurately) of the inadequate appreciation accorded masterpieces and masters on their first appearance, but we ought really to be equally impressed by the fact that they often have to be rediscovered and recanonized. It is difficult for us to imagine a cul-tural world in which Bach was best known as the father of his sons or Florence was not a magnet for the discerning, yet Florence as we know it, the Florence of Giotto, Ghiberti, Masaccio, Brunelles-chi, the Florence which Ruskin and Henry Moore went to see—was discovered (one might almost say created) in the first half of the nineteenth century. Perhaps it is unfair to call the normalities of any world of taste provincialisms, since a provincialism is an ar-bitrary limitation *within* a cultural world, but all worlds of this sort, having individuality also have their limits, limits determined by ne-cessities of time and history as well as by choice and prejudice. The gnomic saying of Hegel, "individuality is what its world as *its* world is," [10] suggests something of the necessarily closed, self-contained, and, so far, limited nature of any personal cultural actuality.

VI

So it must be very cautiously indeed that we might suggest that our cultural world is a novel one in something other than the trivial sense in which we recognize that all cultural situations are unique. Yet is it not the case that the sheer multiplication of effectively avail-able objects, traditions, information, and ideas has created for us a special problem—for us, that is, of the civilized West? The com-bined effects of technological change (from the invention of print-

10. Hegel, *Phänomenologie des Geistes*, C (AA), V, b ("Von der Beobachtung des Selbstbewusstseins in seiner Reinheit"). "Die Individualität ist, was *ihre* Welt als die *ihrige* ist . . . ."

ing to the wonders of television), of 'mass' education (from simple
literacy to the expansion of 'postsecondary' education), and of the
accumulated products of centuries of physical and intellectual exploration and reflection seem to have transformed our world by an
unprecedented enlargement of cultural alternatives and of those
to whom they are available.

It is difficult to measure the change and assess its significance.
Hawthorne had to go to Italy to see pictures which every New En-
glander can now see in reproductions of a quality unimaginable in
his time, and there are available in fifty American museums actual
examples of the same art—not to mention that it is much easier to
visit Italy. It is recorded that just about a century ago the German
pianist and conductor Hans von Bülow (now unfortunately best
remembered because Wagner ran off with his wife) offered a concert at Meiningen in which the first half consisted of Beethoven's
Ninth Symphony and the second of another performance of the
same.[11] It is all very well for us, who can 'hear' the Ninth Symphony
about as often as we choose, to be appalled by such program making, but Bülow's argument that this difficult and complex work was
so rarely performed that performers and audiences could hardly
get to know it is not so easily dismissed in his circumstances. (Most
of his contemporaries, if they knew the work at all, knew it by
score-reading or by hearing parts of it in the piano transcriptions
which were then staples of musical culture. We may be permitted
our doubts about recorded performances, but who would wish to
exchange them for piano transcriptions, even four- hand transcriptions?) A little thought along these lines might suggest that "the
world is so full of a number of things / that I'm sure we should all
be happy as kings." But in fact we may simply be confused and
frustrated. Worse, we might well develop a kind of cultural dilet-
tantism, the symptoms of which would be superficiality of attention
(using Beethoven as background music—a kind of super-Musak),
habits of apprehension and response determined by glibness of
formulation in which the slogans of criticism make the object for

11. The practice is not as eccentric as might be thought. I seem to recall that
Mahler's Fourth Symphony was performed twice on the same program in 1904 in
Amsterdam, conducted first by the composer and then by Mengelberg. And I myself
was present at a concert of the Chicago Symphony Orchestra in 1965 (April 17) at
which Stravinsky's *Variations,* being performed for the first time, was played twice.

us, and a set of preferences at bottom whimsical but consecrated for us by a conviction that the important thing about any judgment or opinion is that it is *personal* and the more personal the more strongly felt. With respect to the arts, we thus flounder somewhere between the extremes represented by knowing all about it and not knowing what we enjoy and knowing nothing about it but glorying in the assertive actuality of preference.

It might be thought, then, that in such circumstances some systematic reflection on the enterprise of forming taste is more appropriate than it might be in a less complex world: that a 'discipline of taste and feeling' is a cultural requisite in these cultural circumstances. But it could also be argued that this felt need and the developments to which it might be a response are themselves indicative of a more profoundly disturbing modern phenomenon. In fact, there are ways (and widely influential ways) of thinking about our situation which would call into question the whole enterprise of 'taste,' of the world of art and imagination, and even of 'culture,' when (as it could be said we have slipped into talking about it here) 'culture' comes to mean that which is possessed by the cultivated. It is not easy to formulate the problem, if only because I find myself fundamentally out of sympathy with many of those for whom it is a problem—a sign that perhaps I have not understood what troubles them. But it is well to face up to it as best I can, since many of the reservations possibly forming in your mind, uncommitted reader, may have similar origins. And therefore we might begin by observing that for most of us, or many of us, the word 'taste' itself is a difficulty.

VII

Though for some reason quite inoffensive when used in such phrases as 'the history of taste' or 'eighteenth-century taste' (perhaps even 'modern' or 'contemporary taste'), it becomes a palpable stumbling block when used adjectivally ('tasteful') and almost repulsive when it becomes 'good taste.' In these uses it has associations not only of some specialized standard available only to the instructed and refined and inaccessible to ordinary mortals, but is suddenly redolent of the pretended privileges and superior, more attenuated delights of special social groups: the middle class, driven by the necessity to meet standards of 'good taste' in order to justify pretensions to join the higher reaches of humanity; the leisured and hypercultivated who have the time (and the money) to devote themselves to the pursuit of 'objects of taste and refinement' guaranteed for them by 'connoisseurs' of these rare (and rarified objects); the aesthetes, whose delicate sensibilities, aroused only by encounters with 'ethereal things,' must not be disturbed by passion or impeded by the intervention of moral imperatives. So 'taste' and 'good taste' have all the earmarks of a bourgeois invention, an arbitrary standard reflecting only a class detachment from life and labor, a conventional badge of status functioning to separate the social herd from the dominant, parasitic social goats in sheep's clothing, a disguised morality pretending to identify approvable pursuits and worthy performances by 'correctness' of appearance and external form.

Worst of all, 'taste' divorces art from life, making it the special preserve of the cognoscenti, probably sequestering it (if not in private mansions) in museums built by owners of mansions and filled largely with their former furnishings, and draining from it the lifeblood of passionate involvement and expression which gave it birth. In such associations, the idea of a disciplinary process designed to develop a discriminating sensibility probably evokes some image of an early nineteenth-century maiden—primly petticoated, wholly innocent not only of amorous experience but of sexual information, expert at needlework, amateurishly decorative at the pianoforte—setting out to 'form her taste on the best models' so that she may number it among the accomplishments which will make her an eligible match for a gentleman of good situation, education, and a capacity for refined conversation. This discouraging picture hardly augurs well for future inquiry, but it is also worlds removed from Masaccio's frescoes, where, after all, we began. Nor does it somehow seem to have much to do with Hawthorne ruminating on a "Dutch fly settling on a peach, or a humble-bee burying himself in a flower," with Walter Scott rejoicing in the fascinations of "ordinary common-place things and characters" in the pages of *Pride and Prejudice,* or even with the official orator on that autumn day in Florence in 1782 greeting the restored Carmine with "this is the Lord's doing; it is marvelous in our eyes."

But, of course, it is dangerous to dismiss the doubts expressed in such a caricature by assuming that they are addressed to a caricature only. And while it may be rhetorically effective to take advantage of the vaguely Marxist tone introduced into the preceding sketch—since Marxism and certain forms of radical egalitarianism enjoy almost as bad a press in some circles as does 'taste'—it is not the case that such doubts always proceed from such an intellectual environment. Nor is it sufficient to protest that engaging in this inquiry does not commit us to any defense of the absurdities and perversions of the world of the cultured, the cultivated, and the cognoscenti. On the contrary, we may join heartily in denunciation of the preciousness, the pretentiousness, and the pedantry of much that goes on in the curiously closed worlds of art-lovers, poets, literati, collectors, lion-hunters, critics, and those markets in which all things and persons are prized by being marketable, that is, by being priced. It may be, that is, that everything is corruptible, but perhaps the gravamen of the doubt expressed is not merely that these admitted vices are the vices of a virtue in the sense that certain external forces have invaded an otherwise legitimate form of human activity, but rather that an extremely important phase of human life has been so cabin'd, crib'd, and confin'd by the intellectual and institutional circumstances in which it is conceived and carried on that the activity itself is impeded and necessarily incomplete—frustrate.

VIII

But it is better to rest the case for this inquiry on assertion rather than on denial. Let us endeavor here to prefigure our stance in terms which seem appropriate. First, we have frequently made use of such expressions as "purposive direction of *ourselves*," and that somewhat vague language was deliberately chosen because it suggests the obvious: namely that 'taste' as here conceived is a functional organization of *all* our capacities, differing in this respect from our cognitive and practical activities only in the way in which they function together in *this* activity. Our intelligence, our knowledge, our physical and sensory equipment and habits, our moral feelings and attitudes, and our practical intelligence are not abandoned or somehow magically inhibited or functionally suspended in 'aesthetic' activity. "[E]very kind of composition, even the most poetical," says Hume, "is nothing but a chain of propositions and reasonings."[12] Any hypothesis which required us to believe that such poetry as

> Some glory in their birth, some in their skill,
> Some in their wealth, some in their bodies' force;
> Some in their garments, though new-fangled ill,
> Some in their hawks and hounds, some in their horse.
> And every humour hath his adjunct pleasure,
> Wherein it finds a joy above the rest . . .[13]

can be appreciated without the exercise of a subtle, discriminating and active intelligence would be simply absurd. Many of the objects which delight us most and certainly those which *move* us most deeply in our world generally and in the arts are 'moral' objects, not in the sense that they are noble or improving, but in the more basic sense that they are objects constituted in a world of choice, of passionate purpose, success or failure, endeavor and consequential action, happiness or misery.

> The expense of spirit in a waste of shame
> Is lust in action; and till action, lust
> Is perjured, murderous, bloody, full of blame,
> Savage, extreme, rude, cruel, not to trust;
> Enjoyed no sooner but despised straight . . .[14]

is intellectually, that is, *conceptually* difficult, but its concepts are moral concepts and its passion and eloquence meaningless (nonexistent) for a reader without moral habits, moral intelligence, and moral judgment. (Nor, we might add, are these cognitive and moral functions the peculiar privilege of literary expression: the drama, the tragedy, and the moral sublimity of Beethoven's Ninth Symphony do not suddenly supervene when words appear in the final movement, and the "tipsy rotundity of flesh" which Hawthorne saw in Rubens' *Bacchus,* while verbalizable, is not verbal comedy.)

It is almost embarrassing to reiterate what seems so simply clear: if there is any mystery, it is what may not seem equally obvious, that

12. Hume, "Of the Standard of Taste."
13. Shakespeare, "Sonnet 91."
14. Shakespeare, "Sonnet 129."

the satisfying objects we seek in the aesthetic organization of 'ourselves' have an integrity of their own, and therefore these satisfactions themselves are not reducible in their objective ground to the satisfaction of knowing or of action and practical judgment. The master of Hardscrabble Farm, homeward plodding his weary way, whose eye is caught by the beauty of a flowering thistle radiantly blue in a whimsical ray of the setting sun is in that moment free from the preoccupations which would, in another orientation of his self, lead him to see yet another weed propagating itself in the struggle to rob him of his livelihood. Can we account for that moment by assuming that he is therein transformed into an amateur botanist suffused with admiration for the perfection of this specimen of *Cirsium pumilum* and its remarkable adaptation to reproductive functions? Must we assume that he is in this act of perceiving decorticated and morally castrate? Is there any point to debating which perceived 'thistle' is more substantial, more real, more actual, more common, more ordinary and everyday—the weed, the specimen, or the beauty?

Fundamentally, human beings are capable of aesthetic satisfactions because they are intelligent, imaginative, active, and percipient beings, not because they are educated, 'cultured,' leisured, or 'artistic.' Our sense of functional priority may be curiously misled if we confuse the cultural (in the broader sense in which the culture of the cultivated is a feature of culture at large), the social, the institutional circumstances within which any actual aesthetic sensibility takes its shape with the conditions which make such activity possible at all. We would do better to regard any actual cultural life—any realization of aesthetic activity in traditions of attentive percipience and crafty embodiment—as efforts to offer concrete satisfaction to a human capability and thus a human need. If nothing else, we should thus be forcibly reminded that the conditions of this demanding capability are satisfied not only in "art" but in the natural and moral worlds in which we all must live. Of course, the question is not really a historical one, but it is not inappropriate to remind ourselves that "rosy-fingered dawn" was beautiful before she was immortalized by Homer and will continue to offer her delight to many who have never heard of him and long after that phrase has suffered from translation into even more recalcitrant languages than English.[15] The grace of Attic vase painting, the sensuous lavishness of Rubens, the searing tragedy of *Lear* offer us so much that we may be tempted to forget that something not unlike these things was there to be perceived before its brilliance challenged the enlarging imagination of artists. To say this is not to require that art is or should be a reproduction of 'nature' or to deny that there are imaginative worlds which never were on land nor sea, rather it is simply to affirm that imaginative perception will satisfy itself wherever it can find or create its occasions. Theories which are essentially theories of art may mislead us by suggesting that aesthetic creativity is only to be found there, thus unwittingly contributing to that isolation of the realm of art from other activities of the human psyche which many of them go on to deplore.

IX

It may be well to reflect upon this matter a bit, since what is at stake is, at least, how we conceive the place of our aesthetic lives in our lives at large and, of course, the importance of that place and that life. Santayana, after an encounter in Venice (1939) with his old friend Berenson (almost the archetypal scholar and connoisseur of art), wrote to another friend.

> [I]t is impossible for me now to regard 'art' . . . as a supreme interest in itself. It is . . . a positive joy when it really reveals something beautiful in the material or the spiritual world. But the social world, the world of convention, to which the criticism of art belongs, has come to seem to me rather a screen that keeps the material and the spiritual worlds out of sight. . . . In order to keep up the game with B. B., however, I mentioned the constant pleasure I find in the light of Venice and in the aspects of the sky. 'Yes,' said he, '*they* were wonderful at catching those

15. In these matters it is not always easy to see on what ground we stand. Consider the following comment by an indefatigable New England (Martha's Vineyard) observer of sunrises. "How often have Graham [a dog, a collie] and I watched for the sun to appear above Chappaquiddick, and how often have I searched for words with which to express the poetry of sunrise. In high school my teacher praised the *Odyssey* for its often-repeated metaphor, 'When the rosy-fingered dawn appeared.' But in all my watching sunrises I have never seen any fingers in the eastern sky—layers, patches, streaks, and singular creatures, but never fingers, and of all the morning hues 'rose' seems to me the rarest." (Henry Beetle Hough, *Soundings at Sea Level* [Boston, 1980], p. 25.) I leave it to the reader to determine relevances.

effects, due to the reflected light in the lagoon of the atmosphere. Paolo Veronese was supreme in rendering them.' I thought of Titian and Tiepolo, but said nothing because I don't really care who *painted* or *saw* those harmonies most perfectly. . . . What I care about are the harmonies themselves, which can't be had at second hand; they are strictly incommunicable; if you can get them out of a book or a picture, very well; but it would be an illusion to suppose that the *same* harmony had been felt by the poet or the painter. He had merely worked in a material, that could offer such harmonies to a properly prepared mind. . . . It is lucky for B. B., in one sense, that he keeps the old flame alive; but I can't help feeling that it was lighted and is kept going by forced draft, by social and intellectual ambition, and by professional pedantry. If he were a real poet, would he turn away from the evening sky to see, by electric light, how Veronese painted it?[16]

Certainly Santayana wrote in a moment of pique, but just for that reason he makes forcibly a point of central importance: the world of art and artists, of scholarship, criticism and connoisseurship is *part* of an organic aesthetic system through which the lifeblood of aesthetic capability circulates, flowing from deeper sources in the human psyche. And it does *circulate*, for, as Santayana's language suggests, there is no contradiction in asserting both that Venetian painting "renders harmonies" which offer themselves "spontaneously" to a "prepared mind" and that Venetian painting may itself be an education or reeducation of perception which prepares a mind to see what otherwise might be hidden. That is, the artistic life of any culture is both a celebration of the imaginative powers of the psyche and a cultivation of them, an expression of our sense of the beauty and the drama of the world and an enhancement of it.

However, in the last analysis all this may be beside the point, or, rather, we may finally have arrived at the point. For it may be that what is objected to in the position we have been adumbrating is that it seems to require that an essential feature of an aesthetically functional organization of human capacities is a certain detachment—almost an attitude of 'contemplation' in which the "material and spiritual worlds" become spectacles rather than arenas of action, sources of an enjoyment innocent of the need to transform.

16. Daniel Cory, ed., *The Letters of George Santayana* (New York, 1955), pp. 341–42 (to Mrs. C. H. Toy, October 10, 1939).

It seems to require, that is, that the psyche find itself at home in an unpremeditatedly responsive world rather than make for itself a world of objects in which it can find itself satisfied precisely because they are an expression of its concerns and prophetic aspirations. The intense preoccupation with agency, action, and achievement which so much of our modern (and postmodern) thinking manifests is bound to generate a suspicion of any philosophy which seems to place a high value on and even make fundamental an attitude which is contemplative—even though it may be contemplative *of* action and achievement. The basic reorientation of thought implied in the aphorism that "the point is not to understand the world but to change it" has ramifications which extend far beyond social science, social philosophy and political action, and history and represents an intellectual shift not confined to dialectical materialism or any other single tradition. It is true that analytically ('theoretically') the treatment of aesthetic activity in terms of categories of action, expression, and creation places upon itself the burden of at once identifying and distinguishing art and action, practical realization and artistic expression. But, also analytically, such thinking tends to reject 'a priori' any analysis of 'aesthetics' couched not in terms of a transformative but of a contemplative activity. Such a 'transformational' analysis does not, of course, commit us to the "professional pedantry" of connoisseurship or to the simple moralizing of the arts demanded by the Moral Majority or the pre-glasnost Soviet Ministry of Culture, any more than an examination of the problems of a discipline of taste and feeling commits us to an effete aestheticism and a debilitated bourgeois culture. And yet the differences are perhaps no less real for all that: the question before us being whether and in what form our aesthetic concerns can constitute and indeed *claim* the status of a "supreme interest," a question to which both modes of analysis in effect address themselves and answer in ways not easily reducible to common terms.

Can we not then, with a sense of at least a common question before us, proceed to deal with our problems reflectively rather than polemically? For the task before us in this inquiry should now be clearer. It is broadly twofold. First, we must endeavor to determine and formulate as clearly as we can the *norms* of aesthetic activity as we conceive it within the framework of the orientation we have problematically distinguished and provisionally accepted. 'Norms' in this sense are simply those identifying demands which articulate our sense that we are engaged in one kind of activity rather than another and, thus, carrying it on well or badly. They are, then, neither standards imposed from without nor 'normalities' descriptive of what does or does not occur on any given set of occasions. In one way they merely identify for us what we are doing, in another they tell us what we are *trying* to do and therefore generate for us more or less fruitful reflection on ways of doing it better. This inquiry will, of course, enable us to understand whether and in what sense aesthetic activity is 'contemplative,' or—what is really the same thing—whether and in what way it may be 'involved,' creative or transformative. It may also help us to understand why and in what way each of us may—indeed *must*—have an individual taste without doing violence to our conviction that our tastes are common and communicable, each comprehensive though necessarily limited. Second, we shall endeavor to determine, so far as is possible within the limits of this inquiry, what claim this kind of activity, with its internal claims, has upon us as human beings: why, in other words, we demand of everyone—and more especially of ourselves—a discipline of taste and feeling. Virtue may be its own reward—and every disciplined activity is so far forth a virtue with its concomitant rewards ("every humour hath his adjunct pleasure")—but there is a multiplicity of virtues, and nothing so individualizes us as the working priority each of us establishes among them.

1

NORMS OF TASTE
AND FEELING

Freedom/Engagement

The first and most astonishing feature of the beauties of the world is that they are freely loved, unconstrainedly enjoyed. The first mark and sign of the 'disposition of the mind' basic to all aesthetic life is this sense (literally 'sense,' for it is a glow of positive feeling) of free engagement with a world which more commonly we are endeavoring to understand or to control. In such moments, our environment seems to favor us with objects, unasked and unsought, alive in their concreteness, so lucid, so stimulating, so engaging as to make them almost the ideal of what experience might be were it untrammeled by desire, need, or obligation: that is, by intrusions in which satisfaction and dissatisfaction, approval and disapproval of objects is constrained by some standard, some norm of utility or good not present in their simple apprehension. So the first 'norm' of aesthetic life would seem to be that it is *without any norm* other than that of the immediate satisfaction offered to us in perception—a satisfaction uncalculated, uncalculating, having the freedom of whimsicality or caprice.

But before we embrace this conclusion, we should take note that what is perceived is an *object,* not merely a sensed quality or an agreeable stimulation. Our experience of beauty is not the satisfaction of luxuriating tired muscles in a hot bath, that caressing of the senses by the sweetness of ripe fruit, or stirring of the loins premonitory or constitutive of sexual desire. These may also seem unasked and sought, but here the world favors us not in the perception of objects but in the pleasures of sensation; it engages us, but by way of attachment to present stimulation rather than by way of

37

a satisfying appropriation of its organized, objectified constituents. In the language of tradition, our aesthetic life is not our sensual life: our sensual life is a life in which we are captured by the world as it is *given* to us rather than captivated by what we find can be *made of it* objectively.

These distinctions are commonplaces of aesthetic analysis that remain, in any formulation, pregnantly ambiguous. This ambiguity is grounded in the phenomena themselves, for aesthetic activity is at once primitive and complex: one of those manifestations of the human psyche which are at once directly simple and yet subtle. Its apparent simplicity is in its character as a *felt* satisfaction, a direct enjoyment—what our simpleminded predecessors made bold to call 'pleasure.' Its complexity is in its character as a satisfaction *among others* from which it is different (yet to which it is inextricably linked) and in the multiplicity of the functions which are so interrelated in it as to yield by their distinctive interplay the character it has as a primitive felt quality. As a felt satisfaction it invites not analysis but continuing engagement. That engagement may, of course, be terminated when the correlative *dis*satisfaction is felt. In that case we think ourselves to have encountered an ugliness, an awkwardness, an incoherence. But it may also be confused with or develop into a satisfaction of a different kind. In that case we may find ourselves—perhaps somewhat shamefacedly—to have mistaken agreeable physical stimulation (at one extreme) or goodness (at another) for beauty. Both situations may stimulate reflection, but in the case of ugliness reflection takes the form of a search for what may have 'gone wrong' *within* an activity of a certain sort. In the other sort of situation reflection is directed to the discrimination of the conditions of one activity or engagement from another.

This is a matter of great importance, for it is a major premise of our inquiry that activities—and consequently the satisfactions which mark them and are their fruits—*are* thus discriminable. This premise is itself a profoundly significant choice. Broadly, the alternatives are fairly represented by, on the one hand, Jeremy Bentham's doggerel mnemonic fixing the "*elements* or *dimensions* of *value* in a pleasure or a pain"—

Intense, long, certain, speedy, fruitful, pure—
Such marks in *pleasures* and in *pains* endure—[1]

and, on the other hand, Aristotle's remark that "without activity pleasure does not occur; every activity is completed by a pleasure"[2] and its consequence that discriminations of ends or grounds of choice can be based, not upon Benthamite measurements of pleasure and pain, but upon discriminations of the activities of which pleasures and pains are at once the marks and the fruition.

Such basic considerations are, of course, not relevant only to our aesthetic life; let us inspect more closely the kind of activity we enjoy there. The traditional answer is, of course, that it is an activity of the 'imagination,' and we might think that in this formula we have found the source of the freedom which seems to characterize the enjoyment of the beautiful, for imaginatively we are free to entertain ourselves in at least the obvious sense that we are bound neither by what we have actually observed, by what we take to be the actual state and nature of the world, or by the necessities of any practical projection of possible behavior. "Poesy," says Lord Bacon,

> is a part of learning in measure of words for the most part restrained, but in all other parts extremely licensed, and doth truly refer to the imagination, which, being not tied to the laws of matter, may at pleasure join that which nature hath severed and sever that which nature hath joined, and so make unlawful matches and divorces of things. (Painters and Poets have always been allowed to take what liberties they dared. [Horace, *Ars Poetica*])[3]

But this sense of imagination is not of primary importance for us, since we are working not from the position of the *creating* imagination of the poet or painter but rather from that of the imagination active in *perception*. From this point of view (literally, one might think), the striking fact is not that we can 'imagine' what is not actually present (and perhaps never could be) in our perceived

1. Jeremy Bentham, *Principles of Morals and Legislation,* chap. 4, note 15. Many editions. In the recent edition of *The Collected Works* (London, 1968—), vol. 3.

2. *Nicomachean Ethics,* X, iv (1175a, 20–21).

3. Francis Bacon, *Of the Proficience and Advancement of Learning, Divine and Moral,* book II. His Horatian aphorism is from *Ars Poetica,* 9–10. (Many editions of Bacon; see, for example, *The Works of Lord Bacon* (London, 1879), vol. 1, p. 32.)

world, but rather that perception itself is intrinsically dependent upon the selective, shaping and sustaining powers which enable us to order our presented world into objects. Bernard Bosanquet, in a remark which reads almost like a commentary on what we have quoted from Bacon, makes the distinction clear.

> There is a tendency to think of imagination as a sort of separate faculty, creative of images; a tendency which puts a premium on the arbitrary and fantastic in beauty, rather than the logical and penetrative. But this, I take it, is simply a blunder. The imagination is precisely the mind at work, pursuing and exploring the possibilities suggested by the connections of its experience. It may operate, of course, in the service of logical inquiry, and of exact science itself. . . . The only difference is that when the mind is operating, for instance, not in the service of theoretical truth, but in that of aesthetic feeling, then it altogether ceases to be bound by agreement with what we call reality.[4]

The mind pursuing and exploring the possibilities suggested by the connection of its experience is no less 'creative' when it is working with what is given in sensation of its present environment or in the materials presented in works of art than when projecting those "arbitrary and fantastic" images we construct for ourselves in daydreams, in 'imagining' worlds that never were on land nor sea. But the immediate paradigm of the former function is *perception*, rather than *imaging*. For, of course, perception is not a passive process in which we simply encounter something or have it given to us. What is *given* in sensation and association is shaped, ordered by complex operations of selection, discrimination, extension, interpolation, and the like into *some-thing* perceived. So habitual, so pervasive, and normally so successful are these functions of discriminating and synthesizing attention that it is only rarely that we may find the world dissolved momentarily into a congeries of minimally organized elements which we refer to as visual fields, auditory stimuli, or streams of images—and even these are already to some extent discriminated. In fact, it takes a considerable 'effort of the imagination' to place ourselves in a situation in which our imaginative activity has not yet taken hold of 'experience,' that is, in a world not yet a world but simply a mass of undifferentiated feeling.

4. Bernard Bosanquet, *Three Lectures on Aesthetic* (London, 1915), pp. 26–27.

"The baby," says William James in a sentence which has contributed a phrase to the language, "assailed by eyes, ears, nose, skin, and entrails at once, feels it all as one great blooming, buzzing confusion."[5] But, of course, the *baby* could not make that observation, since to have done so would be to have already objectified the confusion: for us to put ourselves actually in this situation would require us to abandon the capacity to take note of it, to feel confused, to perceive a situation in which 'what there is' is confusion.

That imagination is an objectifying, formative, synthesizing function active from the lowest limits of perception accounts for the interest which terms such as 'form' have always had for aestheticians and critics. But for the present we are concerned only with giving some account of that quality of imaginative perception which we have called its freedom. Having rejected as fundamental, though not as nonexistent or trivial, the freedom of whimsicality, license, and fantasy (the imagination making "unlawful matches and divorces of things"), we must look elsewhere for illumination. To return momentarily to Farmer Clodhopper of Hardscrabble and the flowering thistle caught in the radiant sunlight of late afternoon, surely the beauty of the flower does not depend upon any perceived abnormality but precisely upon the *normality* of the activity of perception itself, but 'normality' not in the sense of what usually or most often happens in perception, but rather in that this occasion of perception is entirely satisfying *in its own character as such an act*—the activity in which colors, textures, shapes, translucencies and opacities, solidities and airinesses are at once discriminated and fused into *this* perceived object. That mysterious phenomenon, 'aesthetic delight' or pleasure, is nothing other than the joy of perceiving/imagining itself: one might say that the beauty of the flower is its perceivability and our pleasure in its beauty is the felt quality of our perceiving. From this perspective, the whimsicality of the imagination is a manifestation of its freedom to realize the potentialities of its activity without the intrusion of demands inherent in other, even closely related, activities. It is, in other words, a manifestation of its *autonomy*. To say that there are occasions in our relations with our perceived world in which it offers us

5. William James, *Principles of Psychology* (New York, 1890), vol. 1, chap. 13, p. 488.

such a realization of the possibilities of perception is to say that the world contains beautiful things: things the perception of which can be enjoyed *for its own sake,* things which are thus autonomously, freely delighted in—freely loved.

What will be found to be beautiful only experience can tell, provided that we understand by 'experience' the quality and the fruit of this orientation of the mind. In this sense, the quality which is beauty is as varied as the things that are beautiful, or, to put the matter the other way round, as varied as the individual and individually satisfying operations of the imaginatively perceiving mind. No more can be said of beauty in general than can be said of truth or good: one can only endeavor to specify the dimensions of an activity which will be satisfied in each case, but what will in fact satisfy them can only be revealed in the activity. That this seems to be particularly characteristic of beauty and the "art of thinking beautifully" derives from the nature of the function, for perceptive imagination or imaginative perception issues always in a *particularity* in experience. What is perceived is always *this;* what is beautiful is always *this.* There may be relatively reliable regularities—Farmer Clodhopper may confess to his family that "thistles have beautiful flowers"—but ultimately these are predictions we may confidently expect will frequently *fail* the test of perception, and that is the only test which, in this mode of autonomy, our minds will accept. Here lie many questions, but for the moment we are concerned only with that quality of free engagement with the imagined/perceived which differentiates—not beauties or beautiful things—but the sense or sensing of beauty of which these are the objects and this special quality of delight the mark.

I I

This account of the life of the mind as focused in the activity of perceptive imagination cannot, however, be judged complete without abusing words and arbitrarily restricting our data, for it can be argued that the 'works of the imagination' taken most seriously and engaging us most deeply are not easily characterized as beautiful or found to be spontaneously delightful. In fact, it might be objected that our imaginative life seems frequently to be a kind of perverse torturing of ourselves and of our imaginative powers.

Hardscrabble Farm offers not only the joys of beautiful things, but gripping dramas of pain and death, anxiety and terror. It is useless to pretend that Farmer Clodhopper's imagination may not be as firmly captured by the terrifying bloodlust of the weasel on the hunt as by the elegance and grace of the family cat preening in the sun. And the testimony of the arts in which the constructive power of the imagination has expended itself would suggest that its satisfactions are not limited to the enjoyment of beauties. It is a classic problem: this pleasure we take in what would seem to be inherently unpleasant. "It seems an unaccountable pleasure," says Hume,

> which the spectators of a well-written tragedy receive from sorrow, terror, anxiety, and other passions that are in themselves disagreeable and uneasy. The more they are touched and affected, the more are they delighted with the spectacle; and as soon as the uneasy passions cease to operate, the piece is almost at an end. . . . The whole art of the poet is employed in rousing and supporting the compassion and the indignation, the anxiety and resentment of his audience. They are pleased in proportion as they are afflicted, and never are so happy as when they employ tears, sobs, and cries, to give vent to their sorrow, and relieve their heart, swoln with the tenderest sympathy and compassion.[6]

Hume's solution of the problem, broadly stated, depends upon a development of the basic insight of any account of aesthetic and artistic phenomena in terms of the imagination, namely that the *mind enjoys its own activity* in the construction of imagined and perceived objects and that this enjoyment is the source of aesthetic delight and of the joys of artistic expression with which the artist's audience becomes engaged. In other words, what is enjoyed is not the unpleasantness of the object but the intense activity to which the mind is stimulated by the mode of the object's presentation and development, that intensity being in part a function of the initially powerful, passionate engagement. In effect, this solution places the problem within the scope of 'beauty' by arguing that what is admired and enjoyed is that the otherwise unpleasant or repellent object is 'beautifully' rendered, 'beautifully' done.

> [T]his extraordinary effect proceeds from that very eloquence with which the melancholy scene is represented. The genius required to

6. David Hume, *Of Tragedy.* (Many printings.)

paint objects in a lively manner, the art employed in collecting all the
pathetic circumstances, the judgment displayed in disposing them; the
exercise, I say, of all these noble talents, together with the force of
expression, and beauty of oratorical numbers diffuse the highest satisfaction on the audience, and excite the most delightful movements. By
this means, the uneasiness of the melancholy passions is not only overpowered and effaced by something stronger of an opposite kind, but
the whole impulse of these passions is converted into pleasure, and
swells the delight which the eloquence raises in us. The same force of
oratory, employed on an uninteresting subject, would not please half so
much, or rather would appear absolutely ridiculous; and the mind,
being left in absolute calmness and indifference, would relish none of
those beauties of imagination and expression, which, if joined to passion, give it such exquisite entertainment. The impulse or vehemence
arising from sorrow, compassion, indignation, receives a new direction
from the sentiments of beauty. The latter, being the predominant emotion, seize the whole mind, and convert the former into themselves, at
least tincture them so strongly as to alter their nature. And the soul
being at the same time roused by passion and charmed by eloquence,
feels on the whole a strong movement, which is altogether delightful.

Of course it is a condition of this possibility that the object shall
be known to be fictional. There is a "suspension of disbelief"—a
willing and *knowing* suspension. "The passion, though perhaps naturally, and when excited by the simple appearance of a real object
it may be painful; yet it is so smoothed, and softened, and mollified,
when raised by the finer arts, that it affords the highest entertainment."[7]
Though couched in unfamiliar terms and bearing the burden
of what may seem an antiquated psychology, this argument is not
too far removed from currently more popular modes of discussion
of the arts and their interest for us. After all, there are many theories which might not too unfairly be summed as celebrating "what
oft was *felt* but ne'er so well expressed," though of course 'expression' here takes on a considerable burden of meaning beyond what
Hume meant by it. But before we accept some version of this solution and endeavor to translate it into more familiar language let
us consider whether it is a complete account of our 'imaginative'
activity in the sense already developed.

7. Ibid.

III

It is a premise of our inquiry that 'art' and 'expression' are derivative in the sense that the life of the mind (better, that life which the mind is) in the activity and action of the imagination, while *manifested* in the arts, is not exhausted in them. That is, the imaginative activity of the mind is the ground of satisfactions the power and interest of which *account for* the arts but are equally manifest in our experience of the world and its objects unmediated by artistic capacity and expression. Thus the fundamental features of what captures and satisfies the mind ought to be clear in our imaginative engagement with the bloodlust of the weasel, the rush of the wind, or the all-embracing stillness of a winter night—and these as experienced and *felt* by those unable to read these words and therefore to be engaged by whatever poor vestiges of the smoothing, softening, and mollification of the "finer arts" they may retain. The question, actually, is whether the mind, functioning imaginatively, does not *constitute* for us a region of *emotional* experience, objects that *move* us *in virtue of* the form by which they are imaginatively perceived. Such an emotional world would differ in ground and actuality from one in which our passionate engagements with objects are given and then domesticated, so to speak, to the mode of the mind by the operations of art and the satisfactions of successful expression.

We may find a trace of such an alternative in words of Lord Bacon in the same passage from which we quoted earlier.

The use of this feigned history [i.e., poetry] hath been to give some shadow of satisfaction to the mind of man in those points wherein the nature of things doth deny it, the world being in proportion inferior to the soul; by reason whereof there is, agreeable to the spirit of man, a more ample greatness, a more exact goodness, and a more absolute variety, than can be found in the nature of things. Therefore, because the acts and events of true history have not that magnitude which satisfieth the mind of man, poesy feigneth acts and events greater and more heroical; because true history propoundeth the successes and issues of actions not so agreeable to the merits of virtue and vice, therefore poesy feigns them more just in retribution and more according to revealed providence; because true history representeth more ordinary and less interchanged, therefore poesy endueth them with more rareness and more unexpected and alternative variations: so as it appeareth that

poesy serveth and conferreth to magnanimity, morality, and delectation. And therefore it was ever thought to have some participation of
divineness, because it doth raise and erect the mind, by submitting the
shows of things to the desires of the mind; whereas reason doth buckle
and bow the mind unto the nature of things.[8]

Here is suggested a relation of the imaginative functioning of
the mind to the world the paradigm of which would not be *perception* but what might be called *idealization*. (It might be thought that
we have characterized 'beauty' as a kind of idealization, but that is
so only in the sense that it is an ideal *of perception*, rather than the
perception *of an ideal*, an idealized object. The possible confusion
of beauty with perfection will concern us again; for the moment it
is sufficient to note that it is a confusion.) But the kind of idealization most obviously projected in Bacon's words is a subordinate or
derivative function, just as the 'fanciful' quality of the imagination
is subordinate to and derivative from a more fundamental function
in the case of what is beautiful. The function of idealization clearly
suggested might be described as 'Utopian wish-fulfillment'—"submitting the shows of things to the *desires* of the mind." What we
need, desire, and want and cannot find in the world as it actually
offers itself to us we project imaginatively, thus enjoying in imagination that satisfaction of having everything our way which eludes
us in 'reality.' Happy endings (or painful disasters for those with a
sadistic bent), poetic justice, and the removal of confusion would
then yield an imagined world more satisfying with respect both to
its intelligibility and its agreeability "to the merits of virtue and
vice," that is, to the demands of human aspirations.

However, we might construe the proportionate relation of the
"soul" and the "world" ("the world being in proportion inferior to
the soul"), in a different and more radical fashion, one in which
the "shows of things" would be *imaginatively construed by the mind by
reference to ideas as* the *ground rather than consequence of experience*, so
that the mind in its imaginative function as well would not "raise
and erect" itself to something like divinity but *manifest* that "divine"
capacity itself. To see, to imagine the world as taking its shape from
intelligence is to view ideas as the *ground* of actuality, to construe
experience as ordered by ideas with respect to both intelligibility

8. See note 3 above.

and existence, to transform the world into the image of rationality as the theater, the scene, of *purpose* and *purposive* behavior.

The latter function is perhaps the more obvious. In effect it is the making operative in our imaginative life that special kind of final cause which is a purpose, an intelligently projected finality which requires that things do "buckle and bow" unto the mind. The world of behavior becomes purposive and thus a world of *action*—of passionate pursuit, of anxiety, of the agonies of failure and the mixed blessings of triumph, of sympathy and antipathy, of "sorrow, compassion, indignation"—in which beauty plays a secondary role.

What, then, of the bloodlust of the weasel? There is a well-known letter of Keats.

> I go among the Fields and catch a glimpse of the stoat or a fieldmouse peeping out of the withered grass—the creature has a purpose and his eyes are bright with it. I go amongst the buildings of a city and I see a Man hurrying along—to what? the Creature has a purpose and his eyes are bright with it.[9]

Here the "alertness of a stoat and the anxiety of a Deer" (as Keats says a few sentences later) have been imaginatively assimilated into the world of purpose, of endeavor, of action. It need not matter—imaginatively—that 'in fact' stoats and deer do not act or have purposes in the same sense in which intelligent organisms do; the dramatic force of and sympathetic identification with organic *functions* are not to be limited by such considerations. The bloodlust of the weasel can capture the imagination as exciting and moving when perceived as single-minded, passionate devotion to that purpose with which its "eyes are bright" and in the realization of which blood plays its part.

Such 'readings' are immemorially the stuff of our imaginative perception of the world. Hear Homer (in eighteenth-century dress) describing the action of Menelaus after the death of Patroklos.

> So turns the lion from the nightly fold,
> Though high in courage, and with hunger bold,

---

9. To George and Georgiana Keats, March 19, 1819. (*The Letters of John Keats*, edited by Maurice Buxton Forman, 4th edition [London, 1952], letter 123, pp. 315–16.)

Long gall'd by herdsmen, and long vexed by hounds,
Stiff with fatigue, and fretted sore from wounds;
The darts fly round him from a hundred hands,
And the red terrors of the blazing brands:
Till late, reluctant, at the dawn of day
Sour he departs, and quits the untasted prey,
So moved Atrides. . . .[10]

Bloodlust may also be differently perceived and differently move as one of those forces of blind passion, desperation, wanton destructiveness and sheer ferocity radically threatening to intelligently formed behavior.

Glad was I when I reached the other bank.
   Now for a better country. Vain presage!
   Who were the strugglers, what war did they wage,
Whose savage trample thus could pad the dank
Soil to a plash? Toads in a poisoned tank,
   Or wild cats in a red-hot iron cage—

The fight must so have seemed in that fell cirque,
   What penned them there, with all the plain to choose?
   No footprint leading to that horrid mews,
None out of it. Mad brewage set to work
Their brains no doubt, like galley-slaves the Turk
   Pits for his pastime, Christians against Jews.[11]

In either case what is perceived is interpreted with respect to and engages us emotionally by its relation to a demand made upon the "shows of things" by the mind, the demand that they be organized into movements to ends taken to be goods.

Bacon argues that this function of the imagination, as manifested in "poesy," "serveth and conferreth" to "magnanimity, *morality* and delectation." It would seem that—waiving for the moment serving and conferring—he was right, for what seems to be opened up to the imagination in what we have been exploring is not improperly called the *moral* world: the world construed imaginatively in the terms of action and choice and, of course, their negations perceived and felt *as negations or privations*. The much vexed (and

10. *Iliad*, xvii, 657 et seq. in the version of Alexander Pope.
11. Robert Browning, "Childe Harold to the Dark Tower Came," originally published in *Men and Women*, 1855.

vexing) questions of the relation of our moral and imaginative lives, of "morality and art," emerge here with an almost brutal simplicity, for in this function the mind *seeks* a kind of satisfaction in imaginative activity which the world does not spontaneously offer as it does (or seems to) in the delights of perception which are the occasions of beauty. As we have seen, the objects which thus capture the imagination are not those immediately ingratiating but those in which something is perceived and felt to be 'at stake,' and which therefore carry in them inherently the possibilities of frustration, loss, anxiety, fear, contempt and tragedy, as well as achievement, security, sympathy, triumph and "magnanimity." The bloodlust of the weasel, like all lust, is

> . . . murderous, bloody, full of blame,
> Savage, extreme, rude, cruel, not to trust;
> Enjoyed no sooner but despised straight. . . .[12]

But much the same natural force when placed in a different relation to purpose and function can be ennobled and respected.

> Though high in courage, and with hunger bold,
> Long gall'd by herdsmen, and long vexed by hounds,
> Stiff with fatigue, and fretted sore from wounds . . .
> Till late, reluctant, at the dawn of day,
> Sour he departs, and quits the untasted prey . . .

In contrast to the beauties of the world, these are objects for which we have a profound concern, with which we are emotionally engaged, which *move* rather than simply please in offering the realized possibility of a stimulation of our minds to imaginative activity unimpeded by any purpose other than the activity itself. Our relation to such objects is not that of freely loving or favoring, but rather that of *engagement,* for here the mind seeks imaginatively a demonstration, a "showing forth," of the experienced world as subject to (or to be subjected to) the demands of an ordering not given but demanded by idea and intelligence. It seeks in the imaginative constitution and order of things and events the purposive freedom of intelligence, the capacity of the mind to make demands upon experience that are not limited by experience. Fundamentally,

12. Shakespeare, "Sonnet 129."

then, what is felt to be "at stake" and what therefore *legitimately* and
necessarily engages us in this imaginative function is the enterprise
constituted by the presence of freedom in the world.

IV

The discerning reader will have observed that analysis has led us
into a paradoxical situation. The freedom, the autonomy, of the
mind as manifested in the activity of imaginative perception finds
in what is beautiful an object freely loved precisely because it con-
forms so perfectly to the requirements of our activity. The mind
here seems to find itself wholly 'at home' in experience. The 'sense
of beauty,' as Santayana says, is a realization of the "harmony between our nature and our experience."

> When our senses and our imagination find what they crave, when the
> world so shapes itself or so moulds itself that the correspondence be-
> tween them is perfect, then perception is pleasure, and existence needs
> no apology. The duality which is the condition of conflict disap-
> pears. . . . Beauty is a pledge of the possible conformity between the
> soul and nature, and consequently a ground of faith in the supremacy
> of the good.[13]

The suggestion here of a moral dimension to our experience
even of beauty (what Santayana elsewhere refers to as the "moral
dignity of beauty") is worthy of investigation, but what concerns us
now is the apparent discrepancy between a 'freedom' manifested
in creating or discovering a conformity of the mind and the world
and a freedom manifested in a felt *disconformity* between the "soul
and nature" requiring the "subjection" of one to the other. But
reflection assures us that the discrepancy is only *apparent*. In the
one case, the mind flourishes, rejoices in the *freedom of the imagination*, placing in the service of this function, so to speak, all its resources—refinement and richness of sense, the wealth of conceptual possibilities of relation and synthesis: in sum all the functions
of objectification. In what we have called its idealizing function,
however, imaginative activity *serves the mind* in its freedom to tran-

13. George Santayana, *The Sense of Beauty* (*The Works of George Santayana* [Cam-
bridge, Mass., 1986], vol. 2, pp. 166–67), part 4, sec. 67—concluding paragraph of
the work.

scend the limits of what is or can be given in our experience, a transcendence the imagination as such cannot literally achieve. In the first activity, the mind realizes its freedom in the autonomy of the imaginative function unencumbered by the attractions of sensation, the requirements of knowing and truth, or the standards of good and evil. In the other, the mind realizes its freedom by the purposive direction of imagination in the service of the freedom to idealize which *is* its proportionate superiority to 'the world.' Fundamentally, therefore, in one form or another this latter function issues in a felt disparity between what can be empirically grasped and what the mind can conceive.

The ramifications of the difference between these two dispositions of the mind in the constitution of the worlds and communities of the imagination will continue to occupy us throughout what follows. For the moment, what is important is the distinction as it emerges in differentiating our mode of engagement with those objects of nature and of art which are beautiful and those sometimes called 'sublime.' Disregarding for the moment the associations of the latter term, we might formulate the difference we have analyzed as the difference between an orientation toward the free *grasp* of the world in imaginative perception and one toward that free *assertion* (or that assertion of the mind which is its freedom) in which the mind's reach exceeds its imaginative and perceptual grasp. In the one case we are freely delighted and the object is freely, disinterestedly loved; in the other we are moved ('emotioned,' we might barbarously say) by the sense of our freedom, and the object passionately invokes our most profound interests. So starkly put, the distinction may seem metaphysically obscurantist, aesthetically simplistic and constrictive, and morally pompous—not to say overweening. Yet the difference between what delights and what moves—whether in a 'catharsis' of pity and fear, in dismissal "With peace and consolation . . . / And calm of mind all passion spent," or in the blaze of triumphant assertion in which Beethoven realizes Goethe's prescription of a "victory symphony" (*Siegessymphonie*) after the execution of Egmont in his play—is not obscure.[14] Nor does it seem plausible to consider these latter phe-

14. The references are, of course, to the concluding lines of Milton's *Samson Agonistes*, the closing scene of Goethe's *Egmont*, and to Beethoven's incidental music

nomena as extraneous moralizings somehow grafted onto objects aesthetically or 'artistically' remarkable for their ingenuity and taste. As has been said, much remains to be explored within and across this basic difference, but something like this is surely of the stuff of our imaginative experience and must be taken into account by any attempt to give some intelligible and normative articulation to it.

We should take advantage of the emergence in our argument of the notion of the 'sublime' as we have (re)discovered it to point out why it is that we are inquiring into the discipline of taste *and feeling*. A cultivated capacity for the orientation of the psyche toward aesthetic delight is complemented and completed by a disciplined capacity for passionate engagement. Both are 'natural' in the sense that both are grounded in the normalities of those complex functions we call our 'minds,' and both are also *cultivable* and *to be cultivated*: both are not only the products and consequences of 'culture' but *constitutive elements* of culture. Moreover, as the Kantian epigraph to this inquiry suggests, both are presumptively required of everyone as human excellences: even at this early stage of inquiry we may begin to understand that a psyche incapable of being imaginatively delighted and moved is so far lacking in the enjoyment of that freedom which *is* being human.

Reference to the "sublime" and the traditions of its discussion serves to remind us of another feature of our imaginative experience. We have placed some stress on the way in which what we have clumsily called the 'idealizing' work of the mind in imaginative function opens up to our experience of the world and of artistic expression the realm of morality not merely as a world to be perceived but as a world in which we have what is most important to us 'at stake' or 'at issue.' The importance of this fact and the difficulties it presents will be persistently apparent in what follows, but the traditional association of the sublime with what is 'infinite' or 'absolutely great' argues a relation to another conceptual or ideal demand implicating a different situation in which the reach of the mind necessarily exceeds its imaginative grasp.

---

thereto (Opus 84). Goethe's direction is "die Musik fällt ein und schliesst mit ein Siegessymphonie." Beethoven's realization of this direction, faithfully entitled "Siegessymphonie des Stücks," is substantially a repeat of the coda of the overture.

Earlier we referred to the bloodlust of the weasel *and* to "the all-embracing stillness of a winter night." When such an object moves—and can it not?—it does not move as do the defiance of Egmont, the agony of Lear, or the ultimate moral strength of Samson. The night—the starry heaven above—may be beautiful; it may be awe-inspiring and in that sense partake of the sublime; but it may also be intensely calming, inspiring a sense of security and peace which its *unimaginable* immensity might seem to contradict. "The effort after comprehensiveness of view reduces things to unity, but this unity stands out in opposition to the manifold phenomena which it transcends, and rejects as unreal." [15] Positively, that rejection is an *assertion* of the reality of our capacity to conceive a unity which is not and cannot be exemplified in the most comprehensive perception. As such it is an enjoyment, a celebration of the contemplative integrity of the soul, its independence of phenomenal presentation. Again such an account may seem obscure and falsely profound in virtue of its obscurity, but as Santayana suggests in the same context, it is simply the imaginatively emotional realization of what happens whenever we "transcend" the complexity and confusion of our experienced world by moving into realms of thought, of abstraction: we take up—if only for a moment—the position of a 'spectator of all time and all that is,' *feeling* in so doing the 'greatness of soul' which that position entails. [16]

Such, then, in cold outline are the satisfactions which the operation of the mind as ordered in imaginative functioning affords. They are modes of enjoyment of our freedom in activity as living creatures gifted with sensibility, perception, intellectual capacity, and practical disposition. They are thus, as activities and as complex adjustments of these various functions to each other, inextricably related to and yet distinguishable from our cognitive and practical lives—those livings which are knowings and doings. But precisely because they are not satisfactions of knowing or doing (and, like these, but in a specifically different way, also not of enjoyment unmediated by our own activity), they have their own norms or their intrinsic normalities. How these normalities can be

15. Santayana, *The Sense of Beauty*, part 4, sec. 60 (in the edition cited above—p. 151).

16. Plato, *Republic* 486 A.

developed into norms—standards by which we can undertake to function better in these satisfying ways—remains to be seen. Yet in a sense there is no more direct and simple "norm" for the recognition of aesthetic activity—the successful placing of our capacities in which the satisfactions of the imagination become realized—than the quality of that satisfaction itself: the disinterested love of the objects of our perceived world and the felt assertion of the self in our enjoyment of our independence on the perceived world.

2

NORMS OF TASTE
AND FEELING

Austerity/Objectivity

I n Lyon, 1883, George Santayana, nineteen, on his first visit to
Europe since childhood, spent a week "going every night to
the theatre where Sarah Bernhardt happened to be performing. It was a great treat: *Phèdre, La Dame aux Camélias, Frou-frou,
Adrienne Lecouvreur,* and *La Tosca.*" But it was not an unmixed treat.

> In listening to *La Tosca* . . . in the scene where Mario is being tortured
> I found the strain intolerable, and slipped out—being in the pit, near
> the door—for fear of fainting. This experience led me to understand
> that there is a limit to the acceptable terror and pity that tragedy may
> excite. They must be excited only speculatively, intellectually, reli-
> giously: if they are excited materially and deceptively, you are overcome
> and not exalted. The spectacle either drives you away, as it did me, or
> becomes a vice, an indulgence that adds to the evils of life rather than
> liberates from them. Sardou was not a tragedian; he was a contriver of
> sensational plays.[1]

Few readers can be expected to have had the opportunity to
encounter the work of Sardou as a playwright, though *La Tosca*
holds the stage in the operatic version—complete with torture
scene—of Puccini, one of at least three of Sardou's plays adapted
for use as libretti. But all of us have had comparable experiences.
Theatrically the problem is as old as the drama in the West: an
ancient biography of Aeschylus reports that at the first performance of the *Eumenides*—presumably in the scene in which the Furies enter like bloodhounds on the trail of Orestes—"infants ex-

---

1. George Santayana, *Persons and Places: The Background of My Life* (New York,
1944), chap. 14, p. 222.

pired and women miscarried," and the text seems to imply that it
may have been because of this intimidation of his audience that
Aeschylus found it advisable to leave Athens.[2] And, of course, it
would not be difficult to parallel this experience in all the other arts
as well. Nor is it confined to the arts: who is there who has not
found an actual 'rosy-fingered dawn' rather vulgarly sensational or
been violently repelled by the 'bloodlust of the weasel' when actualized in still smoking blood and guts?

But it will have been observed that there are actually two distinct
kinds of aesthetic (or 'anaesthetic') situations implicit in Santayana's
anecdote and his reflections upon it, situations differing markedly
in one respect, for one repels ("drives you away") and the other *may*
guilefully attract ("becomes a vice, an indulgence"). To mark this
distinction in words is not easy, though the existential import may
be clear. Explicit treatment of sexual detail may be disgusting but
it may also be attractively sensational. Nor should it be assumed
that the presence of such materials in themselves necessarily requires either of these modes of apprehension, thus ruling out possibilities of beauty and sublimity. The images of

> The fitchew nor the soilèd horse goes to't
> With a more riotous appetite.
> Down from the waist they are Centaurs,
> Though women all above.
> But to the girdle do the gods inherit,
> Beneath is all the fiend's.
> There's hell, there's darkness, there is the sulphurous pit,
> Burning, scalding, stench, consumption . . .[3]

may well make one wince, but the tortured, mad rage of Lear may
yet be felt to be rendingly moving.

---

2. This ancient (and brief) life of the poet is frequently found reprinted with
the text of the plays, as for example in the various editions of Aeschylus in the
Oxford Classical Text series, the latest being *Aeschyli Septem Quae Supersunt Tragoedias*,
edited by Denys Page (Oxford, 1972), pp. 331 ff. The only complete translation I
have found (the operative sentence is frequently quoted) is in *The Tragedies of Aeschylus*, edited by F. A. Paley, 4th ed. (London, 1879), where it is printed as an addendum
to the "Preface" (pp. xxxiv–xxxvi). Needless to say, some modern scholars dismiss
the whole story. See, for example, H. D. F. Kitto, *Greek Tragedy*, 3d ed. (London,
1961), p. 87: ". . . made boys in the theatre faint and women to have miscarriages—
a silly enough tale but one understands why it should have been invented."
    3. *King Lear*, IV, vi (l. 121 ff.).

These aesthetic phenomena—and both are aesthetic in the sense that they are phenomena of sensation, perception, and pleasure and pain—are instructive because they suggest in different ways the limits and constitutive conditions of perceptual/imaginative operations of selection and judgment. What is disgusting represents a limit of perceptual and imaginative function in the brutal sense that it is destructive of the possibility of perception at all. Literally what is 'dis-gusting' is what is ejected by and from the organs of taste: it is literally not tastable. In other words, in some fashion or other what is presented for perception and imagination as potentially an object or ingredient of an object is found to be incompatible with the operations of our functions of sensation, imagination, and feeling. At one extreme, such a rejection may be a physiological incompatibility, rather than a learned or 'cultural' response. Of course, the latter differ strikingly in their toleration of sights, sounds, smells and the acts and objects of which these are elements and concomitants. Most western human beings find the notion of drinking their own urine or handling human or animal excrement disgusting, while elsewhere the limits within which such objects and materials are found indifferent, tolerable, or even favored are quite different. And one need hardly belabor the varieties of reaction to the consumption of human flesh, to say nothing of that of dogs, insects, and, in some cases, any flesh at all.[4]

---

4. It is perhaps worthy of note that tolerances of this sort vary strikingly *within* cultures, or, put another way, that the same differences may be observable in occupational and social distinctions within a given tradition. They also vary with individuals. Cf. the shrewd observations of Shylock:

> Some men there are that love not a gaping pig,
> Some that are mad if they behold a cat,
> And others, when the bagpipe sings i' the nose,
> Cannot contain their urine; for affection,
> Master of passion, sways it to the mood
> Of what it likes or loathes. . . .
> As there is no firm reason to be rend'red
> Why he cannot abide a gaping pig,
> Why he a harmless necessary cat,
> Why he a woolen bagpipe, but of force
> Must yield to such inevitable shame
> As to offend, himself being offended;
> So can I give no reason, nor I will not. . . .
> (*Merchant of Venice*, IV, i [ll. 47 et seq.])

Physiologically, one may observe that beyond a certain intensity of light (which may vary from individual to individual), the eye simply ceases to function, usually by the activation of some protective mechanism which effectively rejects the intolerable sensation. In their grounds and therefore in their possibilities of variation these cases are very different. The difference is marked, somewhat imprecisely, by linguistic usage—we should hardly call highly amplified sound in a confined space 'disgusting'—and there are many things which in one context we might find disgusting which we are confident we could 'learn to tolerate' if necessary—but for a given individual at a given moment the result is that noted by Santayana: it "drives you away," thus effectively destroying any possibility of perception and imaginative assimilation. What 'turns the stomach,' burns the tongue, or cracks the ear actually interrupts any imaginative/perceptual activity in which it is encountered. For Santayana in Lyon, *La Tosca* as perceived object (and what else is it aesthetically?) ended with the torture scene: when it ended for the actors, the stagehands, and the stronger-stomached members of the audience is another matter.

II

Such responses or reactions are proximately *involuntary*: that is, while most of them are learned and may no doubt be unlearned, in a given instance for a given individual they are uncontrollable. But Santayana's account of his experience in Lyon suggests the possibility of another sort of response which is a *choice*—"an indulgence" which may in time ripen into a "vice," an habitual indulgence, a steady preference for one sort of satisfaction over against another. But what are the alternatives presented for preference, whether or not they present themselves as choices for good and evil, ripening respectively into virtue and vice? For a clue, we might return to one of our beginning points, the traditional distinction between our sensual life and our aesthetic life, between the pleasures of the perception of objects and the pleasures of sensation as such—the satisfaction of luxuriating tired muscles in a hot bath, the sweetness of ripe fruit, or the agreeable excitation of sexual stimulation. This gives a meaning to 'sensational' which is simple enough and yet carries with it complex and far-reaching problems of discrimination, to which problems of choice may be consequently related.

For we see immediately that there are here no simple alternatives of good and evil. It is not necessarily evil to luxuriate in a hot bath (though the vaguely pejorative tone of the verb exemplifies the difficulties of finding a neutral language for such satisfactions), enjoy sexual stimulation, or even to savor wine in its sweetness. But even supposing that somehow all these things—or 'the pleasures of sense' in general—are to be avoided as objects of choice, what is important for our purpose is simply that such satisfaction is *different* from the satisfaction of perception as such, the difference being that between the positive quality (pleasantness) of feeling or sense and the positive felt quality of the activity of perceiving as this is objectified in what is perceived, or (yet again) between an agreeable stimulation and an agreeable object. It is, after all, *things* that are beautiful, not sensations or feelings. What makes the distinction difficult to fix is that the 'thing' in this case is the thing perceived or, if one chooses to make such a distinction, the thing as perceived or as *object* of *perception*. And, since there is no perception without sensation, there is always the possibility that the two kinds of satisfaction may be mingled, confused or both. 'Taste,' in the sense in which it is our object of inquiry, is the ability to discriminate these different sorts of satisfaction in each instance of perception, or (since the *discrimination* is not an end in itself) the cultivated capacity for that kind of satisfaction which is the joy of perception and which, as such, excludes the alternative with which, given its necessary conditions, it may be so easily confused.

However, since our concern is the development and perfection of taste as a stabilized capacity for this sort of satisfaction, what we are concerned with is the *ability to cultivate* or *practice* the activity which has beauty as its object and objective. This requires a reflective ordering of our experience in an effort to make the discriminations required and stabilize the normality which is the satisfaction of perception. That is, it requires us to make determinate for ourselves what sorts of satisfactions (or dissatisfactions) are mingled in a given situation of sensation/perception and to reject—in the interest of stabilizing the satisfaction of objectivity—distracting satisfactions. The normality of what we have earlier called the autonomous activity of perception therefore emerges as a *norm*—a

standard, an end to be achieved, a ground for the reflective questioning of our experience of the world present to us in sensation/
perception in the interest of discriminating satisfactions from each
other.

As an end achieved, this norm might best be called simply the
autonomous *objectivity* of perception, but as it functions as a ground
of cultivating the activity in which this objectivity emerges it may
well be described as an attitude of reflectively effective *austerity*. The
choice of a term here is not easy, though perhaps also not crucial.
Like many of the terms we find ourselves using, its original meaning (Greek, *austéros*) was a sensible or perceived quality: the rough,
the harsh, the bitter, as opposed to the smooth, the bland, the
sweet. (Wine is austere or sweet—almost as we might say *dry* or
sweet.) Presumably, if one prefers or seeks out the austere the immediate point is not that rough is better than smooth or bitter than
sweet or that smoothness and sweetness are bad, but rather that
the rough, the harsh and the bitter, not being immediately ingratiating, must offer some form of satisfaction which differs in kind
from immediate sensory gratification and from which that gratification may distract. And the distinction is thus generalized and extended. Plato, discriminating among the poets admissible to his
well-managed city, invites some to leave, remarking that "we shall
make use of the more *austere* and less pleasant poet and mytholo-
gist," such a poet being allowed to remain.[5] The use of the term for
our purposes amounts to an extension of the austerity of the poet
and of his work to the austerity of a developing preference, the
'taste,' of the 'audience.' Proximately, therefore, austerity is the ability to remain undistracted from the satisfaction or potential satisfaction inherent in the activity of perception by given sensory
agreeablenesses *as such*.

But this norm is necessarily and easily extended to include the
distinction and "rejection" of other forms of agreeable and interesting "affects" which may distract from, be incompatible with, or
be confused with imaginative/perceptive objectivity. Among these
would clearly fall some which are *consequent* upon the emergence
of an object in the activity of perception, an object which in some
way moves or 'touches' us in virtue of its associations as a certain

5. *Republic*, iii, 398A.

thing or a thing of a certain kind. Here, for example, lie those possibilities of confusion of the beautiful not with the literally 'sensational' but rather with what might better be called the 'sentimental.' Degas is said to have remarked of the American painter Mary Cassatt that she was engaged in "painting the Infant Jesus and his English Nanny."[6] Justly or not, what is suggested is the possibility of a confusion of religious and domestic nostalgia with aesthetic satisfactions. And our language contains a variety of terms which— used pejoratively, as they usually are—suggest a range of qualities and characteristics destructive of or not infrequently confused with 'beauty': terms such as 'pretty,' 'charming,' 'sensational,' 'sensual,' 'sentimental,' 'sweet,' etc. And taking into account art, artistic intention and technique generates another range of distinctions frequently associated with these: 'clever,' 'slick,' 'contrived,' 'calculated,' 'trite,' and so on.

In this broadened sense what "austerity" requires of us is not so much the rejection of a kind of satisfaction or interest corruptive of aesthetic satisfaction as a discrimination and careful interrelation of different kinds of interests and satisfactions. Perception and imagination have many functions in the life of the mind, and correspondingly perceived and imagined objects provide many satisfactions, have many uses, and offer many sources of interest. That is, of course, even true of 'natural' objects; language suggests some of the possibilities to be discriminated. A 'beautiful' specimen or example of something—a 'beautiful' case—are usages which are justified by an analogy to the satisfactions of imaginative perception, for they celebrate that lucidity of a perceived, concrete, individual object in which our experience seems to coincide completely with what conception demands. But the fact that there is no contradiction in speaking of a 'beautiful example' of 'ugliness,' vulgarity, or sensationalism suggests that presented intelligibility in this form is not the same as beauty in the sense we have tried to determine. However, such phenomena are not simple and demand careful analysis: we must at least always be asking ourselves what the 'object' is. To say, for instance, that the anecdote of Santayana and *La Tosca* is a 'splendid example' is not to say that it is a splendid example of the sensational or disgusting, for the 'object' here is not

6. Gerald Reitlinger, *The Economics of Taste*, vol. 3 (London, 1970), p. 65.

the torture of Mario but the experience of that represented torture by a sensitive young man, so that if it is 'beautifully exemplary' it is so because it fits so well in its concreteness the demands of a conceptual differentiation of the "sensational" and the "tragic" or because it represents so well a characteristic turning point in the development of a psyche. And in that latter function it might well be imaginatively reshaped into an episode in another story or drama, a story of maturation (a bildungsroman?) in which its aesthetic status might be puzzling. Of course, such reworkings are the apparent stuff of many novels and other works of human art. Thereby hang many questions. As we have argued before, we do not lay aside our intelligence in our imaginative dealings with the world; the beautiful and the sublime engage the whole of the psyche: what differentiates them is the mode of functional engagement, and while the difference may be isolable in crucial cases, the balance of faculties and functions involved is so complex and delicate that discrimination is often far from simple.

III

'Art' in the broadest sense—the purposive, intentional shaping of the world resulting in the production of perceivable objects the existence and form of which seems explicable only by the presumption of purposive behavior—clearly complicates an analysis which grounds itself initially in the discrimination of the objectifying and idealizing functions of the mind dealing with its 'world' as given without such intervention. In part, this is merely an analytical strategy—though 'merely' hardly suggests the consequences such choices (and particularly this one) may have. On the one hand, such an analysis places the generic relation of the mind and its world in the forefront of thought, enabling us to raise questions of teleology in a powerfully broadened way. We need hardly remind the reader that Santayana—in the analytical mode of *The Sense of Beauty* rather than of some of his later considerations of art—found the sense of beauty to be a realization of "the harmony between our nature and our experience."[7] Kant's famous phrase with re-

---

7. For both sentences from Santayana in this paragraph see above, chap. 1, note 13.

spect to beauty, "purposiveness without purpose," is not badly ex-plicated by Santayana's "the world so shapes itself or so moulds the mind that the correspondence between them is perfect . . ." and the problems it raises are suggested by his remark in the same context that "[b]eauty is a pledge of the possible conformity between the soul and nature, and consequently a ground of faith in the suprem-acy of the good." We should hardly find such a conformity ground-ing a faith in the supremacy of the good in the world at large were it to be attributable to human shaping to achieve a conformity with human interests and aspirations, unless, of course, the "supremacy of good" is identical with the supremacy of man. But these ques-tions are not our present concern.

What *is* here our concern is to note that the world of artifacts and art, of institutions, communities, personalities, traditions, and cultures high and low is the world of the mind (*its* world) in the sense that the human psyche is *constitutive* of them, not, of course, by creation *ex nihilo* but nonetheless decisively. Aristotle, discussing the formation of habits good and bad (by tradition quaintly termed virtues and vices) remarks that habits "do not come about either by nature or against nature, rather we are naturally receptive of them [that is, habituable] and this receptivity is realized in habituation."[8] So we might say in general that our world is patient of purposive realization in habits, in institutions, in technique, technology and art, and also in knowledge, wherein (coming full circle) we can at-tempt to differentiate by a traditional distinction the natural world and the world of human culture and artifact. So there emerges as massive fact a world in which the mind finds itself 'at home' not only because the world is in some degree intelligible or beautiful but because it is a world the mind has made and in so making has made and continually makes and remakes itself, for this is the world in which any actual human psyche becomes developed, trained, habituated, educated, acculturated—shaped into a func-tioning intelligence, agency, and sensibility. Proximately this is the world in which we "live and move and have our being,"[9] for to live a human life is to live more or less socially, more or less intelligently, more or less purposefully, more or less problematically, to live *by*

---

8. Aristotle, *Nicomachean Ethics*, II, i (1103a 24–26).
9. *Acts* 17, 28.

culture, tradition, and habit and *in* a world mediated and constituted by cultures, ideas, languages, selves, and artifacts. Increasingly, we may think, even the physical constituents of our world,
those things with which we have biological and physical relationships, the things we eat, work with, sense, perceive, enjoy, and fear
are the incorporated constituents of this world, products of human
living bearing the perceptible marks of human hands, human design, human purpose, and significance. (The 'world' has become
increasingly 'the ecology'—a term etymologically revealing, since it
would seem to mean something like '*home* articulable in speech.')
For us, living among animals selected and purposefully reshaped
to reflect our interests and serve our purposes, landscapes explicable only by cultural geography, buildings, machines, texts, signs
and symbols, nature as physical, perceptible existence has become
a peculiar and relatively rare object which must be sought out, specially and purposefully experienced, preserved for future generations. The 'wilderness' wherein one can commune with nature un-
touched by human hand and mind has to be bounded, controlled
and protected; it has, that is, in a curious way itself become something like an artifact which exists, if not by human agency, at least
by human sufferance and design.

It is easy to view this process with apocalyptic anxiety or yearn-
ing for simpler days, with, that is, a *home*sickness for the days in
which our home was somehow more nature itself, or perhaps,
when we could feel more at home with her.

> Little we see in nature that is ours;
> We have given our hearts away, a sordid boon!
> This Sea that bares her bosom to the moon;
> The winds that will be howling at all hours,
> And are up-gathered now like sleeping flowers;
> For this, for everything, we are out of tune;
> It moves us not.—Great God! I'd rather be
> A Pagan suckled in a creed outworn. . . .

Those who rather enjoy being cosmically distressed by telling "sad
stories of the deaths of kings," more especially that king called Man,
will grimly rejoice to find that in order to make our present situation palpable we should have recourse to a text from which, with
some difficulty, we can recreate the nostalgia of a poet who died

more than a hundred years ago for an age which was for him a mythical antiquity.[10] But our present purpose is neither cosmic nor elegiac. It is simply to point out that 'art' or 'the arts' are at once constituents and products of this our world and therefore are subject to all its conditions. The consequences of this fact remain to be explored; at the moment we may note, without attempting to exhaust the problems, what perhaps is obvious enough. Art and the arts *exist* as the capabilities of individuals and groups, as functions and enterprises in and among human beings. They exist also as objects, artifacts—meaningful structures—and as modes and occasions of enjoyment, appreciation, understanding, expectation, and more or less shared and sharable goods. And all these modes of existence are parts of the life of communities, traditions, cultures, or civilizations—vague words in which we try to point to the interrelations of the many functions and activities which make up the stuff of actual human living. And of course these elements and their more or less systematic interrelations are constantly changing not only in the short term and the small scale but in the large. To this universal law the 'discipline of taste and feeling' in any actual shape is no exception: the search for such a discipline—a complex of *habits* of apprehension and judgment—is itself a cultural phenomenon as historically or culturally conditioned as are the techniques of arts and artists and the *works* which are both discriminated by and contribute to the formation of habits of apprehension and judgment. (Even our 'taste' in natural objects is no exception.) In fact, were it otherwise the discipline of taste and feeling would not be a problem, for there would then be no need to make choices, to consider alternatives, to deal with innovation, to reflect upon the variety of functions and values which emerge, in differing relationships, in any culture. Any actual culture or civilization is an alternative arrangement of human possibilities, the result of 'choices' made within the limits of circumstance. The culture of the individual is equally a choice, however actually arrived at, of capabilities, activities, and their inherent goods and evils, among which we may locate a discipline of taste and feeling with its appropriate satisfactions and achievements.

10. Wordsworth, Sonnet, "The world is too much with us, late and soon," composed in 1802 (?).

IV

In this perspective, an analytical strategy which begins by considering beauties and sublimities in nature has its importance as an
effort to abstract from conditions of purposiveness, of function, objectivity and value that are ineluctably present in cultural products
of the human mind and imagination. Minimally, it is to hypothesize
that aesthetic values are not reducible to other goods and evils pursued, developed and embodied in civilization. This is not to argue
that these values ante*date* the values of art and culture: in the experience of individual human beings in a highly developed culture
that is not necessarily the case, and appeals to the experience of
the human race would reduce the whole question to a matter of
fact rather than an analytical differentiation. The 'practical' problem for a discipline of taste and feeling is that of stabilizing the
integrity of a certain kind of discrimination and satisfaction not to
be confused with other, equally valid interests, satisfactions, and
appreciations which, in the cultural worlds in which we live, enter
into our encounters with the works of humanity and inevitably condition our understanding, apprehension, and judgment of them.
The works of man in all forms—from the simplest gesture of the
hand or the throwing of a pebble on the beach to the most complex
of texts, ritual performances, institutional arrangements, or Wag-
nerian *Gesamtkunstwerk*—can, do, and indeed must incorporate
something like the whole range of human needs, ingenuities, and
activities: moral, technological, economic, political, religious, cognitive, *and aesthetic*. The analytical effort to locate the integrity of
aesthetic value—in old-fashioned language, the irreducibility of
the beautiful to the true and the good—issues in a continual effort
at discrimination of values and goods in their complex interrelations as we encounter them in the cultural world in which we live
and move and have our being.

In our actual world this continual effort takes many forms—
debates of critics, manifestoes of artists, even in legal arguments
searching for "redeeming social value" in objects otherwise found
disgusting or morally corrupting, and so on endlessly—but its
proximate form in this inquiry is the habitually and reflectively discriminating attitudes adopted by individuals in their dealings with

objects. In fact, it is not going too far to say that we are engaged always in constituting different sorts of objects by the different ways in which we orient ourselves in apprehending and judging them. The world (for example) of a literate person—particularly of that peculiar sort of literate person who reads automatically, voraciously, and voluminously—is constituted in large part by objects which are literary objects—texts. But these texts are read for information, for entertainment, for insight, argument and truth, for moral reflection, for aid in 'making up one's mind' on a variety of questions, for literary distinction (beauty?), and because they engage us emotionally. Further, each of these (nor is the list complete) is a relatively vague and ambiguous purpose which may be and in practice is refined and sharpened. And the 'same' text can function in an act of reading which will satisfy all or most of these interests— sometimes simultaneously. In each act what is important in the text, how it is put together in reading—its elements discriminated, its form apprehended and estimated with respect to any of these interests—is different, so that, in fact it becomes in that act *a different object.* The active life of a reader is, viewed in this way, a kind of bewilderingly virtuoso performance requiring acts of discrimination and synthesis so complex as to defy easy understanding of how the capacity to perform them could have been developed.

We might pause to admire our own virtuosity, but the point of our analysis is not to admire but to develop and perfect. And the norm which guides 'developing' is the norm of refinement and discrimination which enjoins us to question our activity with respect not only to its complexity but with respect to the careful discrimination of the fruits that it yields. It is not going too far to call this discrimination a kind of *respect* for the autonomy of these diverse modes of apprehension requiring us to reject any confusion of the goods and satisfactions to which they are individually ordered. 'Austerity' here means a dedication to honoring an activity and its inherent satisfactions in their integrity and therefore by endeavoring to avoid confusion of its goods with others with which it happens to be associated in an actual occasion. One does not honor the nobility of a wine by praising its cheapness, though that is so far forth a good. If we claim honor for ourselves in so praising it, we claim it not for our taste but for our emptorial shrewdness. We may even honor this wine as representative of a noble tradition, but it is a dubious honoring which confuses that relationship with the faded actuality on the palate here and now.

In these simple cases (but reflection may reveal that they are not so simple as they seem), such distinctions may seem easy; but in the daily making of such discriminations which makes up our lives of enjoyment, frustration, and judgment they are harder to make and the objects less perspicuously discriminable. Nevertheless we attempt, even in our simplest (that is, least articulated, least analytical) judgments to make them all the time. The reader who enjoys a novel because "it reminds me so much of the place in which I grew up," but hastens to add either that it isn't otherwise a worthy novel or that just for that reason "I am in no position to judge it as a novel," is making distinctions of value, interest, and quality the grounds of which are in one sense so obvious as to be almost banal but in another way are very difficult to articulate and defend. And rare is the critic who can distinguish between the joy of finding a text exemplifying with exceptional clarity everything required by favored hypotheses as to how such objects are put together and the joy of finding them here *well* put together. In fact the possibilities of confusion seem almost endless and to multiply as sophistication and experience accumulate. Later we may endeavor to explore— with trepidation—some of these possibilities; at the moment we may point to two questions arising not with respect to the actual operation of the norm of austerity/objectivity but about its status as a norm and its relation to other norms.

V

We have come some distance from young Santayana feeling faint in Lyon in 1883, moving from what is intolerable to what is simply distinguishably different, from what destroys or corrupts an aesthetic apprehension to apprehensions sharing some of the same conditions (most notably the occasion and the data with which they are engaged) but are different functions issuing in other objects and satisfactions. It is therefore worth pointing out that these too have their "norms," and that the austerity which requires us to respect the norms of beauty requires equally that we honor the claims of other functions. The historian who says, in effect, "Such is the story as usually told; it is a wonderful story, gripping and complete in its own terms, worthy of a master storyteller. Unfortunately it seems not to have happened, and what does seem to have happened, while less satisfying dramatically, full of improbabilities and bungled eventuations, nevertheless has the merit of accuracy so far as historical inquiry can lead us." Such an historian is honoring the norms of his craft, and if we find his work less interesting in consequence it is not because he has disappointed us as historian but because we find the exercise of the historical imagination and what it discloses less satisfying to us than other functions. Gibbon, describing autobiographically a romantic attachment to which his father objected, says, "I sighed as a lover; I obeyed as a son."[11] So we might say, "I sigh as a poet, I obey as historian," but if Gibbon lost an agreeable association, what have we lost? The original story remains to delight us, once we can separate its poetic cogency from its 'truth,' and we need not give up whatever satisfying associations we have with the historical imagination. In fact, would we not be better human beings if we could say, "having rejoiced with the poet, I now rejoice with the historian"? For there is a discipline of historical inquiry as well as a discipline of taste and feeling. Nor is it impossible that their demands and satisfactions might in a given case eventually coincide; were that always the case our worlds would so far be always beautiful and moving as well as intelligible and instructive. As it is, however, our worlds are more complex and confused and our lives bewildering enterprises of discrimination in coincidence.

Norms are those guiding insights into the conditions of a given activity—a working orientation of the self and its capabilities—which are operative in our more or less self-conscious pursuit of goods. Such an activity is a complex organization of functions purposively defined, the organization being the governing condition of the realization of the purpose—the good. Austerity as norm

11. This famous sentence appears in the first published version of Gibbon's autobiography (1796) as edited by Lord Sheffield. Gibbon left several manuscripts from which Sheffield composed a text. The sentence does not occur in what seems to have been Gibbon's last version. Cf. Edward Gibbon, *Memoirs of My Life, Edited from the Manuscripts by Georges A. Bonnard* (London, 1966), p. 85.

points both to the internal form of that organization—requiring us to ask how it can be corrupted, degenerated, or so impeded as to be effectively crippled—and to its integrity or completeness as over against other functional organizations which are the conditions of other goods. But it will be observed that as we have formulated this demanding guide it presumes that there is a plurality of such integrities and therefore of goods, that they ought not to be confused if their several purposes are to be fully realized, *and* that their fruits are of such importance or intrinsic worth as to make that fuller realization itself important. There are, thus, always two questions about the status of such norms, questions which ultimately have to do with the status of activities and their goods. To recur for a moment to etymological beginnings, it is one thing to point out that the sweetness of wines is an impediment to the development of the appreciation of vinous possibilities and that the austerity of wine requires an austerity in a developing taste; it is another to insist that developing and ultimately possessing a sophisticated taste is an important or essential attribute of a person.

Of course, in a sense such a taste is justified by that to which it gives access by discriminating and constituting experienced objects, but pointing that out simply shifts the burden of the argument to the examination of the place of such *goods* in our lives. Austerity thus implicates directly a question we have suggested from the beginning of our inquiry: on what ground do we, in the words of Kant, "demand of everyone and assume in everyone who has any culture" both *taste* and *feeling*? The question is infrequently addressed, perhaps because for those who are in a position to consider it in virtue of possessing some 'culture' it is rather like asking why joy is enjoyed, enjoyable or, simply, joy. But what is really in question—and the reason the question is peculiarly relevant at this point—is the place of these activities and goods among and in 'competition' with others. We may say, with Hume, that "a delicate taste of wit or beauty must always be a desirable quality; because it is the source of all the finest and most innocent enjoyments, of which human nature is susceptible. In this decision the sentiments of all mankind are agreed," but though possibly sharing the sentiment, we might like some explication. For, even though we may be disposed to grant to Hume that "wherever you can ascertain a delicacy of taste, it is sure to meet with approbation," [12] we might ask whether general agreement in such a judgment accords well with the *practice* of mankind. It is possible that a refined taste is one of those human acquirements honored in general and *for others* rather more than effectively required of ourselves. And there are serious questions as to what we should demand of ourselves. It seems implausible that any special taste—such as a taste in wine or in the wines of France—is required. If that seems absurd, is a taste in the music of the West or of the German tradition or, for that matter, simply in music more plausible? Is a taste, perhaps consequently that of a dilettante, in all the arts or all the forms that beauty might take essential? Perhaps, at the other extreme, all that is required is that we have *some* sort of taste, but at that extreme the demand may seem to be approaching emptiness. Again, we are reminded that in any actual case these problems will have to be solved in given cultural, social, and personal circumstances and that in the necessary limitations of any life—cultural, economic, even physiological (what of the tone-deaf?)—they may present themselves as problems of priority, opportunity, and even as to what is to be sacrificed for what.

VI

Insisting upon the integrity, the irreducibility of the beautiful as over against (most grandly) the good and the true, does not require us to insist that they are wholly unrelated (or incompatible) and cannot form a harmonious system in a personality or an object. In the strictest sense, the question as to the place aesthetic activity should have in our lives is an ethical question, a question as to what sort of person we should endeavor to be, and therefore a question of *good,* and it is not to be wondered at that in general "the sentiments of all mankind" have concurred in suggesting that there is more than a casual association between the capacities to realize these diverse values. As to the mode and efficacy of their association there is less agreement.

12. The quotations are, of course, from *Of the Standard of Taste.* By "finest" enjoyments Hume means 'most subtle' (that is, 'refined').

The man that hath no music in himself,
Nor is not moved with concord of sweet sounds,
Is fit for treasons, stratagems, and spoils;
The motions of his spirit are dull as night,
And his affections dark as Erebus.
Let no such man be trusted.[13]

This seems to assert one mode of relation of aesthetic and moral sensibility, but while we might not wish to reject it entirely, we would probably regard it rash to conclude simply that a good, universal musical education would eliminate from the world treasons, stratagems, and spoils. Read backwards, however, the proposition may be more suggestive: that is, insusceptibility to aesthetic values may be some sort of sign of an insusceptibility to moral attitudes. And the rough converse of that suggested relationship, namely that lack of moral 'cultivation' profoundly limits, if it does not destroy, our ability to apprehend certain aesthetic objects, is also not implausible; in fact it might be thought obvious. All that we need to do, after all, is to reflect upon the changes in our own perception of the 'same' book or story from childhood to adulthood.

These problems thus remain to be explored, not only in the light of the norm of austerity/objectivity but in relation to other norms of taste and feeling. But before we move on in our outline of the normative functions appropriate to taste and feeling probably a word should be said about the bearing of austerity/objectivity on that powerful range of our aesthetic experience traditionally called sublimity. In contradistinction to the beautiful, the sublime is that which *moves,* that which engages us emotionally—that, in other words, for which a discipline of *feeling* is requisite.

The problem is already before us, for Santayana's devastating verdict on Sardou—"Sardou was not a tragedian; he was a contriver of sensational plays"[14]—clearly suggests that 'sensationalism' may corrupt or be confused with the tragic, the moving, the monumental and the powerful as well as, in another guise, it may be austerely rejected as the sensuous, the pretty, or the sentimental. Here we encounter the paradox, noted earlier, that what may destroy beauty would seem to be the life of the sublime—passionate

13. *Merchant of Venice,* V, 1 (ll. 82 ff.).
14. See above, note 1.

engagement, the sense of something overwhelming at stake or realized. Whatever one thinks of Michelangelo's *Last Judgment*, *Othello*, or Beethoven's *Great Fugue*, beauty and its related categories do not seem appropriate to them any more than to a lion's rage or to the madness of Lear.

Yet austerity in these matters seems equally necessary. Not for nothing do critics labor to distinguish the giganticism and pomposity of the architecture of the Third Reich from the monumentality, power, and dignity of the Pantheon or St. Peter's and find themselves bemused by the extravagances of Blenheim or Gaudi's *Church of the Holy Family*. Perhaps the operations of norms of objectivity/austerity emerges most clearly in situations in which there is no question of rejection of emotion—that is, in situations in which being deeply moved is felt to be entirely legitimated but not by the integrity of the object or experience before us. A melody which 'in itself' we would find neither beautiful nor moving may command tears as a patriotic symbol; whatever integrity may justify this response is not to be found in the melody but, if at all, in the quality of the larger event within which it functions. (Again paraphrasing Gibbon, we might say, "I wept as lover of my country, I sighed as lover of music," and the norm of austerity would seem to require us to find suspect any instance in which patriotic fervor and aesthetic merit would seem to coincide.[15])

Such displacement of emotion raises more difficult questions. It is not obvious that all orderings of experience which move deeply and powerfully are occasions of sublimity: first, because to the extent that our *actual* fate is at stake there is lacking that purposive ('willing') active, *imaginative*, free engagement with the world which is a mark of what we have called the idealizing function of the imagination, and secondly because not all emotional qualities—no matter how powerful and deep—seem, *prima facie*, to be sublime. Few emotions are more deeply felt than self-pity or despair. Can they or their occasions—real or imagined—be said to be sublime? Again the constructions of art which seem to aim at tragedy or sublimity

15. A case in point is that of the famous chorus of the Hebrew exiles from Verdi's *Nabucco*, "Va pensiero sull'ali dorati," which became a kind of anthem of Italian patriotism. For many Italians (and Italophiles) whom it brings close to tears it would be very difficult to discuss its 'musical' (in this case, of course, dramatic) merits 'as such.'

are instructive, though they introduce complexities into which we will not now enter. In Puccini's version of *La Tosca* we see (if we have managed to survive the torture scene) the heroine, Floria, crushed by the death of her lover (to save whose life she has killed his torturer Scarpia). But the suicide with which the opera ends is finally invested with an attitude not of despair but of defiance as she leaps from the battlements pursued by Scarpia's avengers. Even without the music the final dialogue makes the point.

> *Tosca* (to her lover):
> Dead! Dead! O, Mario dead! You? Like this! You, dead? (Weeping) Mario . . . (Shouting) Your poor Floria! Mario! Mario!
> [Simultaneously Scarpia's henchmen enter, shouting that his murderess must not escape. The final words follow almost immediately.]
> *Spoletta:*
> Ah! Tosca, you must pay dearly for [Scarpia's] life!
> *Tosca:*
> With my own! O Scarpia, onward to God (*avanti a Dio*)! [She throws herself into space.]

All this no doubt remains sensational and 'affecting' enough, but clearly also Floria Tosca ends with an *act* and that it is an act simultaneously acceptive of responsibility and defiant significantly changes the emotional tone from what it might have been had she simply submitted in despair: "Mario! Your poor Floria!"

These problems may, however, be elucidated by the recognition of another sense of 'objectivity,' that meaning in which it carries with it the notion of what is independent of "subjective" or merely individual, circumstantial, local elements and considerations, the sense in which 'objects' constitute a public, shared world all of us inhabit. This direction of thought would suggest that if what moves us deeply is to be thought sublime or tragic it must be in some fashion not dependent upon our actual circumstantial engagement with what is at stake but in the formal quality of such situations—in, one might say, the ratios and proportions of elements constituting situations of the sort that move. In that sense they would be, insofar as these proportions are the same for all of us, universally moving. How that may be remains to be investigated, but clearly it demands of us a kind of austerity in the estimation of our deeply felt responses—a disciplined assessment of feeling.

3

NORMS OF TASTE AND FEELING

Communicability/Catholicity

Inquiry has taken us far afield; it may be as well to remind ourselves that we began with something almost palpable: pleasure and pain—and, more relevantly, with satisfaction and joy. So far, what we have explored in the interest of cultivating our capacities for this satisfaction would suggest that the special character of the pleasure, the joy, consists in its *freedom* (in the sense that it is not dependent on desire or the realization of purpose in the world) and in its *objectification* (in the sense that this enjoyment is inseparable from the presence of a concrete object). It is hardly necessary to replicate all the subtleties and qualifications which these simplicities have suffered in the course of the argument or to argue again that they entail norms for the cultivation of our capacities. But another feature of this satisfaction seems equally obvious and, perhaps, equally puzzling. Bernard Bosanquet gets at the meat of the matter in a typically direct and challenging paragraph.

> [Aesthetic feeling] is a *common* feeling. You can appeal to others to share it; and its value is not diminished by being shared. If it is ever true that 'there is no disputing about tastes,' this is certainly quite false of aesthetic pleasures. Nothing is more discussed; and nothing repays discussion better. There is nothing in which education is more necessary, or tells more. To like and dislike rightly is the goal of all culture worth the name.[1]

There is here a subtle touch in the use of the word "appeal." Clearly it is not used in the sense of 'beg': in making such an appeal

1. Bernard Bosanquet, *Three Lectures on Aesthetic* (London, 1915), p. 5.

we do not "call for a favour . . . , make supplication, entreaty or request to a *person* for a *thing*." Rather to appeal in this sense is to "address oneself, specially and in expectation of a sympathetic response, *to* some principle of conduct, mental faculty, or class of persons," and it is literally in expectation of a sympathetic response that we address another, for what is expected is the same or similar *feeling* on the part of another.[2] Nor is the "appeal" indiscriminate: we address ourselves here to those who have taste, to another's taste, to those who are capable of discriminating aesthetic activity from other ways of relating themselves to the world, those who are, one might say, capable of conducting themselves aesthetically.

But while admiring such precision in the use of words we may be missing a more important subtlety. It would be extremely tempting in this context to think (however it might be expressed) in terms neither of supplicating or appealing but of *demanding* (if one is thinking of the person or faculty addressed) or *asserting* (if one is thinking of what is being enjoyed or judged. That is, an 'aesthetic judgment,' it is alleged, demands the assent of everyone and makes a claim—an assertion—about its object the validity of which is ('in principle') determinable by everyone. Here hang many issues which have much bemused aestheticians, especially in an age when it tends to be assumed that an 'aesthetic judgment' is a statement or a proposition somehow 'about' the world. From our point of view, however, questions of validity and adequacy are rather questions of the *authority* of judgment, and the use of the word 'appeal' thus serves to separate two sorts of questions arising when an aesthetic world begins to take shape. Such a world would be constituted by psyches in an aesthetic relation to their experienced world (freedom) discriminating valued objects in it (objectivity). That this is a 'public' world requires that the objects be commonly perceptible and their value communicable. Perhaps all that means is that *any* psyche constituted as is the human psyche can function aesthetically and any object constituted in that relationship to any psyche can be constituted by any other psyche. That is, aesthetic judgments—in the sense of feelings of a certain sort inextricably attached to objects of a certain sort—are communicable.

The complete articulation of the elements of this world—

2. *Oxford English Dictionary*, s.v. "appeal."

psyches, objects, and satisfactions—would establish a community which could identify itself either in terms of the objects shared or in terms of the psyches sharing them. The standard—the canon— for membership in the community and therefore for the satisfactions which are shared in it could then be located either in some 'classical' set of objects which would measure the 'taste' of its members or in some authoritative taste which infallibly discriminates these objects and therefore *is* the canon by which *they* are measured. In both cases a universality or catholicity is apparent: an object which universally pleases, a psyche taking up a generalizable—that is, a universally available—position. The reciprocity between these two modes of universality in the search for a standard—an authoritative object or an authoritative judge—may be observed in the elegant argument of Hume.

> But though all the general rules of art are founded only on experience and on the observation of the common sentiments of human nature, we must not imagine that, on every occasion, the feelings of men will be conformable to these rules. Those finer emotions of the mind are of a very tender and delicate nature, and require the concurrence of many favourable circumstances to make them play with facility and exactness, according to their *general* and established principles. . . . When we would make an experiment of this nature, and would try the force of any beauty or deformity, we must choose with care a proper time and place, and bring the fancy to a suitable situation and disposition. A perfect serenity of mind, a recollection of thought, a due attention to the object; if any of these circumstances be wanting our experiment will be fallacious, and we shall be unable to judge of the *catholic* and *universal* beauty. The relation, which nature has placed between the form and the sentiment, will at least be more obscure; and it will require greater accuracy to trace and discern it. We shall be able to ascertain its influence not so much from the operation of each particular beauty, as from the durable admiration, which attends those works, that have survived all the caprices of mode and fashion, all the mistakes of ignorance and envy.
>
> The same HOMER, who pleased at ATHENS and ROME two thousand years ago, is still admired at PARIS and at LONDON. All the changes of climate, government, religion, and language, have not been able to obscure his glory. Authority or prejudice may give a temporary vogue to a bad poet or an orator; but his reputation will never be *durable* or *general*. . . . On the contrary, a real genius, the longer his works

endure, and the more wide they are spread, the more sincere is the admiration which he meets with. Envy and jealousy have too much place in a narrow circle; and even familiar acquaintance with his person may diminish the applause due to his performances. But when these obstructions are removed, the beauties, which are naturally fitted to excite agreeable sentiments, immediately display their energy; and while the world endures, they maintain their authority over the minds of men.[3]

At best, however, the durability, the persistent admiration for any object—any classic—is only ambiguous evidence, a somewhat uncertain sign, of the operation of a generic, a common sensibility. It is better to hold, with Kant, that such a consensus is "only an idea." And as he argues, it is a con-sensus, a common sense, that is thus ideally postulated, for it would be as if the community had the same organs, functions, habits, and forms of perceptive imagination, so that all its members would perceive the same objects in the same enjoyed way. Clearly this would be a world without controversy, without disputation—for what would there be to differentiate one member from another? We would be in that position suggested by a remark of Aristotle's to the effect that if there were something that everyone takes to be good it would be so, presumably because to be a human good is to be functional as an end-to-be-realized and such an object would always, everywhere, and for everyone so function. (It is not accidental that one is reminded in this context of the formula for orthodoxy of Christian belief—*quod semper, quod ubique, quod ab omnibus*—what has been believed always, everywhere and by everyone. That too is a formula articulating the assumption that judgment is ultimately communal, shared.)

It is apparent that this world-in-idea would—paradoxically enough—be a world *without communication,* that is, it need not incorporate discussion, or any of the other sorts of efforts to share by our ordinary devices of communication about the world and our activities—language, gesture, directed imitation of behavior, and so on. Communication in this ideal world would be the shared enjoyment of objects commonly perceived and commonly judged. In

3. David Hume, "Of the Standard of Taste," from *Essays Moral, Political and Literary.* Many editions, many printings, frequently printed by itself or anthologized. The emphasis is mine.

fact, there would be no distinction between the activity of perceiving and imagining and the enjoyment of that activity in its appropriate form. Where perception is unimpeded and satisfying there is judgment both in the discrimination and synthesis of the object and in the enjoyment of that objectification. An empirical image or analogue for such communication might be the rapt, shared, wholly engrossed, enjoying, *silent* attention of an audience in a concert hall, a situation in which, as some performers testify about their audiences, one can almost feel them breathe with the music. In fact, such communication might be described as 'pure judgment,' a statement startling only because of our modern habit of thinking of the *expression* of a judgment in signs as the judgment itself, so that there can be no judgment unless someone says or somehow asserts something to someone. Given the realization of *a common sense*, moreover, judgment could not be other than it is and thus the judgment of each member would necessarily be the judgment of everyone: that is, it would be authoritative. So also would the objects of that world, perceivable by that common sense, exert a corresponding authority "over the minds of men," but authority would be a directly felt cogency, unadulterated with coercion and not requiring to be evaluated as a *claim* to be validated or rejected.

Short of such a perfect adjustment of object and perception on the part of everyone, there will be communication in the shape of efforts to articulate for others and for ourselves perception and what is perceived on the assumption and in the expectation that the mode of our perceptive imagining and what is thus perceived are possibilities for others. It is tempting to think of this move as an 'appeal' to the judgment of a community to which one ultimately submits one's private judgment. But a moment's thought will reveal that such authority is possessed only by that community-in-idea which is not available to us, and therefore it is better to think of communication as an effort to *create, sustain, and more fully articulate* an actual community which can at best be only a partial realization of the community in idea. The communication which is a normal feature of our aesthetic lives is thus primarily functional as an effort to record and reflectively formulate direction of attention in the interest of clarifying and stabilizing activities of perception/imagination and the worthy objects attended to in them. It may be that every such report or recommendation makes a claim

to be authoritative in the sense that it implicitly claims to be a report or recommendation for *rightly* attending and thus to be effectively related to the disclosure of a *rightly* judged object, but proximately it functions as a *hypothesized* way of attending, and the
hypothesis includes its shareability. Earlier we referred to a remark
of John Dewey's to the effect that criticism is best thought of as an
effort at the "reeducation of perception . . . an auxiliary in the process, a difficult process, of learning to see and hear." At this point
we might recognize the force of that remark in a more generalized
form, that is, all communication (whether recognizably 'critical' or
not) about our aesthetic activities and the objects to which they are
directed is educational or directive of activities of seeing, hearing,
perceiving, imagining and so on, functioning as an appeal in the
sense that it is an *invitation* to engage in these activities in a certain
way, a suggestion advanced as a fruitful hypothesis for directing
ourselves aesthetically. It is, in other words, an attempt to offer
means by which a "proper violence"—Hume's pregnant phrase—
may be "imposed" upon our imagination in the interest of accurate
discernment of "beauties and blemishes."

The consequence of all these rather abstract considerations for
this inquiry is that to have taste, to be engaged in the enterprise of
functioning aesthetically, to be in search of a personal "discipline
of taste and feeling," is to enter into a public world the public character of which is manifested in and dependent upon communication. It is, in other words, to conduct one's personal search for aesthetic satisfaction as a member of a community engaged in a
common enterprise. 'Communicability' as a norm of taste and feeling is the effective, the functional recognition that our individual
aesthetic sensibility and activity is developed, sustained, and stabilized in communication. What it requires of us is that we be able to
participate in communication with respect to what are taken to be
common activities directed toward objects in common and issuing
in common satisfactions. Taste as communicable is not merely an
ability to perceive in a certain way or to perceive an object of a
certain sort, it is the ability to communicate the attitude, the stance,
the organization of an activity of perceptive imagination or the relevant features of a perceived object to others and, conversely, to be
receptive to such communication. Simply put, what is required is
that those who have taste be articulate about aesthetic activity and

aesthetic objects. But to be articulable, taste must be organized, articulated. Those who have taste must be thoughtful, that is, *reflective* about it, and in that sense their taste will be an articulated, articulable system.

But all this anticipates, for in the actual development of any individual sensibility such a system is absorbed—so to speak—by us as part of the process by which we learn to see, to hear, to read and to select among objects those which we find peculiarly cogent and entrancing. It is only after such a lore of the arts and the 'cultural' world has become part of us through the learning of any language in which there will be embedded distinctions of kinds and qualities, of satisfactions and disappointments, through selective exposure to certain sorts of objects to which attention is directed in many ways other than by explicit linguistic forms, and through our 'unthinking' participation in shared activities of perception and enjoyment in the many forms of audiencing and doing which are characteristic of even the least developed communal life, that reflection upon the ways in which all these forms of communication can be made use of as resources for further exploration becomes itself an element in the enterprise of taste and feeling. Our personal, individual, reflective taste, that is, is grounded in and perhaps can always be viewed as some variant of a shared congeries of habits. Such a "discipline of taste and feeling" is in some degree the property of everyone in a given society; it is learned and it is taught, but learned and taught in that fashion pointed to by Protagoras when Socrates asked who teaches virtue, or, as we might say, who teaches habits of acceptable conduct, right and wrong ways of doing things? "Everyone," says the sage, "is a teacher of virtue to the extent that each is able to do so, and so it seems to you that no one is. So also if you were to ask who teaches the young to speak Greek, *you* would find no teacher anywhere."[4] The sources of our aesthetic capabilities and our sense of what the world of beautiful and moving objects contains are as varied and pervasive as the linguistic ambience to which Protagoras points; our world is replete not only with voices and words directive of our attention but of objects and ordered environments which, though mute, perhaps speak even more powerfully to a growing sensibility. And Protagoras's analogy

4. Plato, *Protagoras*, 327E.

to the learning of a language is suggestive in other respects, for while not everyone speaks Greek equally well and there are varieties of 'Greek,' nevertheless what we learn is the language of the country, of the time and the place, and it is only later that other languages or even the multifaceted character of *a* language become objects of reflection and potentially problems of conscious choice and individual orientation. And we know that despite comparable variables in the aesthetic and artistic activity of any actual community, what we acquire is always *a* taste, that of a time and a place, a given tradition, a conflation or confusion of traditions, a more or less determinate culture and civilization, skewed as it may be by the particular circumstances of our individual lives. From this rich and powerful context there is no escaping. We cannot confront the world or 'experience' as if no one had ever been there before, like Adam naming the animals in the Garden, simultaneously inventing both an ordered world and the language in which that order can be communicated and (prospectively) shared.

II

We are concerned in this inquiry with the problems confronted by individuals in developing taste and a capacity for disciplined feeling. At this point in the argument our contention is that taste is, or makes a claim to be, shareable, communicable, and that this claim entails that individuals be capable of "participating in communication with respect to what are taken to be common activities directed toward objects in common and issuing in common satisfactions." This claim and its entailed demands are not unique to the aesthetic world. In appropriately diversified forms they have their analogues in the enterprises of knowing and doing, the communities of knowledge and action. And in all these communities there tends to develop a tension, a confusion between two dimensions or functions of communal activity. As enterprises, purposeful *orderings* of human capacities for ends realizable by human beings they are universal in the sense that it is assumed that all human beings, as such, are capable of sharing in them, and also as orderings of our capacities not *given* with those capacities they require to be learned, transmitted, and practiced and are necessarily assumed to be learnable, transmittable, practicable. But as *purposeful* activities they must also be assumed to admit of being engaged in more or less satisfactorily or completely: they admit, in other words, of being done well or badly. (In fact, without such an assumption the notions of learning, of transmission, and of practice would be empty of content, for they would be exercises in trying to do something where there is nothing to be done or to become.) In communities actually engaged in these enterprises ('cultures'), there thus arises a double orientation. On the one hand they function to maintain an integrity of shared activity through the changing circumstances in which it must actually be undertaken by existing human beings. On the other they strive to identify, within the actual community so (imperfectly and perilously) stabilized, instances in which the activity undertaken has been, may have been, or is being more or less completely ('finally') realized. The one is a function of invitational initiation and the other of exemplary achievement and perfection. With respect to forms of communication (many, of course, not verbally formulated) which are instrumentalities of both these functions in the life of actual communities they make correspondingly different demands. The one demands that communication be in the broadest way conductive, educative; the other that it be authoritative, exemplary. From the point of view of the individual psyche (the stance we are trying to maintain), the first is a function of invitational direction: we are invited to orient ourselves, our faculties, in a certain way, to 'try something on.' In the second, communication functions to claim for a given orientation that it has realized or can or will realize more or less completely the end sought in this mode of possible human orientation. Here we are not merely *invited* to try, we are *expected* to find the trying cogent, compelling—more or less fully satisfactory of the conditions of the activity being practiced. In the reflective moment, which is a characteristic feature of an individual development with respect to activities of knowing, doing, and 'tasting,' these two functions are differentiable as two different ways in which we make use of and evaluate communications. In the first, we attempt to use them as guides for exploration, experimentation, discipline; in the second, we join necessarily (or find it impossible to join) in the celebration of what exploration discovers, experimentation confirms,

and discipline requires. But, if only because the end to be achieved
is inherent in, realizable only in the activity, so that learning and
practicing presume an orientation toward that end, all these processes and all communication about and in behalf of them are invested with both dimensions and can function both ways. As has
already been pointed out, the simplest assertion may be heard not
only as directing attention or suggesting a possibility but also as
claiming to direct attention rightly, to be, so far, 'true'—to be correctly asserting whatever modality its form carries with it. If only
that dimension of the communication is effectively heard, *all* communication is dogmatic, coercive—demanding assent and mechanical replication rather than guiding thought or other activity. But
this is to confuse what in this inquiry we are calling norms or problems of communicability and the norms or problems of authority.

But it is thus not surprising that when our aesthetic 'education'
has advanced to the point of reflection on its conditions and results
there should occur moments in which 'life' seems to reduce itself
to romantically agonizing dilemmas of personal freedom and independence. In such phases, the "rich and powerful" cultural context in which taste and a capacity for disciplined feeling emerge as
possibilities appears to us as limitation and coercion rather than as
opportunity and invitation. Fundamentally, these moments and
their concomitant emotions may be puerile, but they are nonetheless actual and perhaps even inevitable. An individual psyche feels
itself to be confronted with an organized world of taste, embodied
in canonized objects, authoritative voices, approved satisfactions,
standardized, conceptualized, firmly formulated modes of analysis
and perception, in all of which, as it may be said, one cannot 'find
one's self.'

> I, a stranger and afraid
> In a world I never made.

In such a stance not only are problems of communicability reduced
to questions of authority but problems of authority become occasions of confrontation: of relative strength and coercive capacity.

> . . . let God and man decree
> Laws for themselves and not for me . . .

> But no, they will not; they must still
> Wrest their neighbour to their will,
> And make me dance as they desire. . . .
> They will be master, right or wrong;
> Though both are foolish, both are strong.[5]

Such pseudo-heroic, pseudo-sublime moods and posturings have little relation to the problems of authority, as we shall have occasion to argue when we turn to consider that norm. For the present stage of our inquiry it is enough to note that if such moments are to be more than simply defiant rejections, 'enjoyments' of self-pitying victimage, they must emerge in the reflective construction of an individually articulated system of alternative activities, responses, and judgments which in its turn necessarily becomes a candidate for shareability and communication. All this is merely to say what should be obvious—that such disillusionments or radical dissents are themselves cultural phenomena, individual moments in a shared enterprise, that they are significant occasions in an individual development not as *mere* rejections or dissents but to the extent that denial rests upon some alternative affirmation, that 'heterodoxy' is not blank rejection of an orthodoxy but an assertion of another stance which in its nature makes a claim to be available to everyone engaged in the same enterprise. As phases in which we become conscious of a radical differentiation of our own orientation from that of others and are stimulated to its articulation for ourselves and others they may be productive and constructive— indeed sometimes profoundly so. Nor need they be—as in the expressions in which we have cited them here—emotionally catastrophic and apocalyptic, 'ontological' and moral crises. A chance remark, a momentary encounter with objects clearly highly esteemed by others but to us trivial or unintelligible, anything in our experience which seems to reveal that what we enjoy and think we understand is viewed very differently by someone else, any of these may serve to precipitate the realization that the world of taste and feeling is ineluctably *our* world, a personal world, as well as one we can share with others. The problem is to react to that realization constructively and urbanely. In this form the problem is not con-

5. A. E. Housman, *Last Poems* (London, 1922), XII.

fined to the world of taste and aesthetic function. F. H. Bradley, writing a preface to a work subtitled "A Metaphysical Essay" observes that

> [t]he man who is ready to prove that metaphysical knowledge is wholly impossible has no right . . . to any answer [in an "Introduction"]. He must be referred for conviction to the body of this treatise. And he can hardly refuse to go there, since he has himself, perhaps unknowingly, entered the arena. He is a brother metaphysician with a rival theory of his own.[6]

"Unknowingly," we enter the world of taste, unreflectively joining a fraternity, or, better, a humanity; in retrospect we may wonder why the discovery that this 'band of brothers' is not a community ideally united should seem intimidatingly destructive. Our alternative is not the abandonment of the enterprise—that would be to abandon in part our humanity—but its reflective reconstruction, tempering our exertions with the recognition that no such effort can, in the nature of the case, be final.

III

Let us return, then—perhaps with some sense of relief—to the problems of a developing and developed taste insofar as these are fructified by and fruitful of communicability and communication.

It is tempting, in the interest of simplification, to reduce these problems to a series of questions about 'criticism'—that is, 'talk about aesthetic objects and occasions' or even 'talk about art.' To do that would be to work in a recognizable tradition in which essays or treatises on the function of criticism, the office of the critic, and the criticism of criticism abound. (Consider, for example, T. S. Eliot, whose work includes essays entitled "The Function of Criticism," "The Perfect Critic," and "To Criticize the Critic.") But we are debarred from this route for three reasons: first because we have refused to confine 'communication' as it is here meant to *verbal* formulation, analysis and judgment; second because we have refused to confine the aesthetic world to the world of art; and third

---

6. F. H. Bradley, *Appearance and Reality*, 2d ed. (Oxford, 1906 [many printings]), Introduction, pp. 1–2.

because, as is in fact implied by the first two considerations, we are discussing a *function* which may be discharged by forms of communication which could not be identified as 'critical' by reference either to what they are ostensibly about or by the purpose to which, explicitly or implicitly, they appear to be directed. From this point of view, in other words, explicitly *critical literature* is but a small fraction of the communication which is aesthetically functional, and it is a small fraction not merely because much of this communication is not verbal (to say nothing of written or published) or because much of it is not about art, but because it is impossible to determine *a priori* what sayings, what acts, what observed reactions may function to direct attention in such a way as to affect aesthetic apprehension and judgment. It could be argued that 'in principle' *any* form of human interaction could so function. But, of course, the same might be said of cognitive and practical activity: only a fool would be willing to maintain that all the communication effectively influential in anyone's scientific thinking comes—and *must* come—from other scientists as such or from explicitly 'scientific' literature. In both regions, however, this might seem to be a trivial or impotent observation, since what we want to know is not that, given the proper circumstances, almost anything may have a consequence of a certain sort or have a significant role in a certain kind of activity but rather what those *proper* circumstances may be, what engagement in what activity generates relevance and fructifies circumstance. And once the matter is put that way, we see that a purposeful context in which what is said and done by others is hypothetically considered as consequential for what we are concerned to do and to be is at least as much something for *us* to provide as it is something to be communicated by others. It is a commonplace that what is heard and what is said or what is meaningful for me and what is meant by you are rarely identical, but perhaps what is less frequently observed is that while this is, from the point of view of the communicator, a problem or an impediment, from the point of view of the 'communicatee,' it opens up plentiful possibilities for the reorganization and reconstruction of 'meanings' for our own purposes. Of course, this may come about 'accidentally' (though not for that reason necessarily less fruitfully), as when we say 'something you just said reminded me of something else' or 'suggested to me, quite irrelevantly, what may be wrong about what I have been recently thinking about such and such.' Such expressions embody a minimal recognition of a distinction between what may have been 'meant' or 'intended' and what is 'heard' and used. And that recognition is important insofar as it points to the possibility of an art of *deliberate*, practiced assimilation of intentions and meanings by one center of activity—a mind, a sensibility—from another.

Thus there emerges the demand for a double discipline of communication in and with respect to aesthetic activity—one for those who communicate and one for those who are communicated to. It would be better to say that there is one discipline to be observed and practiced in the function of communicating and another in the function of making use of or profiting from what is communicated, for both are, of course, functions and roles which may be and are in fact in some degree undertaken by all members of the community. But what we have argued above would entail the conclusion that there is no simple symmetry between these two functions, if what is meant by that is that the problems can be reduced to determining on the one side what are the proper, the right, the useful ways of talking about these matters and on the other to determining how one identifies the right sorts of talk and can undertake to profit from them. At least, from the point of view of those who would profit from communication, the problem must be put rather differently: it is rather that of developing a capacity to profit not only from 'critical' talk which is ineffectively or perversely directed, but, more importantly, from talk which is simply *differently* directed or even not obviously directed at all. (Nor, of course, need any of this in fact be *talk*.) This problem might be formulated as the problem of how we can *make* communications function critically for us, regardless of their origin, their intent, and the other functions they might serve in other contexts and *for us* in other relationships. Lecturing critics on the proper performance of their art and amateurs on how to identify and read good critics seem hardly adequate measures in attacking *that* problem.

But all this is to anticipate. Clearly we need some formulation of the role which communication can fruitfully serve in the development of our aesthetic lives, for it is that formulation which may begin to supply some guidance for functioning critically in either sense or from either side. Of course, it can only provide *guidance;* like all other arts, the art of functioning critically emerges and is perfected in practice. And immediately we realize that we are not wholly unprovided in this respect—our whole argument has presumed and developed, more or less explicitly—the requisite conception. Have we not said that we are concerned with "what sayings, what acts, what observed reactions may function to affect aesthetic apprehension and judgment" and have we not labored throughout to give some differentiated meaning to the notion of "*aesthetic* activity and judgment"? We should therefore find it easy to amplify and refine the question: "what communications, how used, can function to affect the concrete realization of satisfactions inherent in our imaginative apprehension of the world?" The phrase "satisfactions inherent in our imaginative apprehension of the world" carries here a considerable weight of meaning, a burden deriving from the progress of our whole argument. To attempt to articulate it fully would be a redundant recapitulation.

But for our present purpose one emendation might be appropriate—would it not be better to say '*effect*' rather than '*affect*'? Why? First, because 'affect' might simply mean 'making a consequential difference' or 'having consequences for,' but what is wanted here is not just *any* difference or *any* consequence but that kind of difference or consequence which is instrumentally related to the inherent end of the activity. And there arise from this observation further grounds for a choice of terms. That is, secondly, because criticism as a mode of "communication in and with respect to aesthetic activity and objects" is not an end in itself, but is instrumental to, supportive of an activity which issues in satisfaction requiring no further purpose. This is not to say that "communication in and with respect to aesthetic activity and objects" cannot or should not be an activity carried on "for its own sake" but simply that insofar as that is the case it ceases to perform a critical function. And, thirdly, the primary function of critical discourse is to effectuate *satisfaction,* enjoyment, assertion. Fundamentally, that is, the critical enterprise as a whole is a function of guidance to the riches and the joys of the world of the imagination: in aesthetic activity as in conduct the pursuit of what is good is prior; avoidance and rejection of evil is secondary and, if made basic, morbid. This is not to argue that all criticism should be celebratory, that we should not wish to be deprived of our illusions, or that critical activity does not ineluctably issue in discrimination of value—explicitly or implicitly. It is rather simply to assert that all such discriminations are distinctions and differentiations within a world which is constituted by the possibility and the actuality of what can be and is valued—*positively* valued; entrance into that world and the exploration of it, initial engagement in aesthetic activity and the development of our taste are motivated by and realized in satisfying activity—purposive activity is intelligible and practicable only as direction of ourselves for the sake of something, in behalf of something worthily achievable. In this region, at least, "it has been well said that the good is that at which all things aim."[7]

These generic considerations have been rather easily translated into maxims or rules of thumb for the practice of critics—professional or amateur—and for the guidance of those who constitute their audience. It is, for example, not infrequently suggested that critics are at their best or most useful when they are telling us about what they find *simpatico*—what they like, those things in which they have found sources of excitement and interest. T. S. Eliot makes a characteristic observation.

> Perhaps what I want to say now is true of all literary criticism. I am sure that it is true of mine, that it is at its best when I have been writing of authors whom I have whole-heartedly admired. And my next best are of authors whom I greatly admire, but only with qualifications with which other critics may disagree.

And he goes on to suggest that the interest of criticism is really a function of the fundamental and enduring interest of what is criticized.

> As for criticism of negligible authors, it can hardly be of permanent interest, because people will cease to be interested in the writers criticized.

And these ruminations conclude on a note of self-denying disqualification.

7. Aristotle, *Nicomachean Ethics* I, i (1094a 3–4).

I do not regret what I have written about Milton: but when an author's mind is so antipathetic to my own as was that of Thomas Hardy, I wonder whether it might not have been better never to have written about him at all.[8]

What has been argued could also be summarized as maintaining that the most important function of criticism is not to issue a verdict, to praise or blame, reward or punish, elect to greatness or condemn to perdition, but rather to put us in such a position as to share the satisfactions thus judged. (In this respect we may be misled by the terms 'criticism' and 'criticize,' since they tend to become narrowed to the meaning 'finding fault with' or 'blaming.' 'To be critical' is, in much ordinary usage, to be doubtful or censorious.) Some critical writing tends to take on, from the point of view of the reader, of the amateur seeking guidance, a hectoring tone: we are constantly being instructed as to how we may have gone wrong in our enjoyments and browbeaten into assent to verdicts which in our hearts we cannot share or find rigidly limited. Criticism then appears largely as the exertion of an unacceptable and negative, an excluding and inhibiting, authority, and we find ourselves rather more depressed by the perils of the enterprise of taste than exhilarated by its wealth of possibilities. In the mellow Florentine October of 1877, Henry James, waiting for a friend in the church of Santa Maria Novella, passed the time by reading Ruskin's guide to Florence: *Mornings in Florence, Being Simple Studies of Christian Art for English Travellers* (1875–77).

I had really been enjoying the good old city of Florence, but I now learned from Mr. Ruskin that this was a scandalous waste of charity . . . I had taken great pleasure in certain frescoes by Ghirlandaio in the choir of that very church; but it appeared from one of these little books that these frescoes were as naught. I had much admired Santa Croce and had thought the Duomo a very noble affair; but I now had the most positive assurance that I knew nothing about them. After a while, if it was only ill-humour that was needed for doing honour to the city of the Medici, I felt that I had risen to the proper level; only now it was Mr. Ruskin himself I had lost patience with, not the stupid Brunelleschi, not the vulgar Ghirlandaio.

8. T. S. Eliot, "To Criticize the Critic," in *To Criticize the Critic and Other Essays* (London, 1965), pp. 23–24.

Indeed I lost patience altogether, and asked myself by what right this informal votary of form pretended to run riot through a poor charmed *flaneur's* quiet contemplations, his attachment to the noblest of pleasures, his enjoyment of the loveliest of cities. The little books seemed invidious and insane, and it was only when I remembered that I had been under no obligation to buy them that I checked myself in repenting of having done so.

Then at last my friend arrived and . . . we stood a while to look at the tomb of the Marchesa Strozzi-Ridolfi, upon which the great Giotto has painted four superb little pictures. It was easy to see that the pictures were superb; but I drew forth one of my little books again, for I had observed that Mr. Ruskin spoke of them. Hereupon I renewed my tolerance; for what could be better in this case, I asked myself, than Mr. Ruskin's remarks? They are in fact excellent and charming—full of appreciation of the deep and simple beauty of the great painter's work. I read them aloud to my companion; but my companion was rather . . . 'put off' by them. One of the frescoes . . . contains a figure coming through a door. 'Of ornament,' I quote, 'there is only the entirely simple outline of the vase which the servant carries; of colour two or three masses of sober red and pure white, with brown and grey.' 'That is all,' Mr. Ruskin continues. 'And if you are pleased with this you can see Florence. But if not, by all means amuse yourself there, if you find it amusing, as long as you like; you can never see it.' *You can never see it.* This seemed to my friend insufferable, and I had to shuffle away the book again, so that we might look at the fresco with the unruffled geniality it deserves. We agreed afterwards . . . that there are a great many ways of seeing Florence, as there are of seeing most beautiful and interesting things, and that it is very dry and pedantic to say that the happy vision depends upon our squaring our toes with a certain particular chalk-mark. We see Florence wherever and whenever we enjoy it, and for enjoying it we find a great many more pretexts than Mr. Ruskin seems inclined to allow. My friend and I convinced ourselves also, however, that the little books were an excellent purchase, on account of the great charm and felicity of much of their incidental criticism; to say nothing, as I hinted just now, of their being extremely amusing. Nothing is in fact more comical than the familiar asperity of the author's style and the pedagogic fashion in which he pushes and pulls his unhappy pupils about, jerking their heads toward this, rapping their knuckles for that, sending them to stand in corners and giving them Scripture texts to copy. . . . [A]s for Mr. Ruskin's world's being a place—his world of art—where we may take life easily, woe to the luckless mortal who enters it with any such disposition. Instead of a garden of delight, he finds a kind of assize court in perpetual session. Instead of a place in which human responsibilities are lightened and suspended, he finds a region governed by a kind of Draconic legislation. His responsibilities indeed are tenfold increased; the gulf between truth and error is for ever yawning at his feet; the pains and penalties of this same error are advertised, in apocalyptic terminology, upon a thousand sign-posts; and the rash intruder soon begins to look back with infinite longing to the lost paradise of the artless.[9]

We may well admire the wit and urbanity of this reaction, while recognizing that it raises questions about the complexity of taste and tastes and the place of art and aesthetic satisfaction in "life" which fall beyond our present concerns.

IV

But even when the critic is in love with what he talks about and the object is worthy of that love, when he is trying to convey something of his own excitement and satisfaction in it, there are pitfalls. One of these is evident in what James says of Ruskin—the tendency of enthusiasm and ardor to become exclusive. When we are deeply moved and excited by something it is easy to forget that there are other kinds of interest, other qualities of satisfaction and other powerful and charming objects. And inability to bring them into focus under the spell of what we are presently concerned with may emerge in the conviction that all else is paltry, worthless, and wrong. What we see and feel we see so clearly and feel so deeply that nothing else can be seen or felt. But there are other possible distortions or displacements. One recalls the shrewd remarks of Edward Gibbon on reading Longinus *On the Sublime*.

> Till now, I was acquainted only with two ways of criticizing a beautifull passage; The one, to shew, by an exact anatomy of it, the distinct beauties of it, and from whence they spring; the other, an idle exclamation, or a general encomium, which leaves nothing behind it. Longinus has shown me that there is a third. He tells me his own feelings upon reading it; and tells them with such energy, that he communicates them.

9. Henry James, "Italy Revisited," from *Italian Hours* (Boston and New York, 1949), pp. 179–83. (This collection was originally published in 1909; the essay in 1878.)

But there is a suggestion of difficulty in the next sentence.

> I almost doubt which is most sublime, Homer's Battle of the Gods, or
> *Longinus's* apostrophe to *Terentianus* upon it.[10]

Clearly this entails the possibility that the work of the critic may
become as interesting and perhaps even more interesting than that
which it ostensibly intended to illuminate and make accessible.
With respect to art one might say that the critic becomes, in this
case, a brother artist with a work of his own to offer, but the broth-
erliness may appear rather as competitiveness or, at best, distortion. It is, of course, not surprising that in historical, technical,
moral, or practical discussions of works of art we might easily become preoccupied with these alternative values and interests 'for
their own sake': in the case of many works it is fair to say that they
can only profit from becoming thus instrumental to some other
'redeeming' value (not necessarily 'social'), given their aesthetic
quality. But what is strikingly suggested by Gibbon's observation is
that it is possible for the *aesthetic* interest of the critic's work to dis-
place the aesthetic interest of the putative object of criticism. If we
have Longinus what need have we for Homer? Quentin Bell, having quoted Ruskin's description of an Italian landscape that had
been painted by Poussin—a description which ends with Ruskin's
question, "Tell me who is likest this, Poussin or Turner?—re-
sponds: "The answer is, of course, Turner, and this for the simple
reason that Ruskin has, with his pen, painted us a Turner."[11] He
has indeed, and so brilliantly that we may find other actual Turners
something of a disappointment. Ruskin's point is that Turner is
more "faithful to nature" than is Poussin, and Bell's is that that is
so if, as Ruskin does, one sees "nature" as Turner did. But it is, for
our purposes, more interesting that in Bell's account Turner and
Ruskin both emerge as *artists*. And it is interesting not only because
it may constitute a trap for critics and their readers but because
once more it reminds us of the complexity and subtlety of the phenomena with which we are concerned. Surely one would not want
to rule out the possibility that one work of art can be enormously
illuminating 'about' another; is one to quibble because one pur-

10. D. M. Low, ed., *Gibbon's Journal* (London, 1929), I, 155–56 (1762).
11. Quentin Bell, *Ruskin* (New York, 1978), pp. 24 ff.

ports incidentally to be a different sort of enterprise—a 'critical' one?

Turner himself in his will left two paintings to the National Gallery subject to the condition that they be hung "between" two (named) canvases by Claude Lorrain, clearly with some sort 'critical' intent, however ambiguous.[12] So we are reminded once again that we are seeking to delineate a *function,* and that objects, events, sayings, juxtapositions—intentional or accidental—may be thus functional, in an appropriate context, in unexpected, unanticipated, and yet powerful and important ways.

How, then, does this in fact occur? How can we, that is, so orient ourselves that the purposive context in which illumination may emerge from these diverse sources is provided by *our* reflection and *our* observation? How can we make our world potentially and actually a world of illuminating communication? The answer, of course, is 'in many ways,' so many that one is tempted to conclude that they cannot be exhausted or usefully described. But surely something helpful can be said about a matter of such importance.

We might begin by seeking some clues in what we have proximately before us, beginning with Gibbon thinking about what critics say and do and what consequences that has for his activity. Leaving aside, for the moment, what he finds *Longinus* to be doing, what he says suggests two general possibilities. Critics may *anatomize* or they may, we might say, *'encomiumize'* (or 'exclaim'), but while he finds the latter activity "idle" or fruitless—it "leaves nothing behind it," has no consequences for his activity—the interest it may have for us is that he thinks of this sort of activity as *"general"*—that is, as addressing itself to the whole "passage" which is the object of critical attention rather than to its "distinct beauties." Stretching what he says a bit, we might hypothesize that what impresses him about Longinus's criticism is that it does both of these things—that is, it expresses feelings taken to be powerful and moving but in

12. Turner's will and the so-called "Turner bequest" constitute a *cause celebre* in the history of English art. All the standard works on Turner develop this tangled tale, in which the provision mentioned here is only an episode. Thornbury (*Life of J. M. W. Turner* [1862, 1877]) actually prints the will, a fascinating document. The matter may be pursued in Finberg (*J. M. W. Turner* [Oxford, 1939, 1961]), Lindsay (*J. M. W. Turner, His Life and Work* [London and New York, 1966]), Reynolds (*Turner* [New York, 1967]), and further. The pictures are still hung as Turner wished.

such a way as to articulate what is before us in the passage in question. Thus Longinus exclaims and encomiumizes *in anatomizing*, making the connection between the 'anatomized' parts and the felt quality of the whole lucid and indissoluble for his reader. Such "exclamation" is not "idle" or fruitless because it functions to direct attention to what is *constituent* of the object as having a certain quality appreciatively felt. Longinus calls this passage "terrifying" or "fearful" (*phoberos*).[13] Had he merely referred to Homer's 'terrifying description' of the Battle of the Gods, he would have indulged in an "idle" encomium; what he has in fact done is to *anatomize the presented fearfulness*. It is true that he has done it in such a way that he begins to construct an *alternatively* fearful or terrifying imaginable object, another fearfulness, but for our present purpose that is irrelevant.

Generalizing, we may hypothesize that we have discovered two different and intricately related functions which critical language, concepts, and acts (including nonverbal acts such as pointing and leading) discharge, functions we may name 'anatomizing' and, for reasons to be offered later, 'characterizing.' The first of these directs attention to the perceived/imagined object as consisting of, constituted in and by a plurality of differentiable elements or parts, the other to the object as a whole or as *an* object having a distinct perceivable quality as such, a quality, a shape, an identity which is both demanded by and realized in its 'anatomy.' But it would be better to say '*claims* to direct attention to' or '*hypothetically* directs attention to' in both cases, and this for two reasons. First, for the obvious reason that the directing may fail, be inefficacious, either because we cannot in a given case separate out, find the parts or character claimed to be present or because they are not there to find. But we realize immediately that *functionally* these are one and the same. What we cannot see through some failure of our own or because of inadequacy of guidance is, for the purposes of imaginative perception, not there. In that sense, this first reason simply says that critical terms, formulae, concepts, and so on *are* as they *do* and that what they do is enable us to imagine and perceive. Second, moreover, they are hypothetical in the sense that they claim not only to direct us to what can be found but to things findable *and* significant

13. Longinus, *On the Sublime*, ix, 7.

for realizing the purpose of the activity in which we are engaged. They purport, that is, to direct attention to what is *aesthetically* there anatomically and characteristically.

V

This is a rich harvest to be gleaned from Gibbon's laconic remarks. But its wealth is concealed in its abstraction. We may restate it somewhat more concretely by explaining the choice of the terms we are using and, thus, how we wish them to be understood. Briefly, we have chosen them because they can easily be given an 'operationally heuristic meaning.' This fine example of explaining the obscure by the more obscure in fact simply means that they are terms which can be seen to refer to what we can *do* in the interest of *discovery*—in both the senses of that word, invention and disclosure, or 'creation' and 'revelation.' Moreover, we may hope that they may carry with them some sense of the sort of 'heuristic operation' relevant to *aesthetic* discovery. 'Anatomize,' etymologically would mean 'cutting up,' 'cutting apart.'[14] It is therefore clearly operational in intent, but, more than that, a moment's reflection on the practice of anatomists leads us to recognize that dissection is not mere or any cutting apart: it is a cutting apart in search of what can be taken to be the functional parts of the body, its parts as a body, not merely as a physical object that is spatially divisible. As Plato says, we want to cut "at" or "in accordance with the joints,"[15] in such a fashion as to separate the natural parts, the parts of a thing of this sort. If we are successful—if, that is, the operations we are directed to perform turn out to be functionally 'right'—an 'anatomization' will be in its result indistinguishable from an 'articulation.' But, of course, it is some sort of whole which is articulated, so at this point we encounter the other function which critical terms, concepts, formulae, and so on may have.

'Characterizing' is no less interesting etymologically and historically. Etymologically it is also an operational word, meaning to

14. I say "would" because apparently the verb form does not occur in 'classical' Greek. But the noun and analogues to it do. See *Oxford English Dictionary*, s.v. "anatomize."

15. Plato, *Phaedrus*, 265E.

strike so as to leave a scratch or a mark, so that one simple sense of
the Greek noun is an engraver. So to 'characterize' might be taken
to mean 'to impress upon something capable of receiving it an
identifiable shape or form.' This basic sense of the word may be
seen to survive in its use to designate a 'character' in printing,
where of course there is the predictable ambiguity as to whether in
any typeface a 'character' is what makes the mark or the mark that
it makes. And this easy connection with 'type' and 'typical' is also
inevitable (retrospectively), for what is impressed is a certain *kind*
of shape, form, or structure, something representing a type and
therefore typical. To 'characterize' is therefore to *attempt* to make
or give to something an identifiable wholeness, a *typical* shape,
form, or quality as a whole. Thus the tendency of characterizing is
significantly different from anatomizing and might almost be said
to be its opposite. But they remain functionally related: one may
'anatomize' a 'character' or 'type' and one may 'characterize' an
elaborated complexity as 'typical.'

What has all this to do with "aesthetically heuristic operations"?
Much. Critical expressions and acts in their characterizing function
are to be taken as suggesting, hypothesizing, proposing that an
identifiable shape, form or quality can be impressed upon or found
in what we have before us in the interest of imaginative apprehension of it as a whole adapted to satisfying (or failing to satisfy, of
course) the conditions of such apprehension. In effect they say
something like 'try putting what you have together into this sort of
structure, in this sort of way, and *an* object will emerge,' or 'try apprehending this as an object having this kind of form and quality.'
Because of the functional relation between parts and wholes reflected in the relation of anatomizing and characterizing, they do
more than simply suggest that this is a whole of a certain sort we
can attempt to put together imaginatively (indulging in what Gibbon calls an "idle exclamation"); for they also (particularly when
they lean in the direction of characterizing by identifying forms or
shapes) suggest what sorts of functional parts or elements are to be
sought out, since structures or shapes or qualities demand 'characteristic' parts. Even the simplest (that is the vaguest and least
'technical') single terms have this directive tendency. We do not,
after all, look for or expect the same elements ordered to each

other in the same ways in a 'landscape' and a 'portrait,' in an 'essay' and a 'story,' in (to become somewhat more refined) a '*sonata quasi una fantasia*' and a 'great fugue.' In effect what we are being invited to do by such characterizing language, even in these almost primitive forms, is to adjust our *expectations,* place ourselves as best we can on the basis of our experience and our practice in a position adapted to a certain exercise of imaginative perception. It might be thought that this function is peculiar to 'structural' or 'formal' characterizations, but reflection will inform us that 'qualitative' terms have similar functions. When we are told that something is essentially 'entertaining,' we do not adjust ourselves, that is, have the same expectations as to how to deal with what is presented as we do if we are told that it is 'harrowing' or 'moving.'

Surely there is much more to be said about these matters, but before we embark upon some implications we should recognize that what we have said entails a third function of critical activity. For even in the simple forms in which we have cited them critical terms inevitably tend to locate or place the objects to which they are directed in relation to other objects and other possibilities. The most obvious manifestation of this tendency is the use of terms in relation to each other. T. S. Eliot (to take an example we have used before) at one point in his critical career made much of a *pair* of terms which mutually defined each other: romanticism and classicism. Later he was to say that "as for Classicism and Romanticism, I find that the terms have no longer the importance to me that they once had," [16] but for us the significant fact is that they suggest that literary objects can be *systematically* ordered—that they (and other aesthetic objects and experiences) can be constituted into an ordered world in which individual objects and kinds have significantly different places, a *system* of possibilities, forms, qualities, and

16. See the essay cited above (note 8), "To Criticize the Critic," p. 15. One recalls his once famous announcement—apparently deliberatively provocative—that he was "a classicist in literature, a royalist in politics and an Anglo-Catholic in religion." In all these regions the 'placing' of himself, his opinions, and his works in a context of identifiable, 'characterizable' alternatives is clear, even though the context is not immediately or fully elaborated. Eliot says of this pronouncement that he should have "foreseen that so quotable a sentence would follow me through life as Shelley tells us his thoughts followed him: 'And his own thoughts, along that rugged way, / Pursued, like raging hounds, their father and their prey.'"

so on, a world in which they illuminate each other as much by their differences as by their similarities.

So we must add 'systematizing' to our list of functions performable by critical language, concepts, and acts. Again etymologically we have an operational word. The family of Greek words from which 'system' and its active forms derive carry the general sense of 'standing' (in the agent sense of 'standing up' or 'putting/placing') with the addition of 'with' or 'together,' so that 'systematizing' is to put together into some ordered whole differentiable wholes which then stand together. And, again, for us in this endeavor this is a critical function insofar as it serves to facilitate, direct, and make practically self-conscious an aesthetic activity which is nourished and developed by comparison—differentiation and assimilation—and issues in a repertory of possible stances with respect to imaginative activity such that we are able to order ourselves to the apprehension of individual objects with a realizable expectation of appreciating them in their individuality.

Formulations such as the one contained in the last sentence are always difficult and probably confusing, but one hopes that is because, in this case, justice must be done to a complex and subtly organized activity and to it both as it develops itself and as it takes shape at a given moment. To the rapidly developing aesthetic sensibility of a young amateur (in the amateurish novitiate, one might say) an aesthetic world expands in range and variety with bewildering rapidity. Objects, experiences, satisfactions, disappointments, puzzlements emerge as much as problems of assimilating and differentiating rather than as more or less self-contained moments of enjoyment, frustration, boredom, and confusion. Earlier we cited some accounts of such moments. They are strikingly different in their objects and circumstances, but they all share the presumption that sensibility is refined, enlarged and stabilized by *comparative* practice and reflection, a practice in which distinctions and terminologies serve as part of a process of refining and firming our abilities to see, hear and read with delight, awe, and exaltation. Critical activity in its systematic function is an expression of this effort at relating our bewilderingly varied experiences to each other, but it may well perform the additional function of directing us to further possibilities for which we are partially prepared to realize for ourselves in virtue of the relations suggested to what we already have and can do. Walter Scott's review of *Emma*[17] distinguishes different sorts of novelistic possibilities, expresses the excitement engendered by Miss Austen's expansion of his literary world, and anatomizes and characterizes her work. But for the readers who are thus invited to read *Emma,* it directs by its comparative, systematic anatomization and characterization a *readjustment* of expectation, a kind of experimental anticipation which may serve to put them in a position to appreciate what is alleged to be a new source of delight. And it is possible for them to take up this position because it is related to, while different from ones to which they are already accustomed. To the extent that it so serves it discharges the essential critical function. It says then, in effect, 'read this differently but in a way you can approximate from your existing practice of reading and something of a different sort with a characteristic quality will emerge.' And, of course, it also says (in this case) 'do *not* read this as if you were expecting the "Big Bow wow strain" for you will then be frustrated and confused.'

It is wearisome to reiterate that 'expectation' in this sense is not anticipation of something that will occur by itself—in that case criticism as adjustment of expectation would be as functionally idle as the "exclamations" of which Gibbon complains. Here expectation is the boxer's *stance* in defense—a preparation to receive and react; but it is more appropriate to think of an active preparation to engage in a certain kind of activity, more like assuming the right stance, the right equipment, the right adjustment of capabilities adapted to engagement in activity of a certain sort of form and quality. And by consequence a developed taste or a taste at any stage of development is a more or less *systematic* repertory of such "expectations," constituting a kind of mirror image of an ordered world of objects, artists, genres, schools, traditions, and so on in the many languages which criticism has elaborated and experience admitted. We remember Polonius testifying to the versatility of the players.

> The best actors in the world, either for tragedy, comedy, history, pastoral, pastoral-comical, historical-pastoral, tragical-historical, tragical-comical, historical-pastoral, scene individable, or poem unlimited. Sen-

17. See above, Prologue, Part One, note 10.

eca cannot be too heavy nor Plautus too light. For the law of writ, and the liberty, these are the best men.[18]

Our argument requires us to recognize that the virtuosity of the players must be matched by the virtuosity of their audience—as readers, listeners, viewers we demand of ourselves a comparable adjustment of interpretive skills, of appreciative orientations, of active expectations. Without such an articulated, systematized sensibility our aesthetic life is bound to be feeble and impoverished.

VI

Here we have encountered, somewhat unexpectedly, that feature of taste and feeling much prized but perhaps not much discussed—*catholicity*. "One has no taste if one has a one-sided taste," said Lessing. "True taste is universal, extending to beauties of every kind, but expecting from none no more satisfaction and enchantment than it can, according to its kind, provide."[19] We hope to find our aesthetic world a garden of delights: he who finds in it but one flower, no matter how enchanting, sees not a garden but a wasteland capriciously fertile, incompetently cultivated, and precariously redeemed. But before sententiousness overmasters us, we might remember that we are only saying once more that "the world is so full of a number of things / that I'm sure we should all be as happy as kings" and remembering that what there is to see and enjoy in the world is there for those who have eyes to see, now with the further recognition that seeing a varied cosmos requires an eye capable of appreciative discrimination and in that sense *systematically* trained. Our discussion of critical communication as a function in the development and articulation of a discriminating imaginative apprehension of the world (and therefore in the discovery and construction of an individual but sharable aesthetic world) has perforce been elementary, a feature which emerges in a tendency to concentrate on critical *terms* and *concepts* despite frequent reference to 'formulae' and 'systems.'

Even in this limited treatment, however, again we must recog-

18. *Hamlet*, II, 2.
19. G. E. Lessing, *Hamburg Dramaturgy*, "Introduction." (*Hamburgische Dramaturgie*, Erster Band, Ankündigung.) Many editions, diverse translations.

nize that these functions are not confined to our aesthetic life—the life of taste and feeling. Bosanquet, whom we have cited before on aesthetic phenomena, is equally lucid when discussing the functions of naming with respect to knowledge and cognition (taking, one may note, a side-glance at the world of art and its history.)

> To give a name is for civilized thought the first step in knowledge. It at once depends upon, and in a sense creates, a recognisable arrangement of things, qualities, and relations. Wherever new ground has to be appropriated, whether actually or in metaphor, the first necessity is to find recognisable points, by which, being named, we can observe and communicate our whereabouts.
>
> The value of this first step is only to be estimated by experience, now necessarily exceptional, of the attempt to attain knowledge without it. . . . Great discoverers are able to add fresh names to language; ordinary men content themselves with learning the meaning of those in common use. The limitations of popular nomenclature form the limits of popular observation. When we are brought face to face with a scientific classification and the terminology it involves, we are astounded at the blindness in which we had contentedly been living. Every yellow ranunculus we call a buttercup, every myosotis a forget-me-not, every large white umbellifer a hemlock; not merely as an epithet, but *because we really see no difference.* So in the history of architecture or of fine art, popular knowledge is confined for the most part to the application of two or three terms which have gained currency. Few people are able to observe without the help of names. It is true that there is something ludicrous in the tendency of common minds to cling to a name; in the insistence of an inexperienced art critic on superficial characteristics which happen to be nameable, when he ought to be looking into the special significance of a work of art; in M. Jourdain's delight at the discovery that he conversed in prose, or in the sudden zeal of Strepsiades for the correct employment of the masculine and feminine terminations. Nevertheless, the current censure of verbal knowledge is itself largely founded on ignorance.[20]

But Bosanquet would not maintain, nor can we, that anatomizing, characterizing, and systematizing are functions reducible to naming and classification. So before we go on to discuss the effective

---

20. Bernard Bosanquet, *Logic, or The Morphology of Knowledge*, 2d ed., "Introduction," pp. 7–8. The references are, of course, to Moliere's *Le Bourgeois Gentilhomme* and Aristophanes' *Clouds*.

meaning of 'catholicity' or universality of taste we should perhaps say a bit more about critical activity, its language, and its thinking.

First, we must reiterate that we are trying to discuss functions and that they cannot be uniquely located. That is, it is impossible to make a list of terms or concepts or activities which are anatomizing or characterizing naturally and always. Within a given systematic use of terms it might be possible—sometimes—to do that, but when approaching such an context (learning a critical language) it is necessary to assume that all terms and formulae can take on all functions. The notion of 'plot,' for example, may seem to have a structurally characterizing function, but in a given usage it may come to mean one complex which is nonetheless a part among many into which a given work may be anatomized. Santayana, an inveterate anatomizer, has 'plot' as an element among elements.

> The plot, which Aristotle makes, and very justly, the most important element in the effect of a drama, is the formal element of the drama as such: the ethos and sentiments are the expression, and the verification, music, and stage settings are the materials.[21]

In other usages to say that 'plot' is an "element" would be nonsense: it would be to say that the whole is a part of itself. But one may note in what Santayana says not only a common form of critical talk ('The plot is an absurdity, but there are several interesting characters, the sets are almost startlingly elegant, and the dialogue is extremely witty when it isn't pushing the plot along'), but the presence of other terms which seem to have systematic functions—'drama' and 'form,' 'expression' and 'materials.' We should not be surprised to discover that in this analysis there are 'beauties' of material, of form and of expression. (And, of course, in many presently fashionable forms of critical analysis to speak of 'expression' as one element among others is also an absurdity.)

We have already pointed out that 'characterizing' functions usually implicate 'anatomies'—to talk of a 'plot' in the sense of an 'action,' for instance, suggests that there are probably agents, incidents, complications, and culminations with all their concomitant

21. George Santayana, *The Sense of Beauty* (*The Works of George Santayana* [Cambridge, Mass., 1986], vol. 2), part 3, sec. 44.

parts. And such terms, if only because they are universal and therefore carry with them some suggestion of kinds different but related, have 'systematic' implications. Again, however, such functions are not given with the isolated terms. 'Drama,' for example, may in one language function to differentiate one kind of thing from 'novel,' 'epic,' or 'lyric,' all of them constituting 'literary' possibilities. In another, 'dramatic' may be a 'qualitative' term opposed, say, to 'lyrical,' and have no special restriction to 'literary' possibilities, so that one may find these qualities equally distinguishable in music, in painting, and even in 'nature.' What is surprising about the plurality of critical languages is that anyone with any experience in these matters finds it surprising.

But perhaps it is not so much *surprising*—after all, we are confronted with similar problems in every human endeavor, including science—as it is *disturbing*, for it seems to suggest that there is no correct or true anatomization, characterization, systematization. And that would in turn imply, since we have argued that these are functions in the guidance of imaginative perception, that there is no uniquely correct way of seeing, hearing, and reading and, since it is in these activities that objects become constituted for us, that the objects about which different critics talk are, precisely to the extent that their talk is functional in our apprehension, different. That is, they may have the same proper names and in appropriate senses the same physical or 'material' identity—Beethoven's Fourth Symphony, Michelangelo's *Last Judgment*, *Paradise Regained*—but as they take shape in imagination and perception they are not identical and may, on the contrary, be radically different. One of the most striking features of communication about our experiences of aesthetic objects is the sudden realization that others are not seeing, hearing, enjoying, or being bored by the same object at all, even though we have all, so far as one can tell, seen the same picture, 'assisted' at the same performance, or read the same book. Indeed, one of the functions served by critical language is to enable us to identify these different apprehensions and relate them to each other, with whatever consequences that may properly entail for our own apprehension or for suggestion to others. The ways in which this sort of experience and communication can occur are infinitely varied, so that any example is likely to be

misleading. One simple form, however, of this experience is that
in which we think we can detect an extreme limitation of taste, an
error with respect to 'catholicity.' Lessing says (immediately prior
to the quasi-aphorism quoted earlier), "Not every devotee is a connoisseur; not everyone who appreciates the beauties of *one* drama
or the excellent acting of *one* actor can therefore properly es-
timate the worth of all others."[22] This is perhaps the ultimate
case of limitation—one drama, one actor—but even if we say one
kind of drama or one *kind* of acting the limitation is obvious. Neither sort of case is in fact unusual. But perceiving the limitation
and taking steps to correct it requires that we be in possession of
some effective and communicable sense of a variety of possibilities.
Such limitations take many forms. There are those for whom opera
is singing and perhaps only *bel canto*. For them *Wozzeck* is a series
of unpleasant vocal distortions and *Tristan* a dreary desert of emotional ranting with a few oases of recognizable melodic power. But
these are relatively simple cases and do not raise the most radical
questions.

Ultimately these are questions of 'authority,' for even the least
developed critical language and activity implicitly makes a claim to
be right and true, that is, in our terms, to direct, organize, and
interrelate our imaginative activity in richly satisfying ways or, what
is for us the same, to a just appreciation of its objects. From our
point of view the suggestion of a radical pluralism amounts to the
possibility that there may be a plurality of worthy exercises of the
perceiving, imagining mind supportable by 'objects' which in other
senses we take to be the same, or, what again is the same thing, that
different objects may satisfyingly emerge for different 'minds'—
sensibilities, imaginations, understandings—under what are argu-
ably taken to be in part the same conditions of experience. Without
anticipating more any discussion of 'authority' it might be said at
this point that the notion of the real, the true, the finally-correctly-
grasped object is to be taken as a limit which we actively attempt to
approach rather than as what we must take as somehow 'given' all
along. In those terms, the experience of others, as critically communicated, is one of the functions in that active reorientation
which constitutes the development of our imaginative activity in

22. See note 19.

approaching this limit. But this *is* to anticipate. It remains at this point to sum up, with additional reflections, how we see that critical function and to say something more about 'catholicity.'

VII

The functional character of criticism is nowhere more interestingly observable than in those situations in which, as we said earlier, the function may be discharged by "forms of communication which could not be identified as 'critical' by reference either to what they are ostensively about or by the purpose to which, explicitly or implicitly, they appear to be directed. . . . It is impossible to determine *a priori* what sayings, what acts, what observed reactions may function to direct attention in such a way as to affect aesthetic apprehension and judgment." We may now amend that formulation by pointing out that one of the features of a disciplined aesthetic life is the ability to *make* use of a wide variety of "sayings, acts and observed reactions" critically or "aesthetically" even when we are aware that they were not so intended or when we judge that, however intended, they are not *directly* adapted to the task in hand. And, hand and hand with that ability, there goes the ability to discriminate communications which, while ostensibly critical and directed to aesthetic objects, *cannot*—at least for us—contribute to aesthetic judgment, to decide, that is, that they are irrelevant to *this* function. That is, part of a disciplined and thoughtful taste is a capacity to be discriminating about criticism; perhaps most importantly about critical talk and writing, if what is meant by that is the flood of discourse which is concerned with aesthetic objects and more particularly with works of art. We shall have to turn our attention more directly to many of these problems when we discuss 'art,' for the moment it is only necessary to give some concrete meaning to what has just been said, if only to show that it is in fact a vital feature of aesthetic development. In attempting concreteness, however, we must keep in mind that we are only trying to indicate the nature of the *problem* as it presents itself to a cultivated taste, not attempting to offer a prescription which will somehow solve the problems in every case. The questions 'how can I make use of this for my purposes?' or 'can I make use of this?' are, as we said earlier, not subject to *a priori* resolution.

One might begin, without attempting to be exhaustive or absolutely precise, by observing that two kinds of very common talk about art in particular tend to generate this problem with an urgency sometimes issuing in frustration, irritation, and something like discouraged abandonment. Nothing is more likely to irritate and discourage the amateur than the *technical* or *historical* talk to which one finds oneself so often exposed. (Alternatively, of course, one may be fascinated by the discovery that there are so many things to know that mere music lovers and readers do not know: secrets of the connoisseur, the artist, and the historian. The invitation to enter the world of those who know how it is done and what it is really all about is sometimes irresistible. Here again questions of authority rear their Medusa heads.) But it is too easy to dismiss 'technical' talk—talk about how something is done—as merely of interest to artists, performers, or various other sorts of producers, while recognizing, of course, its importance, its indispensability, to them. At the extreme, one might think the distinction easy to make. Consider, for instance, Cecil Forsyth's charming description—in the course of a discussion of the difficulties of making use of bells in orchestral works—of the machine devised at Bayreuth for producing the sound of the bells in *Parsifal*.

> The appearance of this Machine is somewhat startling. It is as if an amateur carpenter had been trying to convert a billiard-table into a grand pianoforte, and in the course of his experiments had left the works outside. There is a deep sounding-board over which are strung heavy pianoforte wires, six for each note required. In each of these sets of six three are tuned to the octave above. The strings are set in vibration by a broad flapper or hammer loosely covered by cotton wool.
>
> How little this sounds like a bell may be judged by the fact that at Bayreuth it was found necessary to employ at the same time four Gongs or Tam-tams, tuned to the pitch of the four notes. Even with this addition, the notes lacked the "ictus" (the *tap*) and the general buzz (the *hum*) of the real bells. A Bass-tuba was therefore requisitioned and made to play [along in notes of very short duration] while a continual roll was performed on a fifth Tam-tam.[23]

How all this must have looked in performance (fortunately out of sight of the audience) intrigues the imagination. In any case, it is

23. Cecil Forsyth, *Orchestration,* 2d ed. (London, 1935), pp. 54–55.

not surprising that Forsyth laconically adds: "This instrument has apparently now been abandoned at Bayreuth in favor of a set of Tubes."

On the face of it, this description might seem to possess no interest or relevance for a listener (however interesting and important it might be to composers, conductors, operatic impresarios, and performers) other than that possessed by gossip, for one of the sources of gossip is an interest in anything and everything associated with something or somebody of importance to us without distinction of its relation to that importance. To the devotee of symphonic music, of Wagner, of *Parsifal,* everything to be known about these objects is easily swept up into an enthusiasm without discrimination of its relation to the origins of their devotion. Talk of the laws of optics which explain rainbows (how it is *done,* so to speak) might well be described by the lover of natural beauty as *scientific gossip* about them.

But let us not thus dismiss even the Bayreuth bell-machine. Read not as an account of someone's ingenuity—in this case probably Felix Mottl—in solving a technical problem, but as an analysis of a bell tone (the pitch, the tap, the octave 'overtone,' the hum, and so on) it suggests further inquiry to sharpen the ear in the interest of that refined perception which is, in one sense, the basic condition of all musical apprehension. And by extension, the conception operating here of *every* tone as a complex which can be *anatomized* by the *ear* as well as by the engineer of sound is a functional notion of incalculable consequence. But the important point to note, of course, is that to serve these purposes Forsyth's account must be read in a certain way and that way is not that for which it is ostensibly intended. And all this says nothing about the possibility that these 'technical' analyses may not themselves point (as is sometimes alleged) to important 'aesthetic' or 'artistic' qualities. There are critical attitudes in which craftsmanship, virtuosity, truth to materials, and generally mastery in execution are important, if not the only qualities valued in art: what is enjoyable and enjoyed, what is appreciatively estimated. Put simply in our terms, it is a question of what I am being invited to *hear.* I may *hear* Mottl's ingenuity (or clumsiness) or I may hear a majestic, sacral *bell.* Both require complex acts of perception and imagination and the relation between them is problematic.

VIII

Similar problems are presented by what might be pejoratively dismissed, for aesthetic purposes, as *historical* gossip, but historical talk and writing about the arts in particular takes so many forms that it is difficult to do more than point to the general character of the problem. One example may suffice.

I go to an exhibition. (Thus I am already in a certain context; but let us waive that for the moment.) I see a painting: a splendid painting, spacious, luminous, with a flowing largess of movement and order. I find it impressively, solemnly exuberant. I am informed by its 'label' that the painter is one Francesco Solimena, Neapolitan (1657–1747) and that the painting is entitled *Saint Bonaventure Receiving the Banner of the Holy Sepulcher from the Madonna* (1710). Fortunately (or unfortunately), I have purchased a catalog and therefore can have all this 'explained.'

> This large painting shows Saint Bonaventure receiving the banner of the order of the Knights of the Holy Sepulcher from the Madonna, who is flanked on either side by Saints Peter and Paul and a host of angels. Three figures, probably members of the confraternity, kneel in devotion at her feet.

This, presumably, is what I am seeing, or am supposed to see, or what the authors of the catalog see, or what might or would have been seen by somebody in 1710. But there is more.

> The banner of the Holy Sepulcher on which this work focuses is the standard of an order of crusaders who wished to battle for the deliverance of this sacred site in Jerusalem, where Christ was believed to have been buried before his resurrection. To join the order, individuals had to apply to the Franciscans who, in 1342, had been entrusted by Pope Clement VI with the custody of the Holy Land. Saint Bonaventure, who here receives the order's banner from the Madonna, entered the Friars Minor in 1238, became its Minister General in 1257, and was named Bishop of Albano by Gregory X in 1273. He was also the author of a life of Saint Francis. His association with the Franciscans and the fact that he established special devotions on the part of this order to the Virgin Mary explains why he is represented here. It is possible that the confraternity which commissioned this composition from Solimena was part of the Knights of the Holy Sepulcher. The picture was initially in

Santa Maria degli Angeli, a small church attached to the Norman fortress of Aversa, which would suggest even more strongly its association with a military confraternity.[24]

And there is yet more, having to do largely with the dating of the painting (now happily established beyond doubt), its influence, the various copies or versions of it extant (one in England), and so on.

It is easy to reduce this sort of thing to absurdity. Clearly, for instance, it is potentially endless. The authors do not feel it necessary to identify further Saints Peter and Paul (or the Madonna, for that matter) but enlighten us about Saint Bonaventure by way of explaining his presence in the picture. But why Peter and Paul? Does not their presence also require explanation? They also see fit to tell us that Bonaventure was the author of a life of Saint Francis, but they do not tell us that he labored with great difficulty to maintain the integrity of the order Francis founded in the midst of intense internal and external controversy and that his life of Francis was written to supersede all others, which he ordered destroyed. Perhaps we would also like to know where Aversa is, how it comes about that it is a *Norman* fortress, whether there is some connection between a church called Saint Mary of the Angels and the host of angels in the picture, and so on indefinitely, that is, infinitely, if only because the historical fabric enmeshed is indefinitely extendable.

But read more sympathetically one may perhaps come to see that this gossip is more methodical, more purposive, than such caviling can reveal. One might read it, then, as an attempt (perhaps a rather clumsy attempt) to tell us what might have been seen by a member of the confraternity which commissioned the painting. Such a person might have *seen* St. Bonaventure in the same way that I see George Washington on a dollar bill, and what I am now told about Bonaventure is a crude sketch of the associations which would make that seeing more than a mere verbal labeling. To see George Washington is to see the Father of my Country, to see concretely integrity, courage, patriotism; so also to see St. Bonaventure might have been to see devotion to the Virgin, dedication to the Holy Places of the Holy Land and the rich heritage of Franciscan

24. *The Golden Age of Naples: Art and Civilization under the Bourbons, 1734–1805* (Detroit Institute of Arts with The Art Institute of Chicago, 1981), vol. 1, p. 140.

piety and heroism as an experienced present and past. Even if one
of those who commissioned the painting had to be told that 'this is
St. Bonaventure,' the impact of that telling would be vastly different for seeing than what it is—at least initially—for me. Do, then,
our catalogers not tell us more about Peter and Paul and the Madonna because it is thought that such seeings of them, such meanings, are still available to us, now, directly? (This may be question-
able, but it is not totally without foundation.) But the question
remains, for me, for us: can I, can we, ever hope to *see* before us
St. Bonaventure receiving the banner of the Holy Sepulcher from
the Madonna any more than a Siamese tourist in the United States
can hope to *see* George Washington? We can *understand,* perhaps,
that for others there are here certain powerful meanings, signifi-
cances, which are, for them, effectively incorporated into their
seeing and what is seen, but can *we* effect that incorporation? Here
there is no single problem—rather a whole bundle of them. One
might begin to think about the relation between the historical and
the aesthetic imagination, or even to question whether such meanings are *ever* properly part of our aesthetic experience rather than
burdens which may be borne by works of art functioning institutionally, socially, morally, as posters, as illustration, acts celebrating
occasions, persons, and objects no longer vital for us. Some shadow
of life, some faint glow of a sense that somebody was once moved
and impassioned about what is before me may be recovered, but
for us there are other occasions, other symbols, other associations
we *can* vitally share that in their turn will become, for others, abstract meanings and attenuated feelings. Are we to argue that time
and circumstance have thus *happily* purged from the work these
irrelevant encumbrances so that we can see certain pure aesthetic
values, see the painting *as* a painting, *as* an aesthetic object? From
this point of view our gossipy historians are not merely irrelevant,
they are subversive; since they would have us get engaged in the
implausible and counterproductive enterprise of becoming someone else.

Nor is this set of puzzles confined to the visual arts—or indeed
to art. We may read with some pleasure the novels of Disraeli, but
what effective use can we make in reading of the keys to the actual
identity of the characters sometimes provided in editions of them.
We may *understand* that 'Lord Roehampton' is 'really' Lord Palmer-

ston or 'Zenobia' Lady Jersey,[25] but can any amount of information
about these people invest our reading with the quality it would
have had for readers who shared with Disraeli the social and political world in which Lord Palmerston and Lady Jersey actually fig-
ured? We may be told and even believe that Beethoven heard in
his *Third Symphony* the revolutionary apostle Napoleon, the bringer
to an oppressed Europe of the practical ideals of liberty, equality,
and fraternity. But insofar as Napoleon is alive for us he is likely to
be a very different figure: what are *we* to hear? But perhaps Beethoven's ultimate choice of a designation for his symphony may
help us: "Heroic Symphony, composed to celebrate the memory of
a great man." Great men and heroic deeds we may not only understand but hear: is it an accident that performances of the *Eroica*
served as commemorations and purgations of feeling on the death
of Franklin Roosevelt? But the puzzles remain, for we would not
like to conclude that even for us, a certain generation at a certain
time, what the *Eroica* is 'about' is *a* death, *a* hero, *our* hero's death,
any more than we might like to admit that "Siegfried's Death Music" from *Götterdämmerung* is to be identified in its significance with
its playing on the Berlin radio prior to the announcement of the
death of Adolf Hitler.

Nevertheless, when Beethoven (or any other 'critic') tells us that
this is a *heroic* symphony, he is performing one of those characterizing acts which are so important in the adjustment of our expectations. So also, when we are told about Bonaventure and the
Knights of the Holy Sepulcher we are, in effect, having the painting *characterized* for us in a way which we can understand *and* make
use of. It is being suggested to us that this is no trivial occasion, but
one we may expect to be invested with a certain kind of emotional
weight. We may then so adjust our expectations so far as we can
and find its special, almost surprising quality of solemn, spacious
exuberance a joy. It is not that therefore we will inevitably find it
so, but rather that we may manage better to take up that imagina-
tive/perceptive stance in which these qualities may be manifested.
In this way, at least, historical talk, appropriately *used,* can present
us with problems we can undertake to solve aesthetically, can point
to possibilities which may become actualities for us. But while we

25. The novel referred to is *Endymion* (1880).

may have said enough for our present limited purpose, clearly we
have barely begun to deal with the questions raised.

IX

Meanwhile, what of *catholicity*? Essentially, as we have argued above,
catholicity is simply the requirement that our taste be a functional
system of anatomizing and characterizing abilities. We may note, in
this immediate context, that 'history' is, with respect at least to the
arts, one of the more powerful ways in which we attempt to system-
atize. It has become a commonplace, for instance, to point out that
every music-lover has a kind of 'historical ear' which makes it possible to attune oneself to extraordinarily different kinds of music-
making and musical artifacts. Without this sort of flexibility of apprehension our musical experience would indeed be an impossible
insensitivity in which, at an extreme, we would hear—or try to
hear—everything in the same way, with the result that much, if not
most, of what we heard would be unintelligible. But it would be
better to say 'unhearable.' And the same may be said of the other
arts. If we insist on reading Milton as if he were writing in the same
language and with the same structural assumptions as Tennyson or
T. S. Eliot we make difficulties for ourselves which we are likely to
end up imputing to 'Milton' with disastrous results for appreciation. Such adjustments of expectation are obvious also in the visual
arts, and these also are frequently expressed systematically in historical terms. Locating works in schools, traditions, styles and periods has or may have the functional consequence of enabling us
to attune ourselves so that, in the words of Lessing, we can derive
from each work no more—and no less—"satisfaction and enchantment than it can, according to its kind, provide." But there are
traps in this form of systematizing as in all others. To these again
we shall return—they are partly problems of authority. For the
present we may simply suggest that perhaps it is important to do
our historical systematizing in its functional form *backwards* as well
as forwards and sideways. That is, in our actual aesthetic worlds we
find it impossible to avoid having our relationship to works of a
given style or period as much affected by what, historically, is consequent upon them as by what is antecedent or contemporaneous.
As T. S. Eliot put it in his once-famous essay "Tradition and the

Individual Talent," we do not find it "preposterous that the past should be altered by the present as much as the present is directed by the past." *For us* it is impossible to read Dickens as if we had never read Faulkner or Henry James, to listen to Mozart as if Beethoven and Richard Strauss and Stravinsky had never composed, to see Goya and Cezanne as if we did not know Picasso.

It follows that catholicity entails or includes an openness to a reordering of that system which is our taste as new possibilities manifest themselves for us. As Eliot says, when novelty supervenes "the *whole* existing order must be, if ever so slightly, altered; and so the relations, proportions, values of each work towards the whole are readjusted. . . ."[26] But "novelty" in the development of an individual taste is of course what is new to *me*, what is new in my history, not in 'history.'

A striking example of the effect of novelty in this sense upon a young and voracious sensibility is furnished by Ruskin, whom we last encountered in Florence at twenty-six rejoicing in his newfound ability to appreciate Giotto. About a month later (July, 1845) he sent his father a letter[27] including an elaborated scheme of painting and painters. (It is only fair to point out that all of this was in preparation for a book which eventually became *Modern Painters*.) The scheme consists of four "classes," each with what is apparently a ranked list of individual painters. Class 1st is "Pure Religious Art. The School of Love." and is headed by Fra Angelico (who, however, "forms a class by himself—he is not an *artist*, properly so called, but an inspired saint") and Perugino. Class 2nd (General Perception of Nature human and divine, accompanied by more or less religious feeling. The School of the *Great* Men. The School of Intellect.") begins with "Michael Angelo" and Giotto. Class 3 is "The School of *Painting* as such." (Titian, Giorgione et al.) and Class 4th the "School of Errors and Vices" headed by "Raffaelle (in his last manner)"—the early manner earned him a place in Class 1st—and goes on to "The Caraccis" and (fifth) to Correggio, whose frescoes Ruskin describes in the same letter as "vulgar,

26. T. S. Eliot, "Tradition and the Individual Talent," sec. 1. This essay was originally collected in *The Sacred Wood* (London, 1920), reprinted in *Points of View* (London, 1941). Also anthologized.

27. Harold I. Shapiro, ed., *Ruskin in Italy: Letters to His Parents, 1845* (Oxford, 1972), pp. 143–45 (letter 85).

coarse, obscure, paltry, petty desecrations of sacred subject." Of this list he says: "I have pretty well now arranged my scale of painters. I shift about here and there a little—I am not sure of the places of all—but I rather regard them pretty nearly in this order, and I shall not alter very much." But two months later he writes that the list requires much amendment; all has changed. What had happened? In Venice on 24 September he visited the Scuola di San Rocco and encountered Tintoretto (who appears in July as seventh in Class III). "I have been quite overwhelmed today by a man whom I never dreamed of—Tintoret . . . it is marvelous lucky I came. . . . I never was so utterly crushed . . . before any human intellect as I was to-day, before Tintoret." [28] The system was never to be the same again; a new planet had swum into his ken and altered the places of every-thing.

As not uncommonly with Ruskin all this may strike us as a bit overheated, but surely it corresponds to events in our own aesthetic lives which, while less "overwhelming" and revolutionary, have a similar impact. But if it does strike us as a bit youthful (adoles-cent?), it is not merely because of the *violence* of the change re-corded. It may also be because the system-making subverted by "Tintoret" is so pretentiously precise, not only in taxonomic form (though, to do him justice, Ruskin points out that "two or three [artists] come into two classes. Bellini was equally great in feeling & color.") but in its concern for an exact *ranking,* for it seems clear that it is intended as a scale of *importance,* of *value* and *greatness.* For Ruskin this is no simple matter. Many factors must be weighed (such as feeling and color), but while one "may shift about here and there a little" one regards "them pretty nearly in this order" and "shall not alter very much." Is there not here some violation of the norm of catholicity as we originally discovered it, not so much a matter of "good, better, best" or (as in the case of the "School of Errors and Vices") of less vicious and more vicious, but rather of looking toward deriving from each no more—and no less—"satis-faction than it can, according to its kind, provide"? It is not that Ruskin does not make distinctions of value and interest according to kind. "The first class is arranged entirely by the amount of *holy expression* visible in the works of each, not by art. Otherwise

28. Ibid., pp. 211–13 (letter 132).

F. Bartolomeo [tenth] must have come much higher, & Duccio [sixth] much lower." But even so it seems important to him that his lists are rank orderings and invested with something like a quantitative precision ("by the *amount* of holy expression"). We argued earlier that "the most important function of criticism is not to issue a verdict, to praise or blame, reward or punish, elect to greatness or condemn to perdition, but rather to put us in such a position as to share the satisfactions thus judged," and we may see here again, perhaps, that confusion of the authoritative and communicative functions of criticism earlier discussed.

This is not to deny that an individual taste, my taste, is a system of values not only in the sense that it discriminates and relates different kinds and sources of satisfactions within its world of activity but also in the sense that it necessarily incorporates discriminations of preference and estimation among them. The enterprise which we have clumsily called the "discipline of taste and feeling" is a discipline in many senses, among them the sense in which it follows the admonition of St. Paul, "Prove all things; hold fast that which is good."[29] A 'catholic' taste holds fast, is bound to all that is good, and a good name for the bond which unites us with our worlds of good is love. We love all good things, but it does not follow that we love them all equally or, what may seem to be the same thing, find them all to be equally lovable. The individuality of a taste is to be found not only in variation in what the loved world incorporates but in the ways in which its constituents are variously loved.

My taste, any individual taste, is a "discipline of taste (in a narrower sense) and feeling," but we are concerned here primarily with the process in which that discipline emerges and is perfected—with discipline as disciplin*ing*. To the extent that this process becomes self-consciously purposive, it may well be called an enterprise, and the norms we have discovered are simply attempts to articulate the nature of that enterprise as a directed development, an effective engagement in this enterprise as one among the various activities in which we, as persons, engage ourselves. As an achievement, a more or less completed development, our taste is free, austere, communicable, and (as we shall see) authoritative; in the process of development we strive to make it so. Communication

29. *I Thess.* 5. 21.

and catholicity point to the fact that the enterprise of taste and feeling is a *human* enterprise publicly shared and sharable, one we did not create *ex nihilo* for ourselves, one to which we are introduced socially and culturally. That is to say, we enter, are inducted into the enterprise at a given point in its career; the special quality of our individual enterprise necessarily takes its shape in the circumstances in which we find it and, so to speak, it finds us. Earlier we discussed this relationship as an apparent dilemma of freedom and authority, it is to be hoped that we may now see it rather as a process in which we incorporate, appropriate, make our own 'property,' an enterprise inherently shared and sharable. We must do that, if only because the enterprise itself *exists* only in the activities of actual human beings, that is, in its 'instantiations.' To say that it is shared, sharable, public, human, is to say that we engage in it knowing that it admits of many instantiations and is exhausted in no one or any actual number of them. In that sense it is, as Kant might say, 'only' an idea, but to the extent that I live in and by that idea I both give it life and receive from it *my* vitality.

Inescapably, then, the contents of *my* aesthetic world will vary with the state of the enterprise as I enter it; what actually emerges as *my* taste will be a consequence not only of what is already there in more or less organized form but of the special mode of my appropriation, my exploration of the aesthetic world I encounter and of which I become aware as a world of aesthetic activity. In one sense I must take the world as I find it; in another I must make my own way through it, redraw for myself the maps furnished by other travellers, and perhaps even rechart its extent. Where I go and what I find may seem to be largely accidental, but that is simply to say that I must start somewhere, make use of what guidance 'happens' to be available *to me,* and find whatever *I* find wherever I may go or be led. In this sense every enterprise is a congeries of accidents, for purposes and purposive behavior realize themselves, become actual in circumstances and on occasions the relation of which to the enterprise in hand is indeterminate and not infrequently obstructive. But events and occasions are only irrelevant, distracting, or recalcitrant if we take as given the purposive activity in which we are engaged: that is, they have these qualities only as they present problems or opportunities of incorporation into that activity.

Thus necessarily the content of our taste, of our individual aesthetic worlds, is largely a consequence of what is effectively available to us, where 'effectively' means not merely present in our environment but actually brought to our attention *and* what we do and do not bring to what is so present in an activity of purposive exploration. No Florentine who died before 1483 could have had a taste for Raphael, for Michelangelo, for 'the Baroque,' but equally not for Greek sculpture as we think of it today any more than for Russian novels or 'the sonata style.' Yet for us to whom all these things are present they may not, nonetheless, be effectively available: that is, they may or may not become loved objects of our individual worlds of imaginative delight and passion. We may or may not appropriate them for ourselves. The norm of catholicity does not require that we appreciate everything that is aesthetically good—that is impossible. Rather it requires that we order for ourselves, out of what we can find and make available, a systematically differentiated sensitivity to sources of joy and passion and that we seek always to enlarge and refine that sensitivity, that, in other words, our taste become ever more coherent, more subtle, and more comprehensive. To say that is merely to say that we do not abandon the enterprise which we have made ours.

X

If we do not abandon it, it will not be because someone has pronounced some norm or standard of taste and feeling, but because we love the beautiful and the sublime and love them wherever they can be found. But while as appropriated by us we love all beauties and all sublimities, we do not find ourselves bound to or bind them to us in love in the same way or the same degree. In these differences the individuality of taste takes on another dimension, another ground of differentiation. To some objects and kinds of objects I am attached by some special bond of affection, delight, or spiritual nourishment such that to them I tend to return, to seek them out, to linger over them, to live with them in a way in which we do not live with all that we love. It is sometimes said that these specially loved things haunt our imaginations, but they are not ghostly or portentous presences. It would be better to say that they people or fill our imaginative life, offering solid and familiar presences which are consistently available sources of refreshment and succor. They are like favorite children in a loving family or objects of personal devotion and admiration among "angels and arch-angels and all the company of heaven." And, as with all such at-tachments, they also are subject to change as the affinities of tem-perament, habit, and activity on which they seem to be based may change. It has long been noted that maturation and aging, by what-ever complex processes, tend to produce such alterations. "When I was twenty, says a French poet, Ovid was my favourite: Now I am forty, I declare for Horace."[30] So also, one can easily imagine some-one who would say, 'when I was younger I preferred Sir Walter's Big Bow wow strain: Now I declare for Jane.' But there are also those who might say that what once seemed to them Beethovenian ranting as against the elegance of Mozart has come to be a mainstay of their emotional/aesthetic lives.

The presupposition of this discussion is that these are not, or at least not always, changes of taste in the radical sense that what was once found good is no longer so, that Ovid is rejected and Horace discovered, Mozart dismissed and Beethoven enthroned, or even a less drastic change in which a reordering of excellences is involved. ('I used to think that such and such a book or such and such a writer was the best, but now I would say only that they are very good but not the best.') The pure case of the kind of differentiation we are pointing to would rather be one we might try to express by saying that 'while I would not undertake to rank such different and remarkable works of genius or their authors, other things being equal *I* would rather read the one than the other.' But of course there are no such pure cases, other things are never equal, and the changes in apprehension always occurring in a living taste are such as to make it impossible to be certain that the works, the objects, have changed for us rather than the preference we give to them. Yet perhaps this is not an important problem. We run the risk of violating norms of catholicity, objectivity/austerity, and freedom whenever we form an attachment so powerful as to become exclu-sive, but is it impossible that one who can spend hours in a state of delight reading *Emma* or "assisting" at *Cosi Fan Tutte* might yet say

30. David Hume, *An Enquiry Concerning the Principles of Morals,* part 5, sec. 2. (Many editions, many printings.)

'on the whole this sort of thing is less important to me than Dos-
toyevsky and Beethoven'? In these terms we might make two observations. First, when put in this way such an individuation of
taste raises questions which may well go beyond the scope of our
aesthetic life alone in the sense that they implicate relations to
other functions, other activities, other standards and norms. To say
that aesthetic activity is autonomous is not to say that it is or ought
to be unaffected by that larger system which is our psychical life—
it is rather to suggest that it cannot be simply reduced to, entirely
assimilated to any other activity. It is possible, in other words, that
here in some wise we touch that bounding question of this inquiry
which we formulated earlier as "what claim this kind of activity, *with
its internal claims,* has upon us as human beings: why, in other
words, we demand in everyone—and more especially of ourselves—a discipline of taste and feeling." That is, if some objects in
our aesthetic world have a personal importance for us it may be
because they are important to us as persons and not merely as
persons of taste. But we are not yet prepared to discuss these problems. Second, the distinction we have made—or tried to make—
may well seem indefensible, for we might put it as trying to differentiate between taste and *my* taste, or my *taste* and my personal
preference. But what is my taste other than my preference? Is not
my preference necessarily *authoritative for me*? So, finally, to "authority" we must turn.

4

NORMS OF TASTE AND FEELING

Authority/Docility

The problems of authority in matters of taste cannot, it would seem, be very difficult. We have argued that the judgment of taste—whatever its antecedents or conditions—is a *felt* satisfaction. And is it not the case that what we feel—like what we sense—is given? However it comes about, it is there and is what it is. To the extent that we understand the conditions of these events of feeling (*how* they come about), we may, of course, by altering circumstances change our feelings, but otherwise circumstances and objects are felt affirmatively or negatively, please or pain, almost as are hot and cold, dark or light. We might *think* that we *ought* to be pleased in a number of different ways, including the simple one that we are surprised that we are not: that we expect a satisfaction which does not accrue. Presumably we might even *imagine* that we are pleased. And we might admit to being indifferent or to having mixed feelings, but do these possibilities significantly alter the case?

For what is the case? If 'authority' is the power to influence or determine opinion or judgment, in that case in which opinion and judgment are what is *felt* how could such a power be exercised? What I *say*—how by saying or in other ways I *express* or purport to express my judgment—or what I *do* may be influenced, even coerced, but how could what I *feel* be determined by anything or anyone except by indirection—that is, by changing the conditions of *my* feeling, most obviously by changing *what* is felt, what it is that is 'charged' affirmatively or negatively, that is, with pleasure or pain? For someone else to be the 'author' of my taste—that is, of this tasting and the taste of this, of my present judgment—would have to mean that I have someone else's feelings and perceptions: effectively be a different consciousness, a different person, a different 'experience.' And if that were, miraculously, to come about, there could no longer be any question of external influence or coercion, since there are no longer two parties to be external to each other.

How, then, does it come about that there are thought to be problems of authority in matters of taste? Because, of course, my 'present judgment'—my taste in the sense of *this* tasting or the taste of *this*—is a product of my past experience and practice, of discipline and disciplined experience. For me, at this moment it is therefore final in the sense that it is where I have arrived, but just because it is a result or eventuation of a development it is also the beginning of another phase of that development. As such it is not final but provisional. And in this inquiry, in which we are concerned with possibilities of *reflective control* of this developing taste, my present taste, my present judgment is authoritative even for me only insofar as I am confident of the integrity and perfection of my disciplined abilities, my trained eyes and ears, my sensitivities and subtleties of perception and imagination. To say that my taste is provisionally authoritative is to recognize that my confidence in myself and my abilities is always relative.

But this is not to say that my present taste is not, *for me,* authoritative and necessarily so. To say that it is provisional is to say that it functions—is accepted and used—in default of something better. But that something better can only be some future satisfaction, some projected judgment having as its condition a better functioning, a better equipped and disciplined 'me': that is, my improved and further developed taste. And in that projected development I must necessarily start with where I presently find myself.[1]

Nor is this a merely schematic or abstract necessity. If I find that what once offered much satisfaction now fails to interest and reward I must seek the ground of the change in the relevant conditions of my *present* apprehension, in all those dimensions of

---

1. Justice Jackson supposedly said of the Supreme Court of the United States, "We are not final because we are infallible; we are infallible because we are final." Of course, even this finality is provisional; there is always appeal to the Court differently informed and perhaps differently constituted. But first one must get their attention.

aesthetic activity which we have been exploring as they are represented here and now. My present judgment is the ruling, the 'authoritative' datum from which I must start, not because there is something absolute about 'givenness' or feeling or pleasure and pain, but because it is the emergent consequence of that complex organization of activity in imaginative perception that is my taste. My present activity—the fruit of a long development and of much practice—has a distinctive flavor enjoyed, satisfying or turning to ashes in the mouth. My present state with respect to enjoyment is thus a sign or index of the functioning state of its 'author' or originator—my aesthetically organized psyche. Any appeal from that judgment must be to a differently organized or differently functioning aesthetic self yielding a different fruit. But if the fruit is my enjoyment or to be enjoyed by me, the appeal must be to another state of myself developed from my present habits, skills, and sensibilities. In brief, to question that authority is *to require me to embark in some degree upon an effort in "reeducating my perception."*

All this is (probably) an overargued way of making the point that for us in this inquiry the 'live' problems of authority must be an attempt to answer two questions. (1) Why should I ever take as sufficient for such practical, reeducative questioning of my present capacities for imaginative perception some ground originating outside of them? (2) What might such sources be and when should I turn to them? Curiously enough, therefore, it might be said that the serious problems about 'authority' are questions about when I have good ground for *docility,* that is, on what occasions of external challenge should I be ready to accept the challenge itself as evidence that I may have something to learn and therefore be willing to undertake to learn? Or, put another way, what claimants to teach me must I recognize and accept as legitimate? As will be seen, the goal of my aesthetic development might be described as the achievement of such a state of my taste as will make *my* taste authoritative in this same sense, namely, justify the docility of others relative to me. To be an 'authority' is to have one's judgments qualify to be taken into account by others in the enterprise which constitutes the aesthetic community. It is to qualify to perform (and so have a 'right' to perform) a function in that community.

But there is in this account so far, however, an ambiguity which must be made explicit before we proceed.

Have we not argued our way into an apparent impossibility? Just as I cannot literally have someone else's sensations or feelings and therefore someone else's judgments in the sense in which they are felt affirmations or denials, so also I cannot literally communicate my judgments to others. How, then, can they be authoritative for others and those of others authoritative for me? The question points to two different forms in which my *present* taste or *present* judgment may exist. If what is meant is my present disciplined *experiencing* it is true that it cannot be literally shared; but my *opinion*—my expressible, verbalizable, conceptualizable memory and anticipation of my practiced experience—is the very stuff of communication. Necessarily, judgments in this their communicable form function at a distance from the experience they record, anticipate, analyze, and categorize. (That is, they are 'mediated' experience.) But they do function, and one of the possibilities inherent in them is a more or less purposively reconstructive return to the primary 'judgings' or appreciations to which they are related. That is, they entail the possibility of reflective reorientation of my aesthetic activity and, consequently, of my aesthetic habits.

In considering the norms of communicability and catholicity we have already explored the way in which our taste develops into a more or less systematically organized whole and the relation of that development to criticism—to anatomizing and characterizing. Clearly everything we said there about the "operationally heuristic" character of these conceptualizations is relevant here as well. From that point of view, the problems of authority and docility can be reformulated as questions about the occasions on which I have reason to take seriously the opinions of others as suggesting to me that my anatomizing, my characterizing, and my systematic placings may require revision. That is what is meant by undertaking to reeducate my perception. To the extent that reeducation takes place, there will be changes in my opinions and some shift, however slight, in my aesthetic universe, my system of taste.

II

Thus, commonly what is identified as a situation in which 'tastes differ' is a difference or confrontation of judgments as *opinions*, that is, as expressed. And commonly as well we assume that the judgments expressed are those of different judges. And thus we may first think of authority as encountered in the cogent operation of a more or less systematic order of opinions forming a traditional, cultural, societal orthodoxy. Such an orthodoxy is more than a register of opinions, formulae, canonic listings, for are not these rather the explicit forms of more subtle directions of attention and habituation in education, in determinations of visibility and availability, in countless other ways in which authority is not mere opinion but cogency, external direction, coercion, power? In this organized world of directing opinion there are of course authorit*ies*, those who in one way or another—as critics, patrons, controllers of media, historians discriminating significance, indeed all kinds of 'taste-makers'—seem to be empowered to make decisions articulating and implementing cultural, traditional, societal norms.

Apparently, then, we were wrong in thinking that the problems of authority in matters of taste and feeling cannot be very difficult. How can they be discussed or even formulated without investigating the actual communities in which taste is formed, judgments effectively communicated, reputations made and lost, artistic activity encouraged or discouraged, and aesthetic canons established, enforced, and revised? It is again characteristic of our ways of thinking about these matters in general that we would be likely to think of the problem as requiring an account of the world of art and artists, of critics and historians of literature and the arts, of patrons and collectors, of performers, editors, publishers and producers—to say nothing of those nebulous groups constituting 'audiences': the reading public, theater buffs, music lovers. Inevitably, in correspondence with each other, there develop (or at least we distinguish) various sorts of arts and audiences: popular, sophisticated, mass, avant-garde, and 'specialized.' And, of course, all these elements and their relations become determinate only historically, changing in response to a set of other developments many of which are remote in origin but rich in consequences for aesthetic and artistic activity. Many of the most obvious of these changes are technological, but there are others which have a more pervasive effect, such as changes in the general level of wealth and power in societies and nations, changes with respect to cultural isolation or in the proportionate weight of different institutional orders (such as religious and secular) within a society.

Here is a fertile field for historical inquiry, for sociological, political, or quasi-political analysis in which—as might have been anticipated from the ambiguities and ambivalences earlier explored—problems of authority tend to be reduced to problems of power and influence, of the controls, institutional and informal, by which the arts, their 'consumption' and enjoyment, their protagonists and followers are disciplined into some sort of relative order of estimation and whatever in the way of honor and worldly goods may be consequent upon it. Necessarily in such an inquiry questions of what 'offices' are effectively discriminating and in that sense 'critical' in a given social order, how they are exercised and how they are acquired by those who occupy them become central. If there is a 'canon' of literature in English or of 'American literature' how did it get established and by whom? How does one become an authority—academic or other—effectively contributing to the determination of a canon decisive for the purposes of education, for the formation of the 'historical consciousness' of a cultural tradition, for the standards of criticism, and for the distribution of honor and profit?[2]

Lurking in the background in such investigations (and in the end usually emerging in the foreground) is, of course, the question of that in the service of which such power is exercised, such influence exerted. It is usually not found to be difficult, in much current thinking, to identify as ultimately constitutive of taste, canonicity, cultural heroism, and other such normalities ruling elites and social and economic power structures, the interests of classes, genders or other oppressors, exploiters and perhaps more benign 'establishments.' In particular, the arts can then be understood as expressions of attitudes and values serving to focus, form, and reinforce

---

2. It is appropriate to relegate to a footnote, as irrelevant to the development of the argument, two questions (suspicions) which persistently arise in my reading of much of the writing about these matters. (1) Is there not a persistent overestimate of the actual influence and viability of these 'offices'—particularly the academic ones—on the part of those who write about them? (2) Is there not a faintly audible note of envy and disgruntlement in much of the complaint about such 'taste-making' and makers? (These grapes may be sour.) Perhaps here are two sides of the same attitude: after all, what is the point of quarreling about positions of no importance?

the attitudes and values justifying and supporting social ordinations and subordinations.

The cavalier way in which we have introduced these considerations should not suggest that the questions being asked are empty and inquiry addressed to them illegitimate and fruitless, though one may properly be skeptical of many of the ways in which they are formulated and investigated. But it is necessary for us to sketch out this region of inquiry primarily to make clear why it is that *our* inquiry into 'authority' cannot orient itself therein.

That is not to say the social milieu there explored is simply irrelevant, that is, it need not be taken into account at all in considering our problems. The question is rather how it becomes relevant on the assumption that the questions we are asking have an autonomous ground—which is merely to say in another way that they originate and make determinate what is relevant to themselves.

Our questions concern the *reflective control*—the adjustment, so far as it lies within our power, by reflection—of our judgments, our enjoyments, satisfactions and emotional responses, under certain conditions and in active relation to certain objects (or, better, objects functioning in a certain way), those conditions and objects being themselves that with respect to which our reflection is directed in an effort to clarify, stabilize, and enrich experience of this kind. Since this experience becomes reflective only after it has already become established in some kind and some degree, reflection, as contributory to its further development, its fuller *emergence* in our living, begins with what is already present, with that of which we are already capable, with an already partially formed and articulated sensibility and emotional life. And, as we have seen, the immediately authoritative, *given* cogency is our own satisfaction or dissatisfaction, our felt affirmation or rejection, whatever at any given point it may be.[3] Any process in which it is to be developed or changed must take it as that which is questioned, that which, provisionally, is authoritative, not in the sense of what influences or determines opinion or judgment but as that point at which the mind has come, however temporarily, to rest.

To the extent, then, that I, an individual psyche, become en-

---

3. It may, of course, be confused or mixed. But a mixed satisfaction or a confusion is still *my* experience and constitutes *my* starting point in *my* reflection.

gaged in aesthetic activity reflectively, 'self-consciously,' knowingly,
the various features and presences of my world which function (de-
signedly or not) to influence and determine judgment become for
me in that activity *claimants* for my attention, *proffered* grounds for
reconsideration, development, or formation of *my* judgment. Official position, institutional certification, traditional endorsement
may all have some weight in determining whether I take such
claims to be justified, that is, to warrant some docility on my part,
but I must weigh them as signs of other qualities and qualifications
and subject their deliverances to the tests appropriate to the activity
which they claim to further. Obviously such an attitude on my part
assumes both the integrity of that activity and my knowing engagement in it—'knowing' meaning no more (and no less) than that I
'know what I am doing or trying to do' and can differentiate in
practice this sort of doing from other sorts. To know that is to have
some comprehension of the conditions, modes, and fruitions of
this sort of activity and therefore to be able in some measure to
determine what furthers and what impedes it, what is relevant and
irrelevant to *this* function. The authority of my judging thus means
that it is that from which I must begin, that I and only I can legitimate any challenge to it, and that any process of development will
end in another act of mine.[4]

The problems of *authoritative* communication here emerge as a
practical, 'existential' form of the relationship between the 'community in idea' and the historical communities in which aesthetic
activity actually emerges among other activities and functions and
seeks to stabilize itself. For, of course, it does not literally stabilize
itself. Efforts to realize and stabilize it are efforts of the human
psyche. The individual psyche, finding itself committed to the activity, seeks to approximate in its own living the activity of a *member*

---

4. If the result of an analysis of the social conditions of the formation of taste
is effectively to deny the integrity of aesthetic (or artistic—for this purpose it makes
no difference) activity, *cadit quaestio*. In that case, those who think they enjoy such
an integral engagement live an illusion, and this whole inquiry is much ado—if not
about nothing—about something at most an attribute or moment of some other
activity. It should hardly be necessary to add that integrity is not the same thing as
'totally without relation to any other' and in fact entails a variety of activities com-
plementing and supplementing each other, frequently in interaction. (Nor is this
integrity as a working assumption of this inquiry a mere act of faith.)

of the community constituted in idea, its activity thus becoming one of the ways in which we endeavor to "create, sustain, and more fully articulate an actual community which can at best be only a partial realization of the community in idea." In *that* community every member is an authority because every member fully exemplifies the activity, fully 'authors' it. The autonomy of the members of the community has as its ground the integrity of the activity itself. Authority and docility as we here consider them are features of our aesthetic lives which emerge as we attempt to take up, in the circumstances of our life and world, something like the stance of such membership, to approach the exemplary autonomy inherent therein. Equally, short of that point (as we always actually are in some respects) we must accept the *provisional* character of our authority and the docility that may entail at a given point.

III

The argument has thus come round to much the same point reached earlier. Let us therefore turn to the question of what legitimate sources of challenge to our provisional authority there may be and how we recognize them. For this purpose the reader must indulge us in yet another visit to Florence and the Uffizi, not this time with Hawthorne but with another pilgrim from New England.

Twenty-five years before Hawthorne traversed these galleries and ruminated about seeing pictures, Emerson arrived in Florence. He had come northward—by way of Malta, Sicily, Naples and Rome, where he had spent nearly a month. He seems to have had eager and rather definite anticipations.

> How like an archangel's tent is this great Cathedral of many-coloured marble set down in the midst of the city and by its side its wondrous campanile! I took a hasty glance at the gates of the Baptistery which Angelo said ought to be the gates of Paradise . . . and then of his own David & hasted to the Tribune [of the Uffizi] & to the Pitti Palace. I saw the statue that enchants the world. And truly the Venus deserves to be visited from far. It is not adequately represented by the plaster casts. . . . I must go again & see this statue. Then I went round this cabinet and gallery & galleries till I was well nigh 'dazzled and drunk with beauty.'

I think no man has an idea of the powers of painting until he has come hither. Why should painters study at Rome? Here, here.[5]

"The statue that enchants the world" is quoted from Thomson's reference to the Medici Venus in *The Seasons*. The sensitive reader may detect in that fact (taken with "I must go again & see this statue") some indication of unease. Another entry a few days later makes it explicit.

> 2 May. I revisited the Tribune this morning to see the Venus . . . and the rest of that attractive company. I reserve my admiration as much as I can; I make a continual effort not to be pleased except by that which ought to please *me*. And I walked coolly round and round the marble lady but when I planted myself at the iron gate which leads into the chamber of Dutch paintings & looked at the statue, I saw & felt that mankind have had good reason for their preference of this excellent work, & I gladly gave one testimony more to the surpassing genius of the artist.[6]

In these years of change and pilgrimage—years marked by the death of his young wife, abandonment of religious orthodoxy and the ministry—Emerson was much concerned with self-reliance, both metaphysically and practically, if in his case one can make such distinctions. A journal entry in the following year, after his return to New England, is unusual only in its generality.

> 22 March [1834]. The subject that needs most to be /presented/developed/ is the principle of Self reliance, what it is, what is not it, what it requires, how it teaches us to regard our friends. It is true that there is a faith wholly a man's own, the solitary inmate of his own breast, which the faiths of all mankind cannot shake, & which they cannot confirm.

---

5. *The Journals and Miscellaneous Notebooks of Ralph Waldo Emerson*, vol. 4, 1832–1834, edited by Alfred R. Ferguson (Cambridge, Mass., 1964), p. 168. Entry under May 1, 1833, but seems to record his activities of several days earlier. As noted in the text, the phrase "the statue that enchants the world" is a reference to Thomson's "So stands the statue that enchants the world. . . ." (*The Seasons*, "Summer," l. 1346). The other quoted phrase is from Byron's *Childe Harold's Pilgrimage*, Fourth Canto, L, a passage written as from the Tribune of the Uffizi and referring particularly to the Venus. Those tempted to reconstruct Emerson's route on this first eager exploration are reminded that "Angelo's" David was at this time still in its original position before the Palazzo Signoria (then, of course, the Palazzo del Gran Duca).

6. Ibid., p. 169. Emerson originally wrote "except *with* that which ought to please *me*" but canceled it, inserting "by." The emphasis on "me" is Emerson's own, if we can trust his editor.

But at the same time how useful, how indispensable has been the ministry of our friends to us, our teachers,—the living and the dead.[7]

But we need not concern ourselves with questions about Emerson: need not inquire whether his evident suspicion of the opinion of "mankind" or the enchantment of "the world" is Yankee crankiness, transcendental principle, or Oedipal rebellion. What we may do is take his account as an approximate paradigm of the elements that enter into situations of the sort we are interested in. Of course, the occasion is only one of the ways in which questions of authority and docility arise—that kind in which we find ourselves in the presence of something recommended to us as remarkable by 'everyone' and are expected by everyone (probably including ourselves) to concur in the recommendation.[8] But what could be clearer than the assertion of what must be the final authority—my seeing and feeling ("I saw and felt") which, far from being legitimated by the preference of "mankind," rather ratifies or confirms *it*?[9] This authority, moreover, is not merely a feeling. That is, it is not my being *pleased* that is decisive but my being pleased by *"what*

---

7. *Journals,* vol. 4, p. 269. (See note 6 above.) Shortly before he suddenly embarked upon his European tour at Christmas, 1832, his journal records a version of the poem later published as "Self-Reliance."

> I will not live out of me
> I will not see with others eyes
> My good is good, my evil ill
> I would be free—I cannot be
> While I take things as others please to rate them.

(Ibid., p. 47. The entry is not dated, but the context indicates a date between the 9th and 13th of October 1832.)

8. But, of course, we do not simply *find* ourselves there—the recommendation is very likely what brought us here and our anticipations as to what is to be remarked, why it is remarkable and in what relation to what else are commonly quite determinate. (Horses athirst are led to water.)

9. There is (for me) a curious air of generous concession, almost of gracious condescension, in Emerson's final sentence: if one must give in, it is ignoble and mean to do so grudgingly. Part of the charm of the passage is its 'innocent abroad' feeling, perhaps better described as a certain sturdy, almost cultivated naivete. By comparison Hawthorne (see above, Prologue, Part One, p. 8) seems much more sophisticated, but one must bear in mind the difference between 1833 and 1858 and that on the relevant occasions Hawthorne was fifty-three, well into his career, and Emerson twenty-nine and still finding his way. But surely he was right in thinking that the "principle of Self reliance, what it is, what it is not, what it requires . . ." needed a good deal of thought.

ought" to please *me*—that is, what satisfies *my* standards, *my* disciplined apprehension. Emerson's language is, from our point of view, strikingly precise: my *seeing* and *feeling* confirm that "mankind have had good *reason* for their *preference."*

IV

We asked as one of our broad questions about authority what sources of external authority there might be. Emerson's account suggests, besides the "preference of mankind," two others: the object itself ("I walked coolly round & round the marble lady . . . & looked at the statue . . .) and the artist (. . . "I gladly gave one testimony more to the surpassing genius of the artist"). If we add to these the obvious supplement of a personal, individual critical voice (in due course, perhaps Emerson himself) rather than some impersonal guidebook allotting stars by what is generally thought, we may have a beginning for an inquiry answering our question.

But only a rough beginning, for it is obvious that we cannot take any of these sources simply, not even the preference of mankind or of the "world" which, in Thomson's phrase, is enchanted by the marble lady. Clearly "mankind" cannot literally mean everyone, nor even everyone who has seen the statue, since this would include many for whom it is at best an odd sort of physical object. Nor can it include all who have seen it as a "marble lady." It is not that we must be literal-minded about unanimity—we can hardly expect more than a 'general consensus'—or quibble about varying warmth of preference, rather we might recognize that many who are greatly pleased cannot be counted. We might flatter ourselves that we are likely to be less prissy than Emerson (and perhaps less susceptible to nudity through what, reluctantly, one may call overexposure) but surely we would not consider approbation in the form of libidinous excitation as contributing to the relevantly authoritative consensus.[10]

10. One might imagine a *Guidebook to Erotic Art in Public Galleries: Northern Italy* ("A Handbook of Soft Porn for Those Bored with ART") in which the Medici's Venus might rate half a star. In its 'data base,' lusty satisfactions would be authoritative. (But even in this case constituencies are not unambiguous: the exigencies of modern opinion would probably require that such a 'Blue Guide' have a rating system recognizing, minimally, the possibly divergent preferences of mankind and womankind.)

The point, of course, is that what might possess some authority for us is agreement of those qualified to judge—a constituency, community, or public not easily identified empirically. The world enchanted by Venus must be the world of those who know something about and love art, the world of the *cognoscenti*, of connoisseurs, of the aesthetically, artistically sophisticated, of the cultivated, knowledgeable amateur. But even these loosely characterized groups do not simply coincide—in these worlds in practice the professionals do not like to be confused with the amateurs, no matter how cultivated, nor is the suspicion only on one side. Further, of course, it is not clear how specific the qualifications are to be; how broad or narrow the circle of the world in which opinion is to be sought and weighed. It is easy to say that the opinions of those who have experience of and have thought about similar objects are relevant but a moment's thought will reveal the impossible vaguenesses of that formula: similar in what respects, what sort of experience and reflection? We have touched upon these problems in considering how we are to orient ourselves to 'critical' discourse; it is hardly necessary to repeat ourselves. And, of course, all the ambiguities and confusions could be restated in terms of the object, since placing any object in the context of each of these publics redefines it, changing the grounds of approval and disapproval, and making agreement or disagreement dubious testimony. But again, we have touched on these matters before.

Yet these are largely theoretical difficulties. In fact, at any given moment in an active cultural environment there will be a rough but working systematization of kinds of objects, contexts of discussion, and interested publics. In this complex world there is commonly also a practical consensus, if not with respect to merits, at least with respect to what is controversial and what are the terms of the controversy. The 'theoretical' considerations just outlined explain why it is possible (and perhaps even necessary) that these groupings and their concomitant placings and judgments of objects, even what is controversial and what about it is in controversy should change, but they do not explain why all these elements are what they are at a given moment—that is one of those things of which we are wont to say that they admit of only a historical explanation.

History—or at least temporal categories—is appropriate for

these phenomena in another way. Broadly speaking, at any moment there is likely to be a kind of temporal foreground for this sort of thinking, doing, and talking—a region where what is important is what is more or less contemporary and those inheritances from the past found to be presently interesting. Correlative with these presences is a congeries of curiously interrelated circles and publics in which a major preoccupation is admitting and assimilating what is thought to be novel. This is, of course, largely a world of artists, writers, composers, performers, patrons, impresarios, publishers, editors, and all the other appurtenances of the oddly varied media and marketplaces of the arts. And it is also the world of fashions, feuds, 'movements,' manifestoes, groups, schools and waves—of "packs and sects of great of great ones / that ebb and flow by th' moon."[11] Nevertheless, in justice one must add that amidst the gyrations of the latest (frequently recommended as the ultimate), the exotic deliverances from some New World, the ringing challenges to tradition and the recurrent discovery that the future is to be found in some past freshly understood, suitably framed and re-presented, there emerge 'secular' trends seeming to separate wheat and chaff, faithful workers in the vineyard from masters of viticulture.[12]

By this process, art and artist (and, less prominently, critics and other citizens of these worlds) come to 'belong to the ages,' moving into the background of the busy worlds of the modern and the contemporary, becoming monuments, ancestors, forerunners and, on occasion, the latest fashion and true contemporaries and prophets. But apart from such resurrections they are the special preoccupation of historians and other academicians, who provide perspectives in which the relations of foreground and background are reversed: the present and contemporary becoming a consequence, a variation, perhaps even a repetition of a history which makes them in these diverse ways intelligible. But again, in justice, one must grant that the net result of this process is a kind of continuing

11. *King Lear*, v, ii ll. 18–19.
12. Here is a fertile field for myth. Thus 'the career of genius' exemplifies in countless variations the movement from early obscurity and struggle marked by public indifference and critical scorn to universal acclaim and canonization, both sometimes posthumous. The young Beethoven was "ripe for the madhouse"; the Beethoven of the Late Quartets lives in or even above the stars.

reassessment in which it is sought to relate our present and our past in some fruitful way—there being, of course, no simple agreement as to how that is to be done or even what it might mean. Nevertheless, again, at any given moment there is something like a practical consensus as to the structure of our history and the consequent estimation of its elements, including general agreement as to what there is to disagree about.

But we have argued that this world—or complex of worlds—is largely irrelevant to our problems, and we must refuse to be drawn into a discussion of these processes of assimilation and discrimination. It would be easy to dismiss them as richly corrupt and corrupting, distorting, manipulated and manipulating, but our concern is not moral or political. But we cannot entirely ignore them, for the individual psyche encounters these ways of the world and their results in the form of a roughly coherent current orthodoxy and a more or less readily available conventional wisdom in 'matters of taste'—at least so far as the arts are concerned. From this point of view it is not so important—in general—that the ways of the world are venal, manipulative, and mendacious as it is that they are *aesthetically* confused, coarse, and imprecisely communicated. That is, in the common wisdom many other grounds of judgment are commingled with aesthetic criteria, all too frequently only the more obvious aesthetic or artistic qualities enter into judgment, and what is pointed to may not be what is actually worthy of interest in the objects and artistic personalities it singles out. In consequence, current orthodoxy and conventional wisdom are triply unreliable. They may be simply 'wrong' because their judgments are not in substance aesthetic; they may mislead because their aesthetic grounds, however genuine, yield only crude discrimination or because their formulae may be quite irrelevant to the qualities which they claim to explicate. And, of course, all these conditions may enter into a given judgment, creating puzzles of fashion, reputation, and criticism which attract attention as such, so that a great deal of the talk and literature of these worlds is devoted to considering why a somebody or something is liked or disliked by somebody or somebodies. [13]

13. It is probably a mistake to take this curiously indirect mode of discussion of merits as specially characteristic of discussion with respect to the arts and 'matters

V

If all this is the case—and the confusions and ambiguities which in fact beset us here could be multiplied to the point of inducing despair—why should we, given our special point of view, be at all concerned with current orthodoxies, acceptations and the terms in which they are conveyed? What possible claim have these things upon our attention?

Let us be clear. We are not here considering the clearly articulated, responsible, individual critical voice and mind, nor the experienced cogency of works and creative energies. No, here we are to take into account the common currency of critical talk, the general opinion which comes to be so reiterated in widening circles that ultimately it seems to be the "judgment of mankind" or what 'everybody knows.' In the shorter run and narrower circles it is what 'everybody' is talking about now, what must be seen, heard, or read, that about which one must have an opinion or the question which must here and now be answered. In short, we mean claims to direct attention and interest inherently vague and generic and having only whatever authority is conferred by consensus, rough agreement achieved at the price of subtlety, precision, and clarity of discrimination.

Further, we are not concerned here with those early stages in the development of an individual taste and emotional discipline in which what we have called the cultural 'background' provides a broad basis for formal and informal educational choice, a general ambiance of functional opinion. Inevitably as this bears upon a developing individual sensibility it will be modified by local and individual circumstance, but its function is none the less indispensable, providing that concrete presence of an organized world of things of human interest—objects, personalities, and institutions—which is a condition of a civilized tradition both in the sense of what is to be transmitted and its transmission. But here we are concerned with an individual psyche which has reached a reflective

---

of taste.' Perhaps it is a phenomenon of 'the media.' A remarkable proportion of political discussion is couched in an indirect mode in which actions and policy are described and justified by their effect—intended or actual—on some constituency or 'body of opinion.'

stage in which these basic data and attitudes have been critically assimilated into a deliberately directed personal enterprise, that stage of 'self-reliance' which Emerson celebrated.

But even such a relatively mature psyche must, after all, live and function aesthetically in an actual public world wherein orthodoxies and conventions are authoritative not merely as influencing what is said and thought but what is *done*. Early in our inquiry we touched upon the importance, in the emergence of an actual individual taste, of the "effective availability" of aesthetic objects.[14] Those availabilities are largely determined by authority of the kind we have been considering. What is preserved, collected, restored, exhibited, produced, performed, published, edited is something which each of us must largely take as given, resulting from currents of opinion and the operation of authorities which may appear, from any individual point of view, to be largely whimsical and capricious. But these choices are none the less consequential for us; in effect they provide the range of our aesthetic opportunities so far as these depend upon what is available outside the narrowest circle of individual existence. The sages will tell us that the heavens above, the lilies of the field, the tiger burning bright, the serpent on the rock, the human form divine, the direct expression of instincts of shaping and adornment, and the dramas of the ritual life offer all the essential riches of beauty and passion, but even these require more than we can provide for ourselves. (There remains the alternative of Walden Pond—but that rests upon more than an aesthetic vocation.) The fact is that the necessary setting of the enterprise with which we are concerning ourselves is a civilization— a 'high' culture—and that it is as foolish to deny ourselves its fruits as it is to allow ourselves to be taken in by its confusions and corruptions.

Moreover, because the enterprise is the enterprise of humanity, of civilization and human cultivation, we have as participants in it not only the right to profit according to our lights from the opportunities it affords us but also the obligation to support and further the realization of its purposes. This is—to make use of 'Kantian' terminology—an end which is a duty, that is, what is obligatory is making the purpose our own. It is therefore a duty of 'indetermi-

14. Above, Prologue, Part Two, pp. 24 ff. Also chap. 3, p. 119.

nate obligation,' compelling to action only as means are available and other obligations taken into account. How in our individual circumstances we are to discharge this obligation each of us must determine: the prescient philanthropy with which the last of the Medici endowed Florence with Raphaels, Botticellis, and the Venus which bears the family name is the privilege of the few, but none of us is entirely without opportunity to exert some influence of patronage, opinion, or example.[15]

VI

But by a quixotic turn we seem to have discovered an obligation to exercise our own authority rather than any ground on which to accede to the "preference of mankind." But a phrase used above— "prescient philanthropy"—may point the way. In hindsight, the collections of the Uffizi and the Pitti Palace were sound, indeed superb, anticipations of the taste, the pleasure, the satisfaction of many generations of "mankind." Is not the persistent interest which they have generated both a confirmation of the opinion which determined their choice and ground on which to anticipate a future in which they may continue to intrigue and satisfy? In fact, such an authority is entailed by what we argued earlier in discussing communicability. It is true that we then argued that "persistent admiration for any object—any classic—is only ambiguous evidence, a somewhat uncertain sign, of the operation of a generic, a common sensibility"[16] and we may now see, also an uncertain sign

15. The "last of the Medici" deserves better notice. She was Anna Maria, the Electress Palatine, who died in the Pitti Palace in 1743 and left all the family property ("galleries, paintings, statues, libraries, jewels and other precious things") to the new line of Grand Dukes, subject to conditions: "these things being for the ornament of the state, for the benefit of the people and for an inducement to the curiosity of foreigners, nothing shall be alienated or taken away from the capital or from the territories of the grand duchy." One should note, as is pointed out by (e.g.) C. F. Young (*The Medici*, 3d ed. [London, 1913], vol. 2, pp. 501 ff.), that the gift included more than the basic collections of the Uffizi and the Pitti Palace. Much of what is now seen in the Bargello, the Medici Chapel ('The New Sacristy') with the Medici tombs of Michelangelo, the nucleus of the Medici Library, and much else also was thus conveyed.

16. Above, chap. 3, p. 78. Of course it can (and will be) argued that collections like those of the Uffizi create the taste by which they continue to be enjoyed by

of a shareable satisfaction. But it *is* still a sign, originally because it is testimony to the occurrence of a value, and the more reliable as a sign of a shareable *aesthetic* value in proportion as that testimony is persistent AND *the persistence is reasonably* attributable *to the replication in otherwise different circumstances of the distinctive features of an aesthetic experience and an aesthetic judgment.* It is because those conditions are so complex and such experience and judgment so closely related to others generating closely related values that the testimony of the traditions and of "mankind" is never to be taken at face value and in fact is never unmixed.

We have touched upon the relevant limiting conditions before,[17] what is important at this point is how they condition the authority of the "testimony of mankind." *In general* the consequence must be that such authority must be—to use an impressive phrase—'hypothetically heuristic.' That simply means that the deliverances of this testimony may establish a presumption that what is recommended is worthy of exploration. The caution of this formula should not conceal its importance. The riches of the world of art in a culture heir to many traditions and open to exotic presences pose serious problems of choice to an expanding sensibility. Some selectivity is necessary; that sort of guidance is one of the offices of tradition. What it offers to a thoughtful taste is, in the broadest terms, the recommendations of experience, mappings based upon the reports of previous explorers, prospectors like ourselves in the realms of gold.

This *general* authority is appropriately modified insofar as we have reason based upon our understanding of the circumstances under which the relevant judgments have taken shape. Thus the judgments which emerge and function in which we have called the "foreground" of the aesthetic/artistic world, being based upon a more limited experience and so more likely to be distorted by ir-

---

functioning canonically, that is, authoritatively. While this ignores the fact that different elements of the collection are differently esteemed at various times—so that at any given moment there is a canon within the canon—there is certainly a 'circular' reinforcement involved. The question is the extent to which the circularity is grounded in arbitrary coercion or autonomous cogency.

17. It is worthy of note that, as usual, Hume has the right terms for the significant qualities of reputation: "durable" and "general" are his terms. See above, chap. 3, p. 77.

relevances and confusions, necessarily are generally less weighty than the more settled conclusions which inform the *background* of 'what is now.' But even here they cannot be entirely neglected. As we have already pointed out, the notion of 'widespread appeal' is ambiguous indeed, but it is not hopelessly ambiguous, since what counts is the opinion of those who are concerned, interested and experienced and these criteria roughly define a 'public' the absolute size of which is not its most significant feature. More relevant is the quality of concern and interest and the depth of the experience. Nevertheless what broadly engages in even the most superficial, transient way 'has something.' What is often not clear is *what* that 'something' may be, what there is that interests and attracts, nor can it be denied that the problem rarely repays investigation. One of the fruits of superficiality of concern (though clearly other factors are involved) is the self-feeding of fashion: proverbially, nothing succeeds like success. (In these worlds it is also well to remember that nothing fails like failure. No dog is more dead than yesterday's lion.) But even so there is usually something 'objective' which starts the process and in the nature of the case it must be something fairly obvious.

Fundamentally these same sorts of considerations are brought to bear in weighing the testimony of tradition. Where we have reason to suspect the operation of bias producing what we, rightly or wrongly, take to be distortion, we discount its authority, but such calculations are rarely simple. (We have already pointed out that tradition is constantly being 'updated': these processes of discounting are part of that revision.) The well-known predilection of the Renaissance for the antique might make us skeptical of the "statue that enchants the world," but the lady's reputation for beauty is not so confined—witness the testimony of our nineteenth-century American pilgrims. And, of course, when the 'background' moves into the 'foreground'—that is, when periods, styles, artists, and works from the past become fashionable, the judgments involved become subject to the doubts we are always entitled to with respect to fashions and enthusiasms. What 'tradition' tells us is that many of its elements are worthy of 'revival' if only as a mode of reconsideration. Anyone with a respect for tradition can only, from that vantage point, deplore the capriciousness of fashion while at the same time being grateful for the opportunities, noted earlier, it may afford.[18]

Of course, the domination of fashion may—more obviously but not exclusively in the performed arts—be such as to produce a sense of limitation and confinement rather than of enriched opportunity. The secular trends of fashionable taste which focus attention more than momentarily are always something of a burden to a sane and catholic taste. In such circumstances a critical voice asserting a well-founded independence of fashion is manna in the wilderness. It is also likely to be prophetic, a circumstance which offers not confirmation but a certain ironic satisfaction. Some thirty years ago a shrewd and thoughtful observer of the musical scene remarked that it was getting a bit boring and irritating to see the energy expended on the preparation and performance of the works of the lesser 'baroque' masters while one rarely heard the music—"which is just as good"—of the lesser 'romantic' composers of the nineteenth century.[19] Our present situation, in which pianists making a name for themselves by playing Liszt encyclopedically and cyclonically is just one phase of a seemingly overwhelming later-nineteenth-century romantic revival, probably pleases him, *as a critic,* no more.

VII

What *is* of interest to us in the present context is the authority of the *individual* critical voice or personality as distinct from the vagaries and vaguenesses of what 'everyone' knows or thinks. Once again we may refer to our earlier discussion of critical communication.[20] In that argument we developed the notion of the "opera-

18. Actually, of course, there is usually good reason for the selections of fashion. They are capricious only because they cannot be understood solely by reference to the merits of what is chosen, being grounded rather by the relevance of those merits or qualities to contemporary needs or preoccupations. Nor need the relevant qualities or interests be 'aesthetic.' Shakespeare's *Henry V* has characteristically been revived when England was engaged in continental war. No simple conclusion as to its merits as a play could be drawn from that history.

19. I heard him say it. He is Leonard B. Meyer.

20. See above, chap. 3.

tionally heuristic" function of critical language and concepts in order to serve the essential function of criticism—the adjustment or
readjustment of expectation, "experimental anticipation," enabling
us to form or reform an aesthetic object in the interest of appreciation, functions of anatomizing, characterizing, and systematizing.
From this point of view what makes a significant critical personality
is the performance of these functions with consistently penetrating
accuracy, subtlety, and lucidity. In contrast, the clichés, reiterated
formulae, and superficial application of routine critical expression
and conventional wisdom are clumsy, mechanical and vague, offering at best a general direction to our perception. In other words,
good critics and good criticism manifest an analytical coherence
and a sure grasp of objects. *Manifest,* that is, in the cogency with
which they enable us to analyze, form or reform, and so firmly
grasp *for ourselves* the objects with which we and critic alike are engaged.[21] The cogency of a critic or of criticism is the power to make
us see, hear, imagine in the presence of the object and in intimate
reference to it a coherent (or incoherent) richness of sense, imagination, and passion which is aesthetic objectivity. It is tempting to
say we are made to see and feel what the critic sees and feels. But
what does this signify other than that we are able to transform critical communication into effective activities of imaginative perception and feeling? And if this is the case is not the authority of the
critic or of criticism the authority of our sensibility, our reflection,
our judgment?

Of course, but as we have argued, questions as to the authority
of critics and criticism arise somewhere short of this point: at those
junctures in which the decision to be made is whether we are in
need of critical guidance, from whom we should accept it, and
whether we should persist in an apparently fruitless endeavor at
(re)interpretation and (re)evaluation under guidance. Such situations may take many forms. I may feel the need of critical guidance
because a critic whom I respect makes a judgment markedly different from my own. If I have always found *Coriolanus* comparatively
rather a dull affair, I would be surprised if I were told that, say,
A. C. Bradley found it as worthy of his attention as *Lear,* and feel

---

21. To 'grasp' is also to place or locate, that is, to perform also the *systematizing*
function, though this may be only minimally explicit or noted.

impelled to reexamine the play in the light of what he might have to say about it. Even if he had never gone beyond expressing a simple favorable judgment one might well take another look.

Such authority is a form of trust, a trust grounded in the conviction (itself reinforced by experience) that experience may be expected to repeat itself when its conditions are similar. This critic and this criticism have been found illuminating and fruitful in the past, there is thus reason to believe that on this occasion too they should be taken seriously. But this trust is not blind. It is not mechanically proportioned to past fruitfulness but rather to our *understanding* of what *relevantly* links this experienced fruitfulness with the present occasion. Our confidence is not simply that what has worked in the past may work again; it is modified by our insight into the conditions of the work—what has worked, how it works, and with respect to what. Does Bradley's insight into Shakespearian tragedy require us to take seriously an opinion of his with respect to Pope, Beethoven, or Delacroix? Of course it *may*, but if it does it will be because we have understood what this critic thinks about and how he thinks critically and have therefore to some extent determined the range within which his thinking may be helpful. In other words, our trust in critics (and therefore their authority) is conditioned by and proportionate to the extent to which we can share in the critical enterprise as thoughtful, that is, reflectively analytical and coherently principled.

In the long run, as our aesthetic experience deepens and expands and our judgment becomes more reflectively systematic—in short as we become more sophisticated aesthetically—we become more adept at detecting those critics and that criticism which is congenial with our own habits of aesthetic apprehension and judgment—so adept, in fact, that we are hardly conscious of the process by which we detect and welcome our aesthetic kin and, correspondingly, ignore alien thought and sensibility. This is one form of 'docility': almost a mutual yielding to each other of co-workers in the same skilled enterprise; "almost" only because in most cases there is not literally the give and take of discussion and because the relationship is usually that of senior and junior. When we feel that we have learned much from critics and their criticism it may be because they have shown us what is for us radically novel, but it is more likely to be because they have given voice to our unarticulated habits, clarified for us what we are already uncertainly attending to, enlarged and confirmed our command of regions already explored, and led us into adjoining fields of which we were unaware or had but dimly discerned.

Just for this reason our own Socratically skeptical reflection may suggest the need for a different sort of docility—a deliberate 'trying on' of alternative, initially uncongenial possibilities—a willing subjection to an alien yoke. We might then turn to critics whose perceptions are differently directed, who do not think and see and hear as we do, who inhabit aesthetic worlds into which we enter only with some difficulty because they require us to reorganize and redirect our imaginative perception.

VIII

But why should we do this? Why, that is, accept—if only provisionally—such disruptive authority? Certainly not on ill-imported 'liberal-democratic' grounds requiring us to take every opinion into account. Whatever else may be clear or obscure it is certainly clear that our docility must be stringently discriminating, that it must rest upon grounds proper to the activity and to that phase of the activity in which we are engaged, that, in short, it is one form of the "proper violence" which initially intrigued us.[22] What we are seeking to determine are the 'proprieties.' We have already considered when the opinion of mankind—what everyone thinks—is appropriately taken into account, but in the relationship we are now considering the *currency* of opinion is not relevant. What we seek is to be sought out because it offers a challenge to our customary aesthetic practice, to the ways in which we engage in and think about our imaginative functioning. A sign of such a difference *may* be a striking difference in judgments of merits, in critical eventuations, outcomes, results. Differences of this sort may point to a different kind of critical thoughtfulness, though they may also merely represent random eccentricity, ill-directed rebellion, or insanity. A more reliable mark of what we seek may be agreement in estimation where the grounds of estimation are markedly different, where, in other words, our attention is coherently redirected so as

22. See above, Prologue, Part Two, p. 14.

to grasp a different object, more reliable because what we seek is a difference of aesthetic functioning that is understood and knowingly practiced—one that is "reflectively analytical" and "coherently principled." Whether that is the case only investigation can determine. But we may still ask why we should even experimentally submit to a discipline so 'against the grain,' much less seek it out.

At this point we may realize that we have approached this problem before: that we are restating here with respect to authority the problem of 'pluralism' touched upon in our discussion of critical communication. There we were interested in the way in which communication broadly conceived might suggest to us the limitations of our experience, but we only touched upon the possibility of a 'radical' pluralism which would entail a systematically different experience. Then we suggested that "the notion of the real, the true, the finally-correctly-grasped object is to be taken as a limit which we actively attempt to approach rather than as what we must take as somehow given all along." [23]

To adapt this earlier language to the present stage of inquiry, we may say that we should by now be fully aware that a 'finally-correctly-grasped object' requires, is wholly correlative with, determines and is determined by a 'finally-correct-grasping.' In turn a 'finally-correct-grasping' presupposes a 'finally-correctly-disciplined-grasp-and-grasper,' and such a finally realized imaginatively functioning psyche is that authority which we all aspire to become and to which we endeavor to conform to the extent that we can identify its operation. We may well doubt that we shall ever encounter this Psyche enfleshed outside the sacred precincts of Parnassus, but everywhere we are often reminded of actual differences between our aesthetic functionings and those of others. To recognize these differences reflectively is to understand that no actual psyche can exhaust aesthetic activity and thus to feel at some point and in some degree the limits of our own activity. Limits are inevitable—no one can explore all thickets or live in all of God's Countries—but there are limits which are self-limitings, the limitations inherent in habituated direction of attention, effective blindnesses, trained insensibilities, prejudices, willful ignorances—all psychic traits rendering the world opaque and us unappreciative of God's

23. See above, chap. 3, p. 106.

Country were we fortunate enough to stumble into it. In practice the only way in which we can clearly identify and remove such limits is experimental—that is, by applying a "proper violence" in our aesthetic operations.

Most such suggestions of limitation we can readily test and respond to appropriately within the range of our own habits and skills. The realization that someone else not obviously insane finds *The Cherry Orchard* outrageously comic or that a respectable critic reads it as a melodramatic satire may surprise those of us who have been finding it tragic, but a reorientation to test out these possibilities requires only that we relocate (functionally, of course) this work within a well-understood range. Such reorientations require no justification other than the satisfactions they promise. Willingness to consider that we have 'got it wrong' or 'missed something' is based upon our experience in following such clues.

But more disturbing are limitations suggested by the possibility of a *radically* different plurality of aesthetic 'points of view,' a phrase hardly suggesting the extent and functional depth of the difference. *'Weltanschauungen'* would be better, were it taken to mean a plurality of experienced *worlds* differently ordered objectively, imaginatively, and conceptually. To each of us this amounts to the possibility that somehow we have 'got it *all* wrong,' or at least that our habits, skills, and understandings are so awry as to mandate a more or less complete reexamination of all that we hold dear, of all that we understand and our understanding of it all. It might be thought that the range and quality of satisfactions yielded by a stabilized, established practice is sufficient warrant for that practice and its assumptions. At least it seems clear that a thoroughly unsatisfying aesthetic practice would justify a search for alternatives, perhaps even abandonment of the enterprise.

But the question raised by the radically diverse alternatives hypothetically before us is precisely what is the enterprise, the practice, the activity and therefore also what satisfactions are proper to it and how are they to be given functional stability in a practice? Satisfactions may indicate that some functioning is successful, that some finality is realized, but cannot by themselves assure us that they are other than the fruits of circumstantial determinations of an individual psyche, not of a purposive individual orientation to the conditions of an activity having an integrity and autonomy resting upon universal conditions, defined by and defining goods claiming to be the objects of human powers as such, inherently shareable in and constitutive of a community. The possibility that we might have 'got it all wrong' is a possibility only if 'it' is an activity and endeavor not exhausted or limited by what we do, by the ways in which we try to give it concrete content. And therefore, too, it is doubtful that we can have it 'all' wrong, if that implies that the alternatives proposed have *nothing* in common with what we are doing and trying to do. They must, in order to be alternatives, be capable of some effective connection with what we do and think, and that within which this connection, this commonality, this relation is established is the idea of aesthetic activity and practice. What obligates us, then, to consider radically diverse alternatives is simply our engagement in this activity as an activity, as an end to be realized.[24] We have spoken throughout of 'finality,' posing the problem of critical or 'personal' authority as that of a 'finally-correctly-disciplined-grasp-and-grasper' but we should see now more clearly than ever that the primary reference of 'finally' here is not temporal, but 'teleological'—namely, functional. That is, 'finally-correctly-disciplined' means, first, 'disciplined as required by the end or function constitutive of the activity' and only secondarily 'in the long run' or 'as a result of a progressive development toward more complete realization.'

What makes the question in its radically pluralistic form difficult to formulate is that it depends upon distinguishing between differences which are limits to our activity but not derived from the way in which we are attempting to carry on the activity and those calling into question the conception of end and function underlying our practice as a whole. As an occasion calling for docility on our part, for an at least provisional acceptance of external guidance, it cannot be our usual state of mind: we cannot always be asking whether what we are doing is right or we should never do it—or anything.[25]

---

24. The reader might recognize here another version of an older formula—"No man would willingly be deceived."

25. We might invoke again Justice Jackson's remark about the U.S. Supreme Court, "We are not final because we are infallible; we are infallible because we are final." (See note 1 above.) That sort of relation generates a kind of *practical* infallibility: for 'practical purposes,' what the Court said must be treated as inerrant and all of us engaged in the enterprise of justice must 'work within it' until it is reconsid-

This radical moment, directing attention as it does to what claim we have to a "coherently *principled*" discipline of taste and feeling, is more a philosophical than a properly critical moment. Such a questioning arises 'naturally' out of reflection on our aesthetic activity in proportion as it becomes more systematically, intellectually reflective; we may become engaged in aesthetics or 'philosophical reflection' as a phase or moment of critical reflection, but we are not concerned—in this inquiry—with critical reflection and aesthetic activity as moments of philosophical reflection. Certainly we need not address here the generic problems of radical pluralism, of the 'dialectic' of warring, apparently exclusive opinions, attitudes, methods, and systems.

IX

We may then turn with some sense of relief to consider other putative sources of authority, and we may begin, following the path sketched out earlier, by asking what might be meant by the 'authority of the object'? Surely there can be no problem here: the business of our aesthetic powers is with objectifying, objects and objectivity. These are the correlates of perceiving, imagining, perception and imagination. Later we stressed the correlation of the 'finally-correctly-grasped-object' with 'grasper, grasping and grasp,' but surely it is obvious that the correlation is complete: that we cannot ultimately distinguish between what is grasped and the object. To grasp by imaginative perception is to objectify, to find, to have something constituted concretely before us—not *merely* that, of course, but *certainly* that. If by the authority of the object we mean simply that imaginative perception works necessarily with the materials of sense and feeling and terminates with these elements coherently ordered in a whole; if, that is, we mean simply that the autonomy and integrity of aesthetic activity can be analyzed in terms of the characteristics of the objects which are grasped in it and that my aesthetic judgment must be grounded in

---

ered by the Court. The relation between finality and (in)fallibility we postulate is analogous. The analogy would be complete were we to argue that the finality of the Court in the sense of 'putting an end to' should rest upon its complete discharge of the function of doing justice.

and attributed to the quality of those objects, have we not simply rediscovered the authority of my taste, albeit in a different form?

Of course—but is that the situation in which 'the object' is invoked as authoritative, or given an opportunity to exert its aesthetic cogency, its authority? Let us recall Emerson—"I reserve my admiration as much as I can; I make a continual effort not to be pleased. . . . And I walked coolly round and round the marble lady but . . . saw and felt that mankind have had good reason for their preference of this excellent work." Here clearly 'the object' is 'appealed' to as an alternative ground for the determination of my judgment, an alternative to the ground offered by the opinion, the preference of mankind. Emerson's coolness is an "effort" to allow or even to *require* that the object make its impression without the aid of a predisposition on my part toward a pleasing ('warm'?) experience and a favorable judgment. That is, it is an effort to avoid prejudgment, prejudice—judgment not the fruit of my experience of the object and likely to distort that experience—the general structure of problems of authority we have already observed.

To interpret the authority of my aesthetic experience as an appeal to the object is thus not to have recourse to the object as somehow constituted outside of my experience; rather it is to insist that aesthetically the object as authoritative for me is to be found only in my imaginative perception, in my encounter with the object in the sense in which it is available for apprehension by me and others as well. In the broadest and simplest sense, then, to appeal to the object is to reject any secondhand or substitute account of it as adequate to constitute that experience which is authoritative for me. It is to insist that any judgment—characterizing, locating, evaluating—not based upon my own encounter with the object is *for me* provisional, tentative, subject to such revision as my direct experience shall demand.

Paradoxically, it may therefore be the most carefully and deliberately executed descriptions or reproductions which are for me the most misleading, for they will be those in which another's view as to how something is to be read, how it is to be seen, what in it is important to be heard will be most evident. But in one way or another and in some degree all such alternatives effectively filter the object through another psyche, through another's experience. It is therefore incumbent upon us not only that our judgment be grounded in our own encounter with the object but also that we be the judge of what conditions are properly imposed upon that experience if it is to be adequate for our purposes. In other words, we must not only read and see for ourselves, we must decide how that reading, seeing, hearing is to be undertaken, what the object demands of us if it is to be adequately apprehended, if—we may say—we are to do it justice.

Emerson in the Uffizi in 1833 is no bad guide in these respects. On his first encounter with "the statue that enchants the world" he saw that "truly the Venus deserves to be visited from afar. It is not adequately represented by the plaster casts." But on this occasion— his first day in Florence, a day of fervid anticipation and rich revelation which left him "dazzled and drunk with beauty"—he reserved judgment, returning when he could walk "coolly round and round the marble lady" in disciplined search of her charm.

In the ordinary conduct of our aesthetic lives and especially in that *systematic* expansion of which the norm is catholicity, these considerations are not trivial. That descriptions, reproductions, and all other modes of *re*presentation, no matter how worthy their intention and how painstaking and expert their technique, may be woefully inadequate to what is found in living encounter with an object is a lesson usually learned at the cost of surprises and shocks, of the embarrassments of error and retraction and the difficulties of more or less radical reorientation and revision. We have all shared, according to our various capacities and situations, that sense of being overpowered by a novel revelation which overcame John Ruskin when he saw what Tintoretto had done in the Scuola di San Rocco—that same Tintoretto the kind and quality of whose work he had so well understood until he saw it.[26] And, as with Tintoretto and Ruskin, while there may be costs, there are also rewards in the shape of additions to our aesthetic worlds of further sources of interest and satisfaction.[27]

26. See above, chap. 3, p. 116.
27. Of course, as we have seen in discussing the criticism of Longinus and Ruskin (see above, chap. 3, p. 94), descriptions and other *re*presentations may be taken to be aesthetic objects in their own right and as such they may be better than the originals they represent. I know of no reason why a photograph of a rather dull building may not be more beautiful than the building—that is, be a better photograph than the building is a building. And that might be in virtue of its misrepre-

However, it may be doubted that these considerations, important as they are, exhaust the force of an appeal to the authority of the aesthetic object. For surely to appeal to the authority of the object is not merely to invoke what is found there in actual encounter but also *what is found* rather than what might be imported or 'read into' what is there, particularly, of course, upon the suggestion or following the lead of alien opinion.

But is such a distinction—between what is found in and what is brought to any occasion of imaginative perception—a comfortable one? Indeed, is it not one of those distinctions which become very puzzling when reflected upon even though 'in practice' they are made 'all the time'? What, actually, are we doing when we appeal to the *object* as to what is there or 'given'? Have we not argued that literally what is given is only potentially *an* object, that is, indeterminate, incompletely ordered, admitting of diverse 'readings'? Is not then any recourse to the 'object' in this sense bound to be either fruitless or deceptive—that is, in effect simply a way of introducing another function of determination, another reading?

Hamlet
   Do you see yonder cloud that's almost in shape of a camel?
Polonius
   By th'mass and 'tis, like a camel indeed.
Hamlet
   Methinks it is like a weasel.
Polonius
   It is backed like a weasel.
Hamlet
   Or like a whale.
Polonius
   Very like a whale.[28]

We may observe (rather solemnly) that this interchange presumes (with respect to perceptual determination) extreme indeterminacy or plasticity on the one side and maximal, schematically lucid 'form' on the other: 'amorphous' clouds and unambiguous

---

sentation. Nor should one rule out the possibility that there may in fact be *aesthetically* indiscernible versions of an object. But we should really say, in such a case, 'aesthetically indiscernible objects.' The possibilities cannot be adequately discussed in a note.

   28. *Hamlet* III, ii.

shapes. Of course complete indeterminacy ('prime matter') is a limit never actually reached, nor are the identifying schematisms of shape or form ever completely determinate, wholly unambiguous. If these limits were ever actually attained, any appeal to an object would, of course, be meaningless, since any and every object would be equally available for perception: that is, there would be no recalcitrance to formation on the part of the material or any uncertainty as to what form it is to take. The data of sense would admit with equal ease of any and every determination, and our faculties of perception would be completely creative of the world of perceived objects. We might then say quite literally that

> . . . imagination bodies forth
> The forms of things . . .
> Turns them to shapes, and gives to airy nothing
> A local habitation . . . [29]

(waiving the question whether 'nothing' is quite the right way to refer to pure materiality). And—curiously but inevitably—this same situation of perception would exemplify what might seem to be the case opposed to that of complete indeterminacy on the part of what is 'given,' for the object in this situation would be—as 'bodied forth,' as instantly and effortlessly perceived—completely determinate, completely unambiguous, so that it is difficult to see how any dubiety or difference of apprehension or interpretation could arise. In any case, any doubt or indeterminacy would be instantly resolved by reference to a so pellucidly distinct object.

X

Any functionally authoritative appeal to the object, then, must assume an imaginative situation which is somewhere between these extremes of determinacy on the part of the 'object' as, at least initially, given. And such, of course, is the situation in which we actually find ourselves aesthetically. That is, we begin with an object partially determinate—or, one might say, with some working assumptions about its objectivity—in order to initiate an imaginatively discursive process of exploration and further determination

---

29. *Midsummer Night's Dream*, V, 1 (suitably adjusted to make the point).

tending toward the emergence of a 'finally' coherently articulated object. In some degree we are always, in imaginative activity , in the situation of Alice after her first reading of *Jabberwocky* (though we might aspire to greater honesty).

> 'It seems very pretty,' she said when she had finished it, 'but it's *rather* hard to understand!' (You see, she didn't like to confess even to herself, that she couldn't make it out at all). 'Somehow it seems to fill my head with ideas—only I don't know exactly what they are! However, *somebody* killed *something*: that's clear, at any rate——'[30]

However, we observe something else: that 'somebody killed something' is clear in the context of other clarities—that this is an object of certain dimensions and kind, a poem, a literary object (otherwise how could one *finish reading* it), that it is a story, a narrative including persons and things, agents and patients, and much else functionally entailed by these 'clarities.' And the entailment *is functional*, for such clarities are *working* assumptions, functional habitudes that do not so much tell us what is there as guide us in exploring and discovering it. That is, they are 'aesthetically heuristic,' a function we have discussed before in relation to critical communication.[31] Further, we see at once that this coincidence is not accidental. It is only when there is such a functioning context within which an object is located and problems of further determination in the terms of that objectivity are felt that an appeal to the object as ground for the resolution of those problems is possible.

Such a situation may or may not be literally and explicitly a situation of controversy—of a difference of opinion as between different judges. (In Ruskin's encounter with the Tintoretto of the

---

30. Lewis Carroll, *Through the Looking-Glass, and What Alice Found There,* chap. 1 (again, many editions, many printings, many commentaries, including that of Humpty Dumpty later in the same seminal work). Cf. Hume: "There is a flutter or hurry of thought which attends the first perusal of any piece, and which confounds the genuine sentiment of beauty. The relation of the parts is not discerned: the true characters of style are little distinguished. The several perfections and defects seem wrapped up in a species of confusion, and present themselves indistinctly to the imagination." In consequence, in the case of "any work of importance," it "will even be requisite that that very individual performance be more than once perused by us, and be surveyed in different lights with attention and deliberation" (*Of the Standard of Taste*).

31. See above, chap. 3, pp. 97 et seq.

Scuola di San Rocco what suffered revision was *his own* prior opinion or judgment. If he had a quarrel it was with himself.) But if there is difference or a controversy, it will be with respect to something (an identifiable object) and (one might say) about that something in identifiable respects. We may all agree that '*somebody* killed *something*.' We may not agree that the poem is "a sorry tale of the destruction of innocent wildlife"—a way of reading the poem dubiously qualifying that killing.[32] But both readings are readings of this text, this poem, this narrative poem, this versified narrative of this fatal action, and so on. Only in an environment, so to speak, of such working assumptions can anything be *found* to be objectively and authoritatively there. Moreover, it is only because these 'contexts' are or can be public—shareable and shared—that there can be objects in common, objects which we may encounter differently, experience differently, of which we may develop variant readings. For the genuinely illiterate there is not only no variant reading of *Jabberwocky*: *Jabberwocky* is not an identifiable object there to encounter, to experience, to appeal to.

Or, at least, it is not a *literary* object. Such a person (a nonreader) might single out in a given printing of the text of *Alice* the visual pattern which *readers* would identify as differentiating verse from prose. The verse pattern so isolated might then constitute a rather limp sort of visual object—a pattern of not very subtly varied repetitions of shaped units possessing a certain magnitude and even, very weakly, a beginning, middle, and end—classical criterion of wholeness.[33] And with respect to this object there might be differences of what, given our context here, had better be called 'seeings' rather than 'readings.' These differences might then in their terms—that is, in the ways appropriate to this sort of visual object—admit of resolution by an appeal to its authority.

But what is the point of such an odd—even bizarre—transformation (transmogrification?) of objectivity? Simply to emphasize that while no process of appeal to objective authority can be undertaken without the working presence of 'assumptions' about objects,

32. Peter Heath, *The Philosopher's Alice* (New York, 1974), p. 139, note 10.
33. Consider Sir Benjamin Backbite on his "love elegies": ". . . you shall see them on a beautiful quarto page, where a neat rivulet of text shall murmur through a meadow of margin. 'Foregad, they will be the most elegant things of their kind!" (Sheridan, *The School for Scandal*, act i, scene 1).

these assumptions themselves are subject in that process to revision
at any point. To put it simply, we must begin somewhere, but we
can move in many directions, all of them, of course, effected from
and affected by where we begin. Within any given context of objectivity there are always alternatives amounting to radically different
hypotheses as to how the data are to be read, seen, or interpreted
and therefore as to what is said, what is seen, what is to be felt and
enjoyed. That *Jabberwocky* is a versified narrative in which a killing
occurs may commit us to a *reading* but to little else. By itself it neither excludes or uniquely selects any of the hypotheses represented
by "tragedy, comedy, history, pastoral, pastoral-comical, historical-
pastoral, tragical-historical, tragical-comical, historical-pastoral,
scene individable, or poem unlimited,"[34] each of which might
yield—in an experimental reading—a very different quality for
that killing which, initially, we take to be baldly given.

It is impossible to develop the implications of what is here
simply touched upon without elaborating a full-dress hermeneutical and critical theory. But some suggestive concreteness may be
given by noting how both the passages from *Hamlet* cited in this
context themselves exemplify the problems and procedures which
they are intended to help formulate. Thus the dialogue between
Hamlet and Polonius concerning clouds and shapes, though
largely intelligible taken point by point, line by line, is, as an episode, itself ambiguous—a cloud, so to speak, awaiting a shape
which might be given to it in a given reading or performance. The
words, the lines, even the pattern of interchange do not tell us by
themselves what either of the interlocutors is to be taken to be
doing. Is Polonius actually being led by the nose or is he simply
indulging the perhaps dangerously eccentric prince? (Of course,
he might be doing both, and these alternatives are not exhaustive.)
What is Hamlet doing, we might ask—what is the 'method of his
madness' here? Such questions, it must be emphasized, are not
mere critical subtleties—they are questions as to how actors are to
act, of what is to be heard and seen to be 'going on' in the scene.
To resolve them actors, directors, and readers have recourse to
other parts of the play as 'given,' but a moment's reflection reveals those data admit of similar ambiguities and that what is

34. *Hamlet*, II, 2. See above, chap. 3, pp. 101–2.

sought (and may emerge) in such recourse is a imaginative (re)construction of the play as a whole, one that takes the fullest account of what is 'given' while at the same time realizing in imaginative presentation a qualitative whole in which the data take on determinate functions.[35] The alternatives represented by "tragedy, comedy, history . . ." simply are the crudest ways of identifying kinds of qualities which such wholes may have.

In that list in this context (our context) the final member—"poem unlimited"—is intriguing, for it suggests a radically 'open-ended' analytical, interpretive possibility, seeming to require only (and even that ambiguously) that we consider our object to be 'literary' without further specification. Such a possibility is theoretically instructive. At first sight it seems to have the great merit of leaving us, as readers, as interpreters, almost wholly free, untrammeled by dogmatic preconceptions. But in proportion as that is the case, of course, it also fails in heuristic power, as a source of hypotheses for exploration and development of the materials before us. Such is the case if we take the freedom it offers as simply negative—as instructing us merely that no direction of exploration is forbidden to us, or, what comes to much the same thing, that there is an infinity of ways to go, all equally open, none sign-posted. We are placed, thus, at a point in an undifferentiated space, deprived of any orientation.[36] But we need not so read it. As a proper culmination of the list which it concludes, it *is* the most positively liberating, the most richly enfranchising of possible ways to go, for then it may be taken to mean that all of these ways are open to us, *and* that we must not assume that they exhaust the possibilities.

It may be observed that this reading is one which emerges when Shakespeare's text is, in effect, incorporated into our text—a reflective, critical, 'theoretical' context. One might pursue the process of interpretation and exemplify its diversity by asking how this 'reading' of "poem unlimited" can be related to its 'original,' 'dra-

35. The reader may identify here that familiar geometrical paradigm—the 'hermeneutical circle.'

36. Of course this is, as stated, false, for we are, after all, in a space defined as 'literary' or 'poetic,' and it is that space which is undifferentiated and with respect to which we are not oriented.

matic,' 'Shakespearian' meaning,[37] but perhaps we have said enough to make our point and to exemplify the complexity of the processes and the difficulties of interpretive and critical practice. Yet criticism and interpretation do little more than make explicit and explicate the processes of imaginative apprehension which are the activities of our aesthetic living.

XI

However, contemplating our versatility and its origin in the formation of our 'taste,' of our individual aesthetic worlds, serves to reveal what, after all, may be the most important, the most basic sense in which the power and authority of objects is manifested. So far we have considered that authority in situations in which to speak of 'appealing' to the object is appropriate, for they are situations taking the form, in a variety of ways, of actual or possible differences of judgment, of apprehension. But prior—both temporally and 'logically'—to the possibility of differences with respect to objects and objectivity is that encountered actuality which reveals to us what is (and therefore what can be) beautiful, what is and thus can be moving, those powerful qualities which make differ-

---

37. A note from Harold Jenkins' edition of the play is illuminating.

[*scene individable*] Usually explained as a play which observes the unity of place, as distinct from *poem unlimited*, which observes no unities. But these meanings are not obvious, and both terms may be more appropriately interpreted as bringing the already ridiculous categories to a climax in an all-inclusive (*unlimited*) and unclassifiable (*individable*) drama. [*Hamlet*, London, 1982 (The Arden edition), note to l. 395, act ii, scene ii]

Without passing on the results of this analysis, we may take its procedure to be appropriate. A range of available meanings is developed (it should be noted that they are reasonably, not whimsically, available), and one is chosen on the ground that it best fits the context *if that context is taken to have as a whole a certain dramatic character which its elements effectively articulate*. The meaning chosen for "poem unlimited" clearly has a relation to one of the possible meanings considered in our 'theoretical' reading, but there 'all-inclusiveness' became heuristic weakness and the freedom of lawlessness—in this reading it becomes the absurd climax of a process of verbal manipulation revealing the ridiculous emptiness of a categorical scheme. If our use of the passage for theoretical purposes is construed as *conceptual* manipulation also an exercise in absurdity, the two absurdities are widely different in ground and effect.

ences of judgment and apprehension with respect to the objects in which we find them worth exploring and submitting to their authority.

Once again we may see that we have encountered in a different form and in a different context, a basic feature of aesthetic activity deriving from its nature as an autonomous imaginative function simultaneously exploring and ordering our experience. The extent and qualitative richness of the world as it comes to be articulated for us individually in objective sources of aesthetic delight and emotion are no doubt the fruit of reflection and directed search, but reflection and direction are initiated and sustained by objects of nature and of art in which beauty is individualized and passion localized. Our experience of them is, after all, what we reflect upon; it is their experienced worth that generates an eager appetite for refinement and further search; and they continue, unless we grow wearily insensitive, to administer those shocks in which 'surprised by joy' or shaken by emotion we are made aware of novel, even revolutionary possibilities for taste and feeling.

It would be indeed a distorted account of aesthetic life to suggest that it consists largely of occasions of controversy, that the things which we find beautiful and moving figure in it as sources of differences of judgment and grounds for their resolution, that, in other words, it is fundamentally reflective and critical, discursive rather than intuitive, an enjoyment of understanding rather than of perception and imagination. Reflection and criticism are, in the end, instrumental functions. Indispensable and essential, nevertheless they are as they do, while that experience from which they begin and in which, if we are fortunate, they terminate needs no further consequence to be rewarding. In some better world in which the discipline of taste and feeling sprang full-formed with the fountainheads of sensibility and intelligence, the world would present itself to us from the beginning as richly furnished with beautiful things inviting not consideration and reconsideration but unalloyed and immediate satisfaction. In such an experience the 'authority' of objects would not be distinguishable from their beauty and their pathos; their aesthetic cogency would be complete, their command over our attention and our love would be freely embraced. Something like that world is what we aspire to create for ourselves by that disciplining in which reflective criticism and the weighing of authorities play their parts.

But in the situation of search and development in which we actually function are there not, over and above this sense in which objects exert a general authority in virtue, one might say, simply of their objectivity, objects which come to possess an especially authoritative role? Are there not objects which are landmarks in a developing aesthetic life, points of reference, 'touchstones,' perhaps 'classics'? If by 'classical' objects we mean those which are identified and endorsed by a consensus (always of course more or less momentary and more or less complete) on the part of 'everyone' or of critical voices, we can only reply that objects as so 'canonized' are indirect manifestations of whatever authority such opinions are justly entitled to, and as such we have already dealt with them. But we may mean by 'classics' not those objects which are identified to us by someone as canonical, nor those which are perceived by us to satisfy some articulated rule, some specified canon, but rather those which *for us*—for an individual reflective imaginative sensibility—function *as the canon*, give the rule not by conforming to it but by being the object the rule *for* which is (no doubt vainly) to be sought, if the question is one of rules. Such objects are exemplary, not as being good or even perfect examples of some given rule but as what-is-to-be-exemplified, as being the rule and in that being *giving* the rule. In the arts, such objects function as objects of imitation and (more rarely but far more significantly) of emulation. In analytical criticism they may function as sources of rules—of formulae and formulable devices—or in the best sense as standards and exemplars. And in our individually developing aesthetic lives they function as objects to which we constantly refer and return as, apparently, inexhaustible in the experience they offer. But if that is the case, is it not because they exemplify not only what beauty or sublimity may be in the materials, the devices, the forms which can be imitated and formulated but also because they exemplify the order of activity in which materials, devices, and forms come to serve the demands of imaginative perception, activity which can continue to spawn other actualities and is thus inexhaustible? It is this which qualifies them as candidates for *emulation* and to which critics may rightly point as exemplary. For this reason—namely that what is 'classically' exemplified is an activity rather than a result (a result evoking with extraordinary power the activity from which it results)—the authority of classics is perhaps best treated not as an authority of objects but of authors, and thus we may now turn with some expectation of profit to discuss the authority of the artist, the last of the putative sources of authority we undertook to examine.

XII

Yet again the first question we must ask is whether in fact such authority differs from the authority of any other critical intelligence or from the authority of an artist's work in such radically significant fashion as to require special consideration? Of course, any artistic work and the work of any artist in any tradition represents in some degree a kind of selection and emphasis which is analogous to explicit critical talk and may in fact have a more profound influence than 'criticism,' and most artists in the traditions which are alive for us not only had opinions about their contemporaries and their predecessors but are likely to have made them explicit. Florentine tradition, for example, preserves many pungent remarks attributed to Michelangelo, some of them supposedly of almost imperial potency. Thus it was he (as Emerson noted) who fixed the opinion of mankind by saying that Ghiberti's second set of doors for the Baptistery of Florence were so beautiful that "they might well stand at the Gates of Paradise" and he whose stinging question about Baccio d'Agnolo's Gallery encircling the dome of Brunelleschi's cathedral ("Why are they putting that cricket cage up there?") stopped the work in its tracks, as one can clearly see even today.[38]

It would be surprising if most or even all artists were not critics

38. Vasari (*Vite,* "Lorenzo Ghiberti," "Filippo Brunelleschi") preserves both of these stories, though not the details of the second one. Michelangelo, of course, had a considerable talent for verbal expression, as his letters and poems witness. Some of his testimony is still cited to influence taste of another sort. There is (or was) a brand of bottled water in Italy which quoted his recommendation of water from its 'source' on its label, and discussions of that noble wine *Vernaccia di San Gimignano* frequently quote his favorable and vivid description of a wine from that ancient city which may be ancestrally identified with it.

in this sense, though few may be as sharply articulate or as influential, but Michelangelo was not a critic in the same sense as, for example, Berlioz, Schumann, Sir Walter Scott, or Bernard Shaw, all of whom contributed to the periodical critical writing of their day, a practice of 'doubling in brass' probably more common than ever. Such writing easily moves into other kinds of critical expression, more explicitly 'theoretical' (as in Sir Joshua Reynolds' *Discourses,* Stravinsky's *Poetics of Music,* or Coleridge's *Biographia Literaria*) or 'programmatic,' in which the chief effort is to advocate or codify for emulation the artistic practice of a 'school,' a group or an individual (for example, Wagner's *Opera and Drama,* the famous "Preface" to *Lyrical Ballads,* or the innumerable 'manifestoes' that enliven the history of the visual arts in the last century or more).[39]

But our question must be whether there is reason to believe that the criticism of artist/critics (or critic/artists) is in the relevant respects so different that it cannot be dealt with as might be the work of critics otherwise qualified. That is, why cannot we welcome their guidance and accept their authority so far as and in those respects in which we find it to be fruitful, with due recognition that fruitfulness is not a simple idea and with no fixed ideas as to the relation of their artistic qualifications to their critical qualifications.

If anything, with respect to that relationship, one might—*in general*—consider the criticism of a practicing artist suspect as likely to be biased to the point of prejudicial blindness. Biased it may be by competition and competitiveness, but more subtly by limitations of understanding and sympathy inherent in that dedicated conviction as to the right (and wrong) way of practicing an art at a given time and place characteristic of so many artists. Of course, such fierce clarity of view may be within its limits an advantage, and we know also that there are many artists, even many great artists, of large artistic sympathy and generous impulse,[40] but it is also true that there are many cases in which what one artist says of another's work, even if only an expression of a general attitude, is likely to be more revealing about the former than the latter. However, if

39. It seems unnecessary to provide documentation for these almost randomly selected works, most of them well known in that way in which writings seldom actually read except by 'specialists' are well known.

40. See, for example, what we said above about Sir Walter Scott. (Prologue, Part One, pp. 10–11).

there is a case in which the critical talk of artists, what artists have
to say about art, is specially privileged and peculiarly authoritative
we have now stumbled upon it, for what they have to say—directly
or indirectly—about their own work or of themselves is likely to be
treated with a special respect.

No doubt this respect is in large part simply a form of that
preoccupation with art, artists, creation, creativity, and creative
expression which is evident in so much of contemporary discussion. When to give an account of our aesthetic life is to give an
account of our experience of art, and to give an account of that
experience is to interpret it as an expressive act ordered by an object bearing the burdens of meaning incorporated in it by the original expressive enactment of the artist, it would be surprising indeed if anything the artist had to say about that expression would
not be taken very seriously. After all, are we not intended to reenact it? But, of course, even on this view of aesthetic experience
it remains true that the best clues to what we are intended to do,
to understand, to feel, to express ought to be offered by the artist's
work rather than by something he or she has to say *about* it, unless
of course that saying helps us to orient ourselves fruitfully toward
the work. And so we arrive again where we started, grateful for
whatever guidance we are afforded, but necessarily the judges of
the worth of any guidance in *our* apprehension, *our* experience, *our*
encounter with the work. On this reckoning in the long run artists
as critics, whether with respect to their own work or the work of
others, will have to make their way with us as do other critics with
other qualifications. The grains of salt with which we take what
they say may be different in source and application, but fundamentally the process of 'judging the judges' will be the same.

XIII

May not we similarly dispose of the other way in which artists exert
their authority, that is, in and through their works? Have we not
sufficiently considered the authority of 'the object'? Why should the
object's being a work of art attributable to an artist make a significant difference with respect to that authority, unless we are to admit
that we are swayed by reputations, by mighty names, by the satis-

faction of joining the rest of "mankind" in giving "one testimony more to the surpassing genius" of this or that artist?

But there may be one case of importance which we have not touched—namely that one in which the name of the artist attached to the work connects it with other works we have experienced and found to be objectively compelling. Thus there may be generated in us an expectation which *in general* we may call an expectation of *mastery* and in the most powerful and significant instances an expectation of *absolute* mastery. By expectations we do not mean, as we have noted in another context, mere vague anticipations that, for example, some sort of satisfaction will accrue, but ways of positioning ourselves functionally with respect to 'objects,' ways in which our powers of imaginative apprehension are adjusted and attuned for the emergence and the special delights of a definite kind of work.

'Mastery' as an authoritative function emerges as our aesthetic worlds expand and our tastes develop along their individual lines. We come to see this or that world of art as consisting not only of individual works of art but of groups of works, more or less definite, including those groupings known as 'styles' and 'schools.' Common origin in an artistic personality may well become, for the purposes of taste and appreciation, as important a linkage among works as we can make. Such a personality is *artistic* because the 'person' is known in the works, known as that characteristic *mastery* of technique, form, and expression which is manifest in these works.[41] The projected continuity of that individual mastery forms and justifies expectations of a work, new to us, linked to some we already know by the shared way of working signaled by attribution to the same worker.

Indeed, in most cases what we effectively know of artists is known through their works and is a 'knowing' of their ways of working and the 'workings' which are at once products and procedures. It is usually accounted a mark of significant cultural sophistication to have accurate information (including pronunciation!)

---

41. It is hardly necessary to point out that one may also be aware, with differential consequences, of a characteristic incompetence, ineptitude, or routine efficiency.

with respect to the names and other biographical attributes of artists, but more often than not our functional knowledge of artists
whom we 'know well' would be most accurately conveyed by adopt-
ing the practice by which historians of the visual arts refer to 'The
Master of the Ghent Altarpiece' or 'The Master of the Cagnola Madonna.' Of course, there are famous cases of authors/artists about
whom we are so ignorant that they are little more than proper
names substituted for such a formula as 'The Author of Waverley.'
Such indeed are Homer—the 'Master of the *Iliad* and the *Odyssey*'—
and even Shakespeare.

But even where there is abundant 'biographical' information
available, the knowledge which works in our interpretive expectations is likely to be largely that of an experienced 'mastery,' so that
Beethoven is effectively the 'Master of the Nine Symphonies, etc.,'
Jane Austen the 'Master of *Pride and Prejudice* and The Other Novels,' and so on. And, in fact, our knowledge of this sort can be so
rich, so powerful, so differentiated with respect to individual mastery that on reflection it may seem odd to say that we know little of
these persons with whose powers and interests we are so familiar.

But we cannot here enter into the problems and 'creative personalities' or the critical practices nourished by biography and 'history.' We must look to our muttons—that is, to 'mastery' as 'authority.'

Commonly the expectations aroused by 'mastery' are positive,
that is, we anticipate a certain sort of *excellence* of performance in
that sense in which 'performance,' like 'work,' is primarily the name
of a thing, an object. Thus the expected mastery is of a certain sort
of thing of a certain order of excellence. This is, of course, a com-
plicated way of saying that we have quite definite expectations of
kind and quality when we are told that we are about to hear a
Strauss[42] *waltz* or are told, in a gallery somewhere, not to miss the
Degas *print* in the next room. These are things that we know how
to appreciate—that is, we know how to approach them so as to
enjoy what they are and therefore also what kind and quality of
satisfaction we may in general anticipate. Yet we must say "in general" not only because each performance has its own individual-

---

42. I refer to Johann Strauss the Younger.

ity—mastery is never entirely reducible to formula—but because there may always be surprises, with respect to both kind and quality. In an important sense we value surprises—violations of expectation—insofar as they turn out to be manifestations of *versatile* mastery. But this has to do with our evaluation of artists, only indirectly of works.

However, were we to be frequently disappointed as to quality, we should appropriately revise our assessment of mastery, which, after all, implies a considerable reliability, a consistency of and in performance. And is not this to assert that whatever authority is possessed by authorship is simply the authority of works, of performances? Perhaps, but there may be a form of cogency inherent in the recognition of artistic origin which we have not yet fully explicated.

In 1836, when Beethoven's *Choral Symphony* had been before the musical public for some ten years (first performed 1824, published 1826) Mendelssohn's friend J. G. Droysen ended a long letter to him by expressing his puzzlement and asking for help. "Recently I heard Beethoven's immense last symphony and was completely at a loss. . . . Yet I'm already acquainted with Beethoven; I've thoroughly enjoyed his wonderful C-minor [symphony] and even understand it in my layman's way." Mendelssohn's reply is exemplary.

> So I'm to talk to you about the grand Ninth Symphony with chorus? In general it is very difficult to talk about music. Before everything you must hear it. The instrumental movements belong among the greatest that I know of in the art; from the point at which the voices enter I also do not understand it, that is, I find only fragments perfected, and when that is the case with such a master the fault probably lies with us. Or with the execution. And so I say, you must hear the first parts as well; I doubt that is likely to be easy in Berlin. But in the choral movement the vocal parts are so positioned that I know of no place in which they might go well, and perhaps that is up to now the source of the incomprehensibility.[43]

43. Carl Wehmer, ed., *Ein tief gegründet Herz. Der Briefwechsel Felix Mendelssohn-Bartholdys mit Johann Gustav Droysen* (Heidelberg, 1959), letters 8, 9, pp. 46, 49–50. I give the German text, if only because there are some phrases almost impossible to

What could be a more striking acknowledgement of the authority of the master? *"With such a master the fault probably lies with us."* That is, if it makes no sense, it is to be presumed that we do not know how to hear it, how to read it, that we have something to learn, and we accept the burden solely because we assume a mastery in the work which demands of us a corresponding discipline. *Or* it may be that the master's intentions have not been realized in presentation, in execution, and we are to assume the burden of fulfilling those intentions, so that again the fault lies with us, with what we have done or failed to do rather than with the work of the master. In either case, it is we who are to exert ourselves, we who are to learn, whether merely as listeners or readers or as literal performers and executants. It may be an odd expression, but is it not quite simply the case that we thus accept the burden of making the work for ourselves? We assume that it is there to be made; we assume (in Mendelssohn's language) that what we now hear are fragments, that is, that they are parts of some coherent and powerful whole and that they can be heard as such, that *we* can hear them as such, that there is potentially a whole to be heard and enjoyed and that actualizing it is our responsibility. We proceed on the assumption (it is important to insist that we *proceed,* that we exert ourselves) that it is not Homer who nods but we who are inept or unready.

For, of course, it must be a Homer: "with *such* a master the fault probably lies with us." Such a masterly status is not easily achieved. But it would be better to say, since what is so obvious here is *our willing docility,* that it is not lightly *conferred.* That is to say that such mastery is a functional place in what might be called our aesthetic

---

translate—notably what I have rendered as "I find only fragments perfected . . .": "Ich finde nur einzelnes vollkommen."

Von der grossen Neunten Sinfonie mit Chören soll ich Dir sprechen? Es is schwer, überhaupt über Musik zu sprechen. Du müsstest sie vor allem hören. Die Instrumentalsätze gehören zum grössten, was ich in der Kunst kenne; von da an, wo die Stimmen eintreten, verstehe auch ich es nicht, d.h. ich finde nur einzelnes vollkommen, und wenn das bei solch einem Meister der Fall ist, so liegt die Schuld wahrscheinlich an uns. Oder der Ausführung. Und darum sage ich, Du müsstest auch die ersten Stücke hören; Ich zweifle, dass es in Berlin leicht der Fall sein kann. Im Gesangsatz aber sind die Singstimmen so gelegt, dass ich keinen Ort kenne, wo er gut gehen könnte, und daher kommt vielleicht bis jetzt die Unverständlichkeit.

economy: to be 'a Homer' is to play this role, to exercise this power for someone. But what is the role and who is qualified to play it?

XIV

To an extent, of course, any mastery once recognized and accepted carries with it such an authority; if our expectations of quality are disappointed, we are willing to consider the possibility that we might have been inattentive, that the conditions for appreciation were not propitious, that we might have missed something. But where the mastery is clearly restricted to 'a certain sort of thing of a certain order of excellence' we are not particularly surprised or troubled by an occasional failure—usually characterizable as a 'performance' not up to the master's usual standard. But in proportion as it is less clear what these restrictions may be the mastery approaches what we called above an *absolute* level, reaching a point at which only with the greatest reluctance, only after we have tried our best to locate and correct our own deficiencies of appreciation, are we willing to consider that Homer may in fact have nodded. And even then we are uneasy in our judgment and would welcome the discovery that we are wrong.

To outline an explanation of this phenomenon of taste is not really difficult, though any explanation will point to the limits of our understanding of art and its conditions. Those who are masters of a sort and with respect to a kind of artistic possibility are so because for us they set or powerfully contribute to setting the standards for such a kind: they have shown us what can be done in this vein, what the possibilities are, what, actually, this kind of thing is. Those who achieve for us the status of absolute mastery are those whose work has served to discover to us what the standards, the possible achievements, the range and depth of an art or of art itself may be. Of them we may feel that they do not so much set standards and realize new possibilities within the human enterprise of art as almost to constitute that enterprise. In that sense they *are* its demands and its standards. Thus we do not expect them to *meet* our standards, our expectations and demands, rather to mold, define, redefine, and enlarge them.[44]

44. What is said here is a translation into authorial terms of our earlier discussion (p. 161 above) of classical *objects*.

Naturally enough the force of this function is most obvious when we find 'such a master' making novel demands upon us, demands we cannot meet with our existing skills, as Mendelssohn found that he could not grasp the choral movement of the "grand Ninth Symphony." Now we may be surprised that he had difficulty hearing it and explain that to ourselves (rightly enough) by noting that we are the heirs of a training in listening to it to which Mendelssohn and other musicians have richly contributed by performance. But 'with such a master' and such a masterpiece can one ever be certain that 'now we know' how to read it, how to hear it, what it finally is? The persistently inescapable challenge of works of such masters is another form of the *absoluteness* of their mastery.

Indeed, in these works and their mastery we may think ourselves to be in touch with the root, the source of those luxuriant growths and rushing fountains which constitute the garden of art. Any mastery, no matter how restricted in its kind, manifests these vital impulses; that mastery in which they seem to us to be subject only to self-imposed restrictions manifests them absolutely. Of course no such manifestation is ever entirely without limitation, never literally absolute. But nevertheless in every individually articulated aesthetic world there are masters whose works come close to showing us what this art and art itself may be and therefore are not subject to our judgment as are the works of less architectonic masters. With respect to them the burden of proof, so to speak, has shifted. Our taste is judged by them, and it is we who must show that they have failed rather than they who must satisfy us.

Since our concern at this point in this inquiry is with these functional moments of authority in individual worlds of taste and feeling, we need not enter further here into these perplexing questions about the roots of human creativity. It is enough for us that there are for each of us such masters and such masteries and their corresponding docilities. It remains only to ask whether the radical character of our docility in this case does not so far limit (and thus destroy) the autonomy of individual taste upon which we have so far insisted.

Again, in direct and simple terms, the question is easily answered. This magisterial office is, in each aesthetic life and practice, *conferred* by us individually, and, since it is based upon our experience with masterworks (the works of the master) it might even be said, with some imprecision of language, to be earned or deserved. What confuses here is what qualifies for the status in question and the mode of its conferring. That is, what qualifies is superiority in that very functioning by which the status is conferred and the mode of conferring is better described as recognition of what is revealed than election among alternatives. (And certainly it is unsought.) In the Roman communion the privilege of canonization—the identification of heroic and exemplary virtue which is to be honored—is reserved to the pope, but it has been well said that the pope does not cause or create sanctity but merely recognizes it. And it is further clear that in conferring this status the popes do not act, with respect to the possession of heroic qualities, *de haut en bas*: they recognize holiness not in virtue of their own attainments in it but in virtue of their office—their responsibilities with respect to the life of a religious community.[45] With respect to our individual aesthetic worlds, each of us might thus be said to exercise papal prerogatives, prerogatives *which no one can exercise for us,* powers *reserved to us alone.* And in that world we may even do what popes perhaps cannot do with respect to canonizations: we can unmake them, difficult as that decision may be.[46]

Analogy to canonization should serve, however, to emphasize differences as well as homogeneities. Canonization is a public, official act of an authority empowered to ordain attitudes and acts of honor on the part of members of a community institutionally organized. It is to make a binding rule for a public whose interests rule-making authority serves, whose integrity it is to preserve, and whose conformity to rule it enjoins and expects—not without sanction. In these aspects—in which it is a function in an actual com-

45. Eric Waldram Kemp, *Canonization and Authority in the Western Church* (Oxford, 1948), p. 111. "The pope does not cause holiness, he merely recognizes it, and this he does in virtue of his office, not because of his personal character." Kemp is here following very closely—if not literally quoting—Augustinus Triumphus, *Summa de potestate ecclesiastica* (Rome, 1582), Quaest. xiv, art. 1, a fourteenth-century work I have not been able to consult directly.

46. Popes have "unmade saints" if by that we mean that the Roman calendar has been revised and many names removed from it. But with respect to saints actually papally canonized questions arise from doctrines of papal infallibility. If acts of canonization are infallible, clearly they cannot be reversed. Perhaps we had better refrain from entering into these issues. (See, for example, Kemp, *Canonization and Authority,* chap. 8, pp. 151 ff.)

munity—it refers us analogically rather to those processes in the aesthetic and artistic world which are also institutional or quasi-institutionalized and thus to what we described above as "the actual communities in which taste is formed, judgments effectively communicated, reputations made and lost, artistic activity encouraged or discouraged and aesthetic canons established, enforced, and revised."[47] Within my own world I may be as absolutely authoritative as any pope, but my office is not institutional and my authority is efficacious only within my world *so far as it* is *mine*. Only for myself can I decree what is classical and canonical, and *insofar as these terms designate actual cogencies in my aesthetic activity* only I can do it. Otherwise what is classical, canonical, and masterly is a social and institutional fact that may be taken account of by me as a more or less well-supported claim to shape my authority.

XV

But we cannot leave the matter in a formulation seemingly radically subjective—private, personal, idiosyncratic—in which autonomy simply means independence of what is external, the capacity to resist external coercion. To do so would be to appear to accept the view that taste is but personal preference and autonomy bare self-assertion. We remind ourselves that earlier we argued that the norm of authority requires of us that we aspire to a taste which is authoritative, that is, qualified to command the docility of others not coercively but nonetheless cogently—not, we might say, by power but by right of excellence in an enterprise inherently, necessarily shareable. And have we not argued that to join in that enterprise is to aspire to activities and satisfactions inherently communicable, catholic and in common? Is it not for these reasons that all problems of authority can equally well be stated as problems of the proper occasions of docility, a form of that self-imposed 'proper violence' which is at once condition and fruit of the discipline of sensibility and feeling which is taste?

In other words, throughout our discussion of authority we have posited communicability and the community that communicability postulates, and what we have said about individual docility in re-

47. See pp. 127 ff. above. The quotation is from p. 127.

lation to the authority of mankind, of criticism, of works and of masters is simply an attempt to set forth the problems of treating the actual community in which we find ourselves actually functioning as a resource for more effective engagement in a human activity that no actual community fully sustains or finally realizes. To assume that our actual environments contain resources that make possible and nourish aesthetic activity is to assume that there are traditions, institutions, and practices in which it is embedded, sustained, and projected. To assert the authoritative autonomy of individual taste when it has matured to reflective direction is to assert that the identification and use of these resources is one of the functions of individual reflective direction. But assumption and assertion share a common ground: aesthetic activity is an activity engaging us as human beings, an activity (like knowing and acting) in which our capacities are so 'activated' as to actualize, so to speak, what it is to be human.

To be human is to engage in this activity and to seek its satisfactions, and therefore it is manifest in every human community. Each of us comes to it in and through the 'cultural' circumstances of our maturation; each of us may also come to some reflective appreciation of the value and importance of this activity to us and concomitantly of what it is that we are doing and trying to do in it. That which we set before us as the richer and clearer practice of it in our own lives is what is articulated in norms for its discipline. *Their* authority, which is necessarily absolute for me, is mine as explicating for *me* what *I* am engaged in doing; it is also the authority of an activity and an enterprise which in my own understanding of it I assume that I did not and could not invent, that I may practice and even contribute to but not exhaust, an expression of a common humanity.

We shall return to these reflections. For the moment, let us ask—since we have reminded ourselves of it—what this extended peregrination through the thickets of authority and authorities comes to in the terms originally proposed: that what is required is that we aspire to a taste that shall be authoritative, that is, qualified to command the docility of others by right of qualification. We need not repeat, save to mention, that this is an internal norm: it requires a certain way of looking at ourselves and is in no way dependent upon how we are actually regarded or treated by others. But as a way of looking at ourselves it projects a growth in aesthetic sophistication, a taste broader and deeper, more practiced and subtle, more flexible and discriminating, more articulated and articulable, clearer with respect to its limits and its strengths—in a formula, more *confident* of its powers and their use; in a word, more *free*.

Neither growth nor confidence are, of course, ends in themselves. That in which we grow and with respect to which we are more confident, that activity more richly, purely and more securely initiated and sustained, those satisfactions which are inherent in that activity and are stabilized for us in the measure of its perfection—are not these ends requiring no further warrant? Authority, confidence, freedom signify our own sense and understanding of our powers, of what we seek in the world through their discipline, of what our world is as a locus of goods and satisfactions—of all these not as adjuncts or accidents of *a* self, or *our* self, rather *as* our *selves, this* actual center of disciplined, human vitality. If we claim any authority among our fellows it is in right of the exemplary humanity of that disciplined vitality.

In summary form these reflections have an air of pretentiousness and a false profundity partly veiled in and partly caused by tenuous abstraction. We should remember that we began—in Florence—with accounts of individual experience which we unashamedly called adventures of taste. To attempt to articulate some of the moments in the development of an authoritative taste is, after all, simply to give an account of our lives and our living as an adventure in and of taste. And is there, then, a better expression of what we have in mind than Hawthorne's direct and elegant prose?

> I am sensible . . . that a process is going on . . . that puts me in a state to see pictures with less toil, and more pleasure, and makes me more fastidious, yet more sensible of beauty where I saw none before.[48]

We may hope to achieve something of the same directness (but not the elegance) in completing our survey of the normalities of aesthetic activity by saying what 'good taste' may be—of course in that broad sense in which it comprises the just discrimination and

48. See above, Prologue, Part One, note 10.

appreciation of both the delightful and the moving, of both beauty and sublimity. A good taste is a taste which is free and freely engaged, austere and objective, systematically catholic and communicable, docile and authoritative. Its 'content' is the articulable system of those objects which spontaneously and freely engage it in virtue of their perceived formality and which function canonically in its activity. Good taste is thus everywhere and always the same and everywhere and always unique, just as its objects are both canonic and irreducibly individual.

5

Aesthetic Life

In April of 1934 Prince Pu-Ru, cousin of the last Chinese Emperor and the only member of the imperial family then allowed to live in Peking, gave a garden-party. Among the guests, mostly those Manchu former imperial officials and dignitaries who remained in the ancient capital, was Osbert Sitwell, who has left us an account of the occasion—something of an exercise in nostalgia, but intriguing and instructive.

According to Sir Osbert, the party was the first Manchu social event since the child-emperor had been forced to flee Peking some ten years earlier, but its occasion was otherwise identified: "the object of this party was to see the crab-apple trees in bloom." So, after the generally aged guests had been greeted by their host and hostess, they

> passed on, beyond the pavilions, in the direction of the orchards. Perhaps they could hardly be termed orchards, because the trees, being grown for their blossom rather than their fruit, were irregularly disposed, and were fewer to the given area than is our custom. Bent, contorted with age ... they must have been planted some two centuries before. . . . [E]ach was as exquisitely placed upon the green turf as any figure upon a scroll by the hand of a great artist. Perfect in their balance and grotesque posture, some inclined, at the precise angle best calculated to display their unexpected and singular grace, while one tree, even, lay on its side and blossomed on the ground.
>
> Slowly, painfully, the old men hobbled along the crooked, paved paths that zigzagged to these trees. When they reached them, they were conducted up small flights of stone steps. . . . These flights, their tops level with the tops of the trees, are thus placed . . . so that the connois-

177

seur can obtain a perfect view of the blossom. Even to a newcomer . . .
the particular view of the tree for which the step had been constructed
offered a revelation of a new world; of the same kind as when you first
fly in an aircraft above the clouds . . . except that clouds disperse, are
opaque, and do not favour an ordered development.

Once there, [the old men] would remain for a full hour, matching
in their minds the complexion and fragrance of the blossom of previous
years with that before them. Then . . . came the more intimate tallying
of one branch, one flower, one bud, with another, and finally it was
necessary again to consider the entire grouping and design. But the
bees . . . got in the way, and even the less industrious butterflies ob-
scured the view . . . Critical appreciation of this high order could not
be hurried. After all it was better fully to use now the powers of judgment with which the years had enriched them . . . for, in the order of
things, they could scarcely hope to see many more of these flowery har-
vests. . . . [E]ven tomorrow this perfection would be tarnished and it
would be too late to form a considered opinion, even one day would
have made all the difference; each old man waited, thus quietly under
the immense blue dome, as though he were a watcher on a tower, or a
guardian of an ancient shrine calling the faithful to worship.[1]

Some of the salient features of aesthetic activity as it emerges in
our lives are apparent in this hauntingly intriguing picture—so exotic and so nostalgic even for a 'Western' reader. And yet also so
familiar, for here, under what are for us rather surprising circumstances, we can see realized a constructive aesthetic impulse,
what in our terms we should think 'art' to be—the attempt to secure some stability for satisfactions of imaginative perception by
the control of their occasions. In these venerable crab-apple trees,
so carefully arranged and pruned for two centuries, we may see the
intimate relation in their aesthetic potencies of what is naturally
offered and what is deliberately sought. In the words of John
Dewey, nature "lends itself to operations by which it is perfected,"
giving "not always freely but in response to search, means and ma-

1. "Old Worlds for New," originally published in *Life and Letters Today,* vol. 33
(April, 1942), subsequently reprinted in two of Sir Osbert's collections of essays and
occasional pieces, *Sing High! Sing Low!* (London, 1944) and *Pound Wise* (London,
1963). I have relied entirely on this source. There seems to be no reason to doubt
that there was such an occasion, but in any case I do not see that it would affect the
argument were it to be largely or entirely invented.

terial" for the "embodiment" of satisfactions otherwise only fortui-
tously available.[2] And we may also observe the complementary condition of the occurrence and the security of those satisfactions, the
disciplined capacities of human beings, also the product of a cen-
turies-old cultivation, though not of trunks, boughs, and twigs, but
of sensibility and perception.

Of course, the security sought and achieved is only relative, at
the mercy of the conditions of embodiment—in this case the natural vicissitudes of the seasons and biological processes of growth
and decay, but also, of course, of economic and 'sociopolitical' conditions hostile, favorable, or indifferent to continued investment
not only in orchards bearing such special fruits, in the training of
gardeners to design and care for them, but in the traditions of critical training and appreciation issuing in the individual "powers of
judgment" of these venerable Manchu connoisseurs. All these have
their conditions and corresponding vulnerabilities; in Prince Pu-
Ru's garden there seems to be no new generation of connoisseurs
to maintain the tradition.

However, aesthetic activity in this natural and cultural ambiance
is hardly to be understood merely as the material and instrumental
dependence of complementary activities of aesthetic impulse and
aesthetic discipline, of art and its appreciation, not only because (as
we have noted before) beauty and sublimity are not to be found
only in the arts, but because the evidence of the arts, taken at face
value, would rather suggest that this activity—both as impulsion
and as discipline—is so deeply embedded in other pervasive human activities and pursuits and the traditions and institutions into
which those are shaped, that an autonomous content, shape, intent, and function can hardly be distinguished. In some cases such
shaping—as seen in the products of what might seem to be aesthetic impulsion—is obvious. The demands of other human enterprises seem literally, for example, to have shaped the monuments
of architectural art: are not the forms of the Parthenon, of the Po-
tala of Lhasa, or the pyramids of Egypt those of temple, fortress,
palace, treasury, bureaucratic beehive, royal tomb? Architecture—

2. John Dewey, *The Quest for Certainty*, chap. 11. (*John Dewey: The Later Works,
1925–1953*, vol. 4, 1929 [Carbondale and Edwardsville, Ill., 1984], p. 241.)

an art making usable things—may be a special case, but these monuments are not only functional in that restricted sense. Are not all of them also in their diverse ways expressions and symbols of power and wealth, of political, national, and religious beliefs and practices, to say nothing of power and pride?

Moreover, the disciplined activity of Prince Pu-Ru's appreciative guests is subject to similar ambiguities. These old men contemplating flowering trees, as engaged and intent in their way as the bees and the butterflies which momentarily impede their perception, seem like "guardian(s) of an ancient shrine calling the faithful to worship," but surely it would be a mistake to think that the shrine is only that of art and connoisseurship. Were revolution to sweep away these orchards and make obsolete the sensibilities on which they depend it would, presumably, not be simply in the interest of efficiency in the production of crab-apples or of a rejection of antiquated ideas about aesthetic satisfactions. What would be rejected, transformed, extinguished would be an institutional order, an organization of human activities and persons, a 'way of life' of imperial, Manchu China which these old men themselves enshrine and, in their faithfulness to this special tradition of privileged satisfaction continue, no doubt feebly and in vain, to guard. Are they, then, enjoying the autonomous pleasures of aesthetic apprehension or enacting a ritual of social order?

II

It may be that sometimes art really has been—at least in motivation and intention—'for art's sake,' designed, that is, to function solely in relation to disciplined capacities of taste and feeling, but far more commonly its works bear almost on their surface discernible marks of other functions, other ancestries, other interests, and even if the intent be pure the product may be co-opted to serve other purposes.

> Art should be independent of all clap-trap—should stand alone, and appeal to the artistic sense of eye or ear, without confounding this with emotions entirely foreign to it, as devotion, pity, love, patriotism. . . . Take the picture of my mother, exhibited as . . . an "Arrangement in Grey and Black." Now that is what it is. To me it is interesting as a

picture of my mother; but what can or ought the public to care about the identity of the portrait?[3]

But while "the public" may not have been interested, as Whistler does not deny that he was, in *his* mother, their interest was not confined as he intended. Eventually, in fact, there appeared, among other manifestations of a broader interest, a Mother's Day postage stamp reproducing the painting (improved for the purpose by the addition of a modest pot of flowers easily procurable from any neighborhood florist).[4]

Alternatively Prince Pu-Ru's orchard and its admirers—aged guardians and ancient shrine—may be equally significant of the resistance offered by aesthetic functioning to domestication, assimilation, or reduction to the terms and conditions of other human activities. In this space there has been created by human craft and ingenuity a place of fantasy, a landscape as exotic in its way as any encountered in a dream—a scene in which there emerges from what is otherwise perceptible as distortion and abnormality an "unexpected and singular grace" and the possibility of a "revelation of a new world" for trained perception. Here, in other words, we find quite literally embodied the privilege of art to be "imaginative" in the sense which, as Bosanquet says, "puts a premium on the arbitrary and fantastic in beauty."[5] It is precisely because the objects here are so clearly 'natural' in their material existence that their 'artificiality,' the origin of their forms in human operations guided by human activity and preference, is so obvious. And these operations of art, while they may "perfect" nature, do so with respect to the realization of purposes which nature knows not of—the perfection of blossom which so efficiently attracts the industrious bees is hardly the same as that so carefully cultivated to attract and fruitfully engage the "powers of judgment" of the connoisseur. This power of the arts to body forth objects thus radically novel, to make actual things and worlds dominantly anthropocentric, is certainly not their least remarkable feature. Indeed it is sometimes thought to be almost definitive of art and artistic activity: the arts are to be

3. James McNeill Whistler, *The Gentle Art of Making Enemies* (London, 1892), pp. 127–28.
4. May 1934.
5. Cf. above, chap. 1, p. 40.

understood best as a special case and a special interest among those activities in which the human environment is arranged not only to serve human purposes, but to reflect, so to speak, human preferences, and to embody satisfactions peculiarly human. These are not arcane considerations—they may be observed in complex combinations in such mundane actualities as cultivated fields, windbreaks, or golf courses as well as in something (to alien eyes at least) as exotic or monumental as Prince Pu-Ru's crab-apple orchards or the boulevards of Paris, which offer magnificent vistas to the eye, while serving also to move traffic and facilitate riot control. And thus by a different route we arrive again at that embroilment, concurrence, coincidence, cooptation (it is difficult to find words which do not begin to suggest judgments and preferences) of aesthetic goods with or by other human goods in the web of human activity, a massive fact which an inquiry into the normality and integrity of aesthetic activity can hardly ignore.

From the beginning of this inquiry, in the legend of Farmer Brown and the Ambiguous Thistle, we have in fact taken note of these ambiguities, which might better be called multivalences. It should come as no surprise to note again the potential multiplicity of functional bearing in any occasion of experience, a potentiality which (short of that radical reduction in which 'experience' disappears into William James's "great blooming, buzzing confusion") may be identified as an ambiguity in or with respect to empirical objects. In this respect the arts do not constitute a special case. The empirical elements apprehended by us in that complex occasion which is an encounter with a work of art may be ordered to a diversity of functions, a possibility which is interpreted as the presence of a multiplicity of 'meanings' of or responses to the 'same' object or simply as a multiplicity of objects. In Prince Pu-Ru's orchard are not what we crudely identify as 'crab-apple blossoms' one thing to the bees and another to the connoisseurs—and yet another to "the less industrious butterflies" or the unenlightened bureaucrat from the Ministry of Agriculture estimating this year's crab-apple crop?

But it is not that we have simply moved from thistles to cultivated apple blossoms: we have made a contextual shift as well. In the context in which we began these distinctions were appropriately made so as to emphasize the diversity of purposive orientations of our perceptual capacities and thus to isolate for analysis that orientation which is aesthetic. Within that analysis such ambiguities were explored as problems of critical functioning, considering how attention may be directed so as to dis-cover a diversity of objects. In the context of authority they reemerged as we considered what might be meant by having recourse to the authority of the object.[6] Here, having articulated as best we can the 'normalities' of aesthetic apprehension—norms which formulate, one might say, its autonomy—we return to consider briefly that activity as what it 'normally' is: one of the activities in which human beings are engaged among others, one of the things we do.

In this inquiry we have taken as the proper starting point the normalities of apprehension, but throughout we have assumed that aesthetic activity is not exhausted in apprehension. As an activity among others, as something we do, as a direction of human energies, aesthetic goods enter into the constitution of our worlds not only as we apprehend it but as we literally construct it. Both these forms of aesthetic functioning are contexts of 'objectification,' one of objectification as a process and product of imaginative perception, the other of objectification as production of an artifact—a making issuing a 'work,' that is, a publicly available object which may in turn become an occasion for objectification in perception. But there is hardly any human activity—any of the things we do—which does not leave behind it some such 'product' (or 'byproduct'), all of them bearing in their diverse ways some marks of human purposefulness, to that extent becoming expressive of what human beings intend and what they value. In this human world, then, it is no less difficult from the side of constructive aesthetic impulsion to sort out, so to speak, the purity of aesthetic function in the welter of objects than it is from the side of apprehension. Certainly it is no remarkable discovery that the multiplicities and ambiguities which are apparent from, so to speak, the side of perception are equally evident from the side of production and in the product. Beyond that, however, we have also provided some ground for the expectation that the problems arising in the relation of aesthetic activity to all other things we do will arise equally and be indifferently formulable with respect to both apprehension and construc-

6. See chapters 3 and 4.

tion, that is, in terms both of the arts and their appreciation. If there are problems they must be generated by the very integrity, autonomy, and consequent multiplicity of kinds of human good and satisfaction we have insisted upon, since only where there are multiplicities can there be options, choices, conflicts, incompatibilities or distortions. In a given situation goods of the same kind may create options and conflicts—uncomfortable necessities to choose—if only to sacrifice the lesser good for the greater according to some more or less complex calculation of means, ends and consequences. But far more serious questions of priority may arise between radically different kinds of goods, especially when they are not merely options in a particular situations in competition with goods of another sort but function so pervasively as to give a characteristic shape to the whole of our living. On a given occasion we may all prefer the satisfactions of understanding to the joys of action, or the pleasures offered by the "concord of sweet sounds" to the cognitive triumphs of harmonic theory, but when scholarship, artistry, or connoisseurship become vocations—ways of life—more serious issues of human good and human personality arise. Since we have argued throughout that aesthetic activity is an orientation of all our capacities, of the whole self, the potentiality for such more profound and perhaps disturbing choices and priorities is surely there.

But before we turn to consider these possibilities of incoherence should note that the pervasive entanglement of aesthetic goods with others admits of another interpretation, for we might just as well have noted that the situation in which these goods reinforce or enhance each other in the result is no less typical than that in which they are felt and thought to be at odds. In fact, one might argue that, at least in the case of many of the arts, the separation of aesthetic goods from others—of what is beautiful or moving as such from other satisfactions offered by what may be here beautifully, movingly rendered, expressed or constituted—is one that is rather forced upon us than sought. Thus it is only when certain ways of worship have ceased to engage us as such that we insist upon the satisfactions of euphony, of drama, of sublimity to be derived—without the necessity of religious commitment or, at least, not of the commitment of its original associations—from music originally inspired and in intention controlled by the liturgy and credal content of a religious tradition no longer, for us, alive.[7] And, *mutatis mutandis,* might not the same be said with respect to the patriotic intention of the *Aeneid,* to the gods of Homer, to the social usages of Jane Austen's Bath, to the many 'vanished worlds' of human behavior, ideas and values which constitute much of the stuff of many still enjoyed objects of our literary traditions? But of course it is not only in the development of the tradition or culture we call our own that such disassociations occur and such distinctions are found useful and necessary. They must, of course, be appropriately brought to bear if we are to make intelligible to ourselves and facilitate the appreciation of much, if not all, of the art of traditions other than our own.

From the side of aesthetic impulsion the separation of aesthetic intent from other functions to be served may seem in such a perspective equally unsought. Surely the intent expressed by Stravinsky—"One hopes to worship God with a little art if one has any . . ."[8]—is no radical innovation in the artistic world, nor has such artistic aspiration been confined to the worship of God. To aspire to and even to attempt to achieve a human world in which everything was beautiful and appropriately expressive as well as

7. This example might remind one of the opposite process—one in which artistic resources are deliberately deployed in conjunction with forms and contents to which the artist, at least, is no longer committed. Consider, for example, Verdi, writing the so-called *Manzoni Requiem* (first performed 1874 on the anniversary of Manzoni's death). There are few who would now assert with confidence that Verdi was a believing (to say nothing of a practicing) Catholic or perhaps even a Christian, yet in his full maturity, under no apparent external coercion, he employed the traditional text of the requiem mass in mourning for a man about whose religious attitudes much the same could probably be said. Was it his sense of his composition as a public rather than a personal act that dictated this course? That is, was it because the public forms of memorializing available to him were still those of the Latin, the Roman mass? But the matter is undoubtedly more complex than that. (There is a well known letter of Boito—the librettist of *Otello* and *Falstaff*—which shrewdly and sympathetically suggests some of the complexities. Cf. Frank Walker, *The Man Verdi* [Chicago, 1982], p. 506.) Interestingly enough, about the same time Brahms produced *A German Requiem*—apparently intending nothing more by that title than that this was a requiem in German employing what had become a classical German text, Luther's Bible. In a sense this is a move in the opposite direction—an attempt to have newly available resources of 'meaning' serve purposes previously served by other texts and other symbols no longer functional. But the whole subject cannot be dealt with in a note—if, indeed, it is a subject at all.

8. Igor Stravinsky and Robert Craft, *Dialogues and a Diary* (Garden City, NY, 1963), p. 79. Stravinsky was discussing the *Symphony of Psalms*.

useful, good and intelligible is perhaps no mean ideal. In the nature of the case, however, how and when such coincidence and reinforcement can be achieved is something only experience can
teach and criticism attempt to illuminate. It is therefore properly
beyond the scope of our inquiry except as it bears witness to a possibility to be kept in mind as we consider those relations of aesthetic
activity to other things we do in which incoherence and conflict
seem to arise.

III

Traditionally, of course, the issues that arise are very broadly formulable as doubts concerning the relation of aesthetic values and
aesthetic activity—whether manifested in the love of beauty or in
the practice of the arts—to 'morality.' Far short of any final determination of what is to be meant by 'morality' and 'moral value,' one
cannot ignore the recurrent suspicion that a devotion to aesthetic
values may somehow have destructive consequences for the pursuit
of more fundamental human goods, that cultivating aesthetic activity may replace, weaken or even destroy devotion to those human goods upon which all others depend—if only because they
are essential to the preservation of orderly human communities—
and therefore may radically disturb the ordering of our lives and
be destructive of our humanity by subverting the priority which
such goods necessarily enjoy. But we cannot attempt here any complete account of such matters—that is surely another inquiry. On
the other hand, our whole inquiry has been concerned with the
conditions of an integral human activity, a human enterprise realizing significant satisfactions, and it would be strange indeed if we
had not said anything, therefore, which ought to be taken into account by any serious inquiry into the whole range and order of
human good and human activity. Perhaps, then, all we can accomplish in addition to what we have already said is to suggest some of
its implications for that broader inquiry, or, to put it another way,
briefly restate what we have said in a fashion more directly relevant
to the consideration of aesthetic activity as one among the 'things
we do.' Throughout we have approached our problems as problems of more or less mature and reflective individuals, and consistently, thus, we might begin by asking what we are 'doing' when we

'deliberately' or 'consciously' adopt toward our worlds an 'aesthetic' attitude, the attitude of individuals with some discipline of taste and feeling.

As an actual psychological phenomenon the taking up of this attitude is a commonplace event; that is, it is an attitude which all of us can and do take up on occasion. What is involved in the ordinary way of things is well illustrated by De Quincey's charming anecdote about Coleridge.

> One night . . . I was drinking tea with [Coleridge] . . . and, amidst some carnal considerations of tea and toast, we were all imbibing a dissertation on Plotinus from the Attic lips of S. T. C. Suddenly a cry arose of 'Fire—fire!' upon which all of us . . . rushed out, eager for the spectacle. The fire was in Oxford Street, at a pianoforte-maker's; and, as it promised to be a conflagration of merit, I was sorry that my engagements forced me away . . . before matters had come to a crisis. Some days after, meeting with my Platonic host, I . . . begged to know how that very promising exhibition had terminated. 'Oh, sir,' said he, 'it turned out so ill that we damned it unanimously.' Now does any man suppose that Mr. Coleridge . . . was an incendiary or capable of wishing any ill to the poor man and his pianofortes . . . ? On the contrary, I know him to be that sort of man that I durst stake my life upon it he would have worked an engine in the case of necessity, although rather of the fattest for such fiery trials of his virtue. But how stood the case? Virtue was in no request. On the arrival of the fire engines, morality had devolved wholly on the insurance office. This being the case he had a right to gratify his taste. He had left his tea. Was he to have nothing in return?
>
> I contend that the most virtuous man, under the premises stated, was entitled to make a luxury of the fire, and to hiss it, as he would any other performance that raised expectations in the public mind which afterwards it disappointed.[9]

The mock-defensive tone of this tale is, of course, a response to the common assumption that there is something 'morally' insensitive or at best 'amoral' about this mode of apprehension, so that its

9. Thomas De Quincey, "On Murder considered as one of the fine arts." The relevant portion of this remarkable piece (Part 1) was first published in 1827; Part 2 and a "Postscript" were added in 1839 and 1854 respectively. The episode of the fire in Oxford Street may have, of course, been invented in whole or part by De Quincey, but surely it is *ben trovato*. The essay has been much reprinted. See, for example, the passage cited in *Collected Writings of Thomas De Quincey* (Edinburgh, 1870; reprinted New York, 1968), vol. 13, pp. 13–14.

deliberate assumption on a given occasion—as in this case—requires justification. Is it significant that even in our own formulations the aesthetic attitude has been defined by the setting aside of the demands made on imagination and perception by other functions? "More commonly," as we said at the outset, we are endeavoring to understand or control the world than to enjoy its beauty or follow its drama, possibilities which may seem by comparison frivolous, fantastical, and even irresponsible. In particular it tends to be assumed that we are moral/practical beings first and 'contemplatively' cognitive or aesthetic beings second. Moreover, this sense of priority itself tends to have a 'moral' tinge. That is, it is not only the necessities of survival and prudential considerations which make the gratification of taste a 'luxury.' It may be that we more commonly adopt a practical attitude toward the world under the lash of biological and social necessity, but the case is felt to be one not only of 'needs must' but of 'ought.' When we are dutifully certain that duty has been discharged, taste becomes an option; it may be *virtuously* indulged when virtue is no longer 'in request.'

Now there is here important insight as well as no little confusion. What is 'moral' or 'ethical,' as we noted earlier, in an important sense falls outside the scope of our concern, but in another sense it is basic to it. This whole inquiry is an attempt to articulate the conditions of an ordered development of the capacities of individuals giving access to peculiarly human goods. Such a development, to the extent that it is complete, is a realization of human potentialities, a human perfection actualized in individuals. So far as ethics and morality are concerned with human good—in what ends human activity is fulfilled—it is necessarily also concerned with what constitutes 'good humans,' since, as we have contended throughout, ends are realized only in activity, and the ability to carry on human activities is acquired and stabilized in practice and mediated by reflection. That is, human goods are dependent upon the perfecting of human beings. It is in that sense—as being concerned with human perfection and human good in their reciprocity—that our concerns are entirely ethical.[10]

10. This apparent paradox that human good is realized only by good humans has dogged ethical inquiry from the beginning, becoming acutely disturbing when it seems to entail the consequence that only those who are already good can come

But, of course, there is another sense in which our concerns are clearly not ethical or moral: that sense in which it is behavior, conduct, action, choice and our dispositions and judgments with respect to them that are right or wrong, ethical or unethical, moral, vicious, amoral, or 'morally' indifferent. Along this line to adopt an aesthetically 'contemplative' attitude is to abstain from action, from practical engagement with circumstances in which goals are sought and goods are at stake, even to treat action and moral engagement as simply another kind of spectacle or imaginative construction, to opt, in other words, for a relation to the world in which 'morality devolves,' if not upon the insurance office, surely upon agents and actors other than ourselves. So viewed, to take up an aesthetic attitude is to abjure agency and so to appear, at least, to abandon responsibility for the world so far as it is shaped by human endeavor for the sake of human well-being.

To 'abjure,' 'abstain,' and 'abandon' may not be to act, but certainly it is to choose and to choose, as in the case of Coleridge and his friends, 'deliberately.' As a functional stance with respect to the world the aesthetic attitude as we are concerned with, it is surely *chosen*, and chosen in a double sense. It is chosen as Coleridge presumably chose it—that is, functionally assumed in a given situation—and it is chosen as a discipline to be achieved, as a practice to be cultivated in the interest of perfecting in habituation—that is, as an acquired capability available for implementation in particular situations. As object of choice in both senses it falls within the scope of 'morality.' As an attitude habitually or deliberately assumed in a given situation it is to be chosen responsibly. So to choose requires, among other things, that due consideration be given in this situation to what other ends might be realizable, what values may be stake, what legitimate demands on us as agents are present. As a form of activity to be acquired, developed and perfected it is to be chosen as a form of human goodness by which human goods are realizable, both being unities within a plurality of human goods. But this plurality is not a mere collection; it is an ordered whole. 'Morality' in the determination of choice no doubt

---

to *know* what is good. The number of those who over the centuries have 'kicked against the pricks' of Aristotle's remark that only those who have been properly brought up and have good habits can with profit *think* about human goods is legion. (Cf. *Nicomachean Ethics*, I, 4 [1095b 1 et seq.]).

means many things, but not least it means the effective implementation in choice of an order among human goods. Thus to say that
the demands of morality must be satisfied before those of taste is
to say the assigning of priorities to human goods in choice is not
the function of 'taste,' though it would be better to say that 'taste' is
not that function. To function practically is, among other things,
to assign those priorities. To do so correctly is to be morally practical and being morally practical in that sense may require, in a
given situation and for a given individual, giving priority to aesthetic goods and therefore to the activities in which they are realized and the attitude toward the world they require.

To put the matter entirely in terms of priorities may, however,
be seriously misleading, for we may forget that questions of priority
arise only when there are multiple claims—claims different from
each other and yet all 'legitimate.' But of course to appear as a
legitimate claim upon the direction of our attention and our energies in particular situations is to have the status of an end, a good
to be realized, and in this case, as we argued already, of a realization, a perfection of our faculties. In the self-disciplining of individuals or in the organization of a culture all these goods—the
goods of action, of knowing and of taste—have priority in the sense
that all are to be sought, all cultivated, all practiced and even institutionalized. We must, as we say, do justice to them all; *doing* justice
requires that we allocate resources to their pursuit *proportionately*
and in that sense assign priorities, but thus stating the problem
does not by itself determine those proportions. As human goods,
the goods of free activity, all are 'absolute,' that is, sufficient unto
themselves, irreducibly integral finalities. In Kantian language
they are all ends that are duties; to adopt them as our ends is a
duty. But in that same language the obligations entailed are indeterminate: how the end is to be attained and honored in the context
of other ends which are duties becomes determinate only in responsible and conscientious choice.

However, our own account of aesthetic activity might require us
to pause before assuming that aesthetic values and moral values,
aesthetic activity and moral choice can be so clearly distinguished.
Have we not argued that a feeling of and for the sublime, in one
of basic forms of that complex but powerful phenomenon, depends upon a deep moral sensitivity—and 'moral' sensitivity in the

sense in which morality is an engagement with human action, human endeavor, human fate? The tragic emotions of pity and fear can hardly be the fruit of an entire disinterested contemplation. We argued earlier that what is beautiful *delights;* it is dwelt upon because it so satisfactorily engages the imagination; its satisfactions are those of the unimpeded activity of imaginative perception itself; concerns of 'reality' and truth as well as of what is desirable and right are (or may be) impediments to that free activity and must be austerely put aside if they corrupt it. But we also argued that the freedom manifested in 'sublimity' is not simply the autonomy of imaginative perception but a willing, a demanding engagement with the empirical world as that wherein freedom is to be realized. That is, it has its roots in a search in experience, in imagination and perception, for a manifestation of the freedom of the mind as intelligence and as agent.

Surely such an engagement of intelligence with the world includes, if it is not exhausted by, 'morality,' the ordered realization of human purposes and human goods in the world. Thus it would seem impossible that the distinctions, the discriminations, the evaluating judgments of 'morality' could not enter into the very constitution of objects in which the enterprise itself is felt to be at stake. For what it is worth, criticism has from the beginning, at least in the West, confirmed this view. The tragic dimensions of poetic action as analyzed by Aristotle thus depend upon proportionate relationships among the worth of agents, their responsible choices and their fortunes,[11] and it has often been pointed out that an audience incapable of these distinctions or perverted in its moral sentiments would be unmoved or 'perversely' moved.

We would not wish to deny that the moral orientation of the audience is essential to the tragic consummation; our question is about their aesthetic orientation, their mode of apprehension. It may be a difficult saying, but is it not the case that engagement with an object of tragic sublimity is 'disinterested' while nonetheless an engagement with a moral object? We said above that what engages us in sublimity in all its forms is the *enterprise* of freedom in the world. To the extent that our engagement is a commitment to an *actual* enterprise, to this or that end which is actually to be

11. Of course, that is not all it depends on.

achieved, to values, goods and persons as actually at stake, that
engagement is to that extent 'interested,' for to that extent our
imaginations are engaged with action *existentially* ("materially")
rather than formally, that is, as a shape or structure in which our
freedom is manifested in the world. The ratios of eventuations
which constitute, in 'classical' analysis, the tragic quality of action
are among moral elements—the goodness of agents, their responsibility and their consequent fates—but it is those *proportions* which
excite the tragic emotions as such. Otherwise Hamlet's question—

> What's Hecuba to him, or he to Hecuba,
> That he should weep for her?—[12]

would always be relevant, that is, it would normally be presumed
that our emotional engagement with the fate of any individual
must be dependent upon a concern for that individual as agent or
patient in our practical world, that somehow our actual fates are
taken to be intertwined, even though the connection may be in
another sense 'imaginary.' In that case the tragic 'fear' would be an
anticipation, however obscure and confused, of actual menace, so
that it would be akin to the terror of the audience at the entrance
of the Furies at the first performance of the *Eumenides* of Aeschylus.[13]

IV

But it is not really necessary to have recourse to tragedy and Aristotle in order to grasp the essential features of this aesthetic relation to the world of doing and suffering, success and failure, good
fortune, disaster and all the other categories of events and persons
in their relation to action and fate—in short, to the world as the
'scene' of action. The basic adjustment of attitude was apparent in
the episode of the fire at the piano factory on Oxford Street. To
treat that conflagration 'morally' is to treat it as a process in the
world which may put in jeopardy life and property and accordingly
to perceive it in the terms of what might be done to alter its course.

12. *Hamlet*, II, ii.
13. Cf. above, chap. 2, I (p. 55). We might make the same point out of *Hamlet*.
Is the reaction of the King to the 'play within the play' the tragic catharsis of fear?

Naturally that deliberation will proceed in terms of some assumptions about what is at stake and what resources are available for directing that course, that is, in terms of ends and means.[14] With the arrival of fire engines under the auspices of the "insurance office" we may judge that, given efficient means for the protection of life and property being present, our relation to the fire has so altered that the fire ceases to be—*for us*—a practical problem. The perception of it as a dramatic process, more or less satisfying insofar as it has a *form* realizable in such a sequence of events, may then proceed unimpeded by other demands. Perception and imaginative organization then function not primarily with respect to means and ends but to the conditions of such a formal coherence— appropriately articulated parts: beginnings, middles, ends.

Indeed one suspects that in this case the early stages of the conflagration aroused expectations of a satisfying pyrotechnical climax which were not fulfilled. (In the jargon of the theater, the fire had 'second act problems.') But it might also have been that the fire had the shape of an ill-managed farce, simply 'fizzling out' in a sodden mess of debris and dirty smoke when it might have terminated in an elegantly unanticipated comic anticlimax. In both cases it would have "turned out so ill that we damned it unanimously." And, of course, there are other possibilities.

We are here in danger of entering the province of criticism; it is no part of this inquiry to examine the actual possibilities of imaginative coherence except by way of example. Thus our interest in *Samuel Taylor Coleridge and The Great Piano Factory Fire* is to show how the alternative modes of perceptual apprehension we have pointed to are not empty abstractions but functionally different in ways that would be manifest at every point in any actual perceiving, or, in other words, to suggest that constituting practical and aesthetic objects in a given occasion of experience is not simply a matter of changing names or interests but is a radical, 'objective' reordering of matter and form. We have already seen, in Prince Pu-Ru's orchard, something of the resulting objective multiplicity/ambiguity, but here in Oxford Street with S. T. C. we see clearly

14. Note that we need not make any assumptions as to the morality of the ends (or means). The world of action is the moral world only in the sense that it is the world within which moral distinctions are made.

that this multiplicity of objects, of values and judgments, this radical ambiguity of any actual occasion of our experience, is an immediate consequence of the multiplicity of human enterprises in which we find ourselves engaged or can discern as possibly or actually comprehensive of any given occasion. That is, it is because we—percipient, reflective individuals—are as human beings engaged in a multiplicity of ways of ordering ourselves and our experience that its particular occasions present us with the multiplicities which may alternatively appear, in radical ambiguity, as a richness of possible fruitions or a frustrating confusion.

In fact, of course, to the extent that we can confine ourselves to one mode of functional engagement with 'the world,' these ambiguities and the tensions they may entail are radically reduced—'radically' because it is possible to reduce all choices to alternatives characterizable within the scope of one enterprise, of one way of ordering our experience into a world. At one extreme all situations, all problems, all choices and all objects may be grasped the terms of action, and for the purposes of characterization it would hardly matter whether it was said that for a so single-minded a 'man of action' many things in '*the* world' do not exist or that such a person lives in '*a* world' drastically limited and impoverished. But it is probably impossible in actuality to achieve such a single-mindedness as would effectively exclude all other possibilities: even the most dedicated of us have at least some intimation of things in heaven and earth other than the objects that predominantly preempt our attention, though they may be only encountered as in dream. The harsh 'realities' of Hardscrabble Farm may require that Farmer Brown live primarily in a world pretty much made up of wheat and tares, of fertile soil and stony ground, and thus a world into which the beauty of the flowering thistle and the elegance of the mousing cat enter only as fleeting, detached and inconsequential encounters with insubstantial objects.

By contrast, of course, were it possible to live solely in an aesthetic world (that is, to live purely aesthetically in the world), such a life would seem to the practically minded as rather like living solely in a dream-world, for all situations, all problems, all choices, and all objects would be grasped in the terms of aesthetic—and thus imaginative—coherence and cogency. Such a life would be comprehensively disciplined and ordered, so that to be an 'aesthete' in this sense would demand much more than a devotion to the arts, a dedicated connoisseurship, and a disdain for politics, conventional moralities, and commercial pursuits. It would, more radically, be a way of life in which these other 'worlds' would be comprehended in imaginative transformation. Santayana claims for monarchy, as a form of government, "imaginative and dramatic superiority," but also adds that this "somewhat ethereal advantage" would constitute a ground for choice only when "monarchy was as apt, in a given case, to secure the public well-being as some other form of government." [15]

But what is one to understand by an "ethereal" advantage? For those as single-mindedly aesthetic in their way as those for whom the world is perceived only as a theater of action such an 'advantage' would be the only sort of advantage enjoyed by any object. It would be as authoritative, as supreme, as cogent for such as psyche as 'public well-being,' self-interest, or moral worth is or could be for the single-mindedly active. But, of course, if our account of aesthetic judgment—preference and worth—is correct, it would not be cogent—as are these other forms of preference and advantage—with respect to choice. For if by choosing is meant search for and selection of means to make actual, to bring into existence what is preferred—the initiation of action ordered to an end—a satisfaction in and a preference among objects of imaginative perception is by contrast fulfilled in that apprehension itself and requires no further determination of our world. That is, it is not a 'desire,' an apprehension of something as not-yet-but-to-be fulfilling, not an apprehension of an object as an 'objective,' but the enjoyment of what is apprehended as an object of apprehension, a 'contemplative' act in which apprehending and the apprehensible are indistinguishably enjoyed. The advantage enjoyed by such an aesthetic object might fairly be called 'ethereal' provided we are clear that it does not consist in disengagement from 'the world' but is a form of engagement with it.

But as human beings we are inevitably participant in both action and aesthetic judgment, not to mention other forms of activity. Aesthetic judgment—indeed the whole of our aesthetic activity— does not so coexist in schizophrenic, external isolation that to move

15. Santayana, *Sense of Beauty*, part I, sec. 6.

from one kind of functioning to another is to move from one psyche to another.[16] It is because they are activities of a single psyche, differently ordered and developed deployments of the our capacities of sense, imagination, intelligence, and feeling, that we were able to argue earlier that fundamentally this whole inquiry is an ethical one. Only as an alternative disposition of our 'selves' can this deployment of our powers be an object of choice, whether as a stance to be assumed in a given situation or as a discipline to be perfected in habituation.

Both these choices are moral or ethical choosings in that they are decisions about how to deploy our powers in the interest of achieving—in our resources for living and here and now—what is taken to be a human good among others. We saw (in *The Great Piano Factory Fire*) that these options may present problems of priority among goods (or of duty and responsibility) on a given occasion; we may see here that as habitual priorities among activities and goods they may be constitutive of a radical diversity of personalities as well. Any full-dress consideration of these alternative ways of life or personal orientations as constitutive of human goodness in general is beyond our scope, but 'intuitively' we might suggest that insensitivity to the beauties of the world and an inability to be deeply moved by the sublime in nature, in action, and in art are as much deprivations and failures of our humanity as are the absence of a sense of mercy, of a deep abhorrence of violence, or of an enlightened devotion to equity in human relations.[17] Extreme cases of truncations of human potentiality in either direction may result in an almost visible distortion of personality—persons so maimed, so corrupted, or so perverse as almost to seem not to

16. In an earlier discussion of such discriminations of function and value, we had recourse to yet another anecdote—what might be called Edward Gibbon's *Sons and Lovers*. (See above, chap. 2, p. 69.) Here we may simply note that it is the same Gibbon who sighed as a lover and obeyed as a son; the differentiation is impossible and meaningless without the identity. It is only because he is both that the necessity for distinguishing these functions arises and that the problem presented by their conflict can be formulated for resolution. So also it is only because 'Coleridge,' in *The Great Piano Factory Fire*, can distinguish between utilitarian/moral considerations and aesthetic ones that he can rejoice with the fire fighters and commiserate with the disappointed lovers of dramatic spectacles.

17. *Mutatis mutandis* the same may be said of purely cognitive activities and goods, but that is another story.

be human at all. As human specimens the single-minded 'moral' fanatic, the wholly devoted pursuer of the 'main chance,' and the completely amoral 'aesthete' hardly seem admirable or emulable. Are they not all of them, their different ways, rather to be pitied, despised, or feared?[18]

V

We shall return to these questions in an epilogue to this whole inquiry, but for the moment we may turn to consider these same ambiguities and multiplicities as they emerge with respect to aesthetic impulsion, that is, in artistic activity and its products. For, of course, the same ambivalences and ambiguities of function and result that may make an apparent muddle of the world as a world of percipience are also discoverable in the world as a world of 'creative' agency, the world of artifacts and as artifact: the world as we find it shaped by human activity, the world in which our activity is given a distinctively human shape, and the world which our activity in its turn may in some measure shape anew. To put it directly, 'shaping the world' is not only *describable* or *analyzable* as cognitive, moral/ practical and aesthetic/artistic functioning; it *is,* in actual function, all of these. Nor is it the case that a given act or instance of activity is unambiguously identifiable as an instance of cognitive, practical, or aesthetic shaping; each is—partakes, admits of—all these iden-

18. It is an interesting exercise in the distinction between the two 'moral' or 'ethical' points of view we have developed to consider how the estimations of these different distortions might change were they to be evaluated simply in terms of their 'practical' tendency—that is, with respect to the consequences for the welfare of themselves and others which their habitual behavior might, in varying circumstances, usually produce. In these terms, for example, it might be argued that moral fanaticism and totally unscrupulous 'entrepreneurship' are in general both more dangerous to the public weal than amoral aestheticism. Nonetheless, somewhere short of extremes a moral/political single-mindedness in the pursuit of justice and liberation is sometimes thought to be a necessary, if not wholly admirable, human condition perhaps indispensable for human progress. So also, there are many versions of the notion of 'private vices, public virtues,' in which devotion to personal aggrandizement becomes a social benefit in productive energy and assiduous marketeering. Even so, I confess that I have often mourned over those whom fate has so visited with injustice that their lives have become almost wholly a working- out of outrage at manifest wrong. The distortions of intelligence and sensitivity in those that devote themselves to righting injury are not the smallest part of the price mankind continues to pay for oppression and systematic injustice.

tifications. And thus it is that to say that one is a shaper of the world, a maker, a point of origination of artifacts, of created objects more or less permanent and publicly available bearing the traces of their origin in human pursuit of human goods is not to identify oneself and one's activity as uniquely, specially, or even primarily aesthetic. The extent to which the objects which constitute our 'cultural'—what might be called our 'artifactual' environment—in fact can function satisfyingly as 'aesthetic' (that is, as resulting from artistic choices designed to satisfy the demands of taste and feeling) is limited indeed. Were this not the case we could expect that everything resulting from human agency would be beautiful or charged with the dignity (and depth) of feeling consequent upon the perception of the presence in it of human endeavor as such, so that there would be, in effect, a complete coincidence of our practical and aesthetic worlds. Short of that situation, we must recognize that 'artistic activity' serves many purposes other than the stabilization of opportunities for aesthetic satisfaction, that artists, artistic activity, and artistic objects ('art') necessarily and properly have functional places in many human pursuits and take their characteristic shape and value from those functional places. Thus there is no way in which artistic, 'creative' activity can be identified by its materials, devices, even 'forms' as unambiguously 'aesthetic' (or, for that matter, practical or cognitive) without specifying how these elements are being used, that is, in what functional context they are deployed. Constructing narratives, making pictures, forming images, patterning sounds, manipulating symbols, striking attitudes, and articulating gesture are functional elements of the primal stuff of human activity—of working, communicating, teaching, and learning, inquiring, entertaining each other, of loving, fighting, and playing, in short, of living as human beings live.

Such an account might seem to refer primarily to forms of human society and culture in which there is not the more explicit differentiation of art, the arts and what we may recognize as artistic traditions, communities and institutions which we might think characterizes our own situation.[19] In fact, however, we might argue

19. Had I said "there is not *yet* the more explicit differentiation" the reader would presumably have recognized a reference to some form of the common presumption that such differentiation or specialization constitutes a basic developmen-

that the ambiguities of 'artistic' function become more obvious as 'the arts' become occupationally specialized professions. For inevitably the continuity of practice required for such institutionalization (its 'traditionalizability') is to be found in transmittable techniques, standardizable materials and instrumentalities, and those generic traits of artistic products which make them recognizable and reproducible—'forms' in an appropriately vague sense. Thus there emerge 'novelists' and 'the novel,' 'dramatists' and 'the theater,' 'composers' and 'the musical world,' 'painters' of kinds and schools—each of these (and there are others) functioning in a complex institutional world with a variety of members performing diverse functions—including, of course, that of reader, connoisseur, audience, patron, consumer.

These are in themselves fascinatingly institutionalized communities, but what is relevant here about them is simply that the resources which each commands (including the trained capacities of artists) are deployable in a variety of different directions in the larger communities of which they are parts. What is most obvious about them, one might argue, is not that they are single-mindedly engaged in the autonomous pursuit of the aesthetic goals on which their integrity as communities might seem to depend, but rather that they are ancillary to processes and functions of 'society' at large. That is, is it not far easier to see novelists and the novel, dramatists and the stage, screen writers and the cinema, painters and painting as working elements in those complex networks of communication by which we inform and educate each other, formulate and discuss issues of social/political policy and moral attitude and choice, struggle to identify and respond with intelligence and clarified feeling to felt changes in the conditions of our living— in short, to articulate in communicable form the bases, the limits, the problematic shape of a communal life? The ways in which the arts so conceived perform these functions are, of course, articulated within the commonplaces of much—if not most—of critical discussion of them and the accounts we construct of their history.[20]

---

tal pattern from a more 'primitive' to a more 'advanced' or 'higher' cultural condition. However that may be, it is not essential to the point here.

20. It is perhaps worth noting that such 'classical' theoretical ('philosophical') accounts of art as expression as those of Croce, Dewey, or Collingwood (in which

And, if nothing else, they account for the recurrent controversies in which art and artists find it necessary to defend themselves against social control. When it is felt that art can and must be defended as indispensable social criticism and artists as messengers from the future pointing the way to new forms of human living, liberating from tradition, convention, exploitation, and domination one may reasonably infer that it and its devotees may experience some social pressure. But of course another side of such potential for influence is that the arts can be perceived as embodying (and thus inculcating and reinforcing) existing values and prevalent cultural 'myths,' and therefore as in effect instrumentalities of social control and of that oppression from which, in another guise, they may, by way of prophetic revelation, offer liberation.

Obviously it is not easy to determine with precision the actual influence of the arts in these communal processes. Clearly this will depend on a variety of circumstances, but certainly it is easy to overestimate the power of those forms of artistic endeavor which are thought to be technically and substantially most sophisticated, most serious, and most demanding of their audience and therefore in the nature of the case generally enjoying limited constituencies.[21] George Eliot's young Doctor Lydgate (*Middlemarch*) did not think "the complexities of love and marriage" required serious study, since these were "subjects on which he felt himself amply informed by literature, and that traditional wisdom which is handed down in the genial conversation of men."[22] Presumably he might have been better informed had he read the works of George Eliot,[23] something for which he was at least intellectually qualified. Over the years there have certainly been many appreciative readers of *Middlemarch* who may have learned much, but that 'many' re-

---

'aesthetics' is generally indistinguishable from 'the philosophy of art') carefully avoid identifying art—as expression—with communication. The reasons are complex; one might say in aphoristic nutshell that art is showing (not of course literally) and being, not telling. Yet, in such views art is preeminently communicative and a primary bond of communities.

21. Naturally, it can be argued that this relationship is suspiciously, if not viciously, circular: elite artistic institutions and circles constituting a closed circuit with economic and political elites.

22. George Eliot, *Middlemarch*, chap. 16.

23. Of course he could not have, since the date of the action of *Middlemarch* is in the (early?) 1830s, before they were written.

mains after all comparatively but a few. The rest of man and womankind may have dubiously profited from more 'popular' literary
sources, and probably in the end formed their ideas of love and
marriage as much from the "conversation of men" (and women) as
from any artistically shaped medium.

VI

However, if we are not specially concerned with the influence of
the arts in the formation of our ideas on such important matters as
love and marriage, the more 'popular' arts might interest us for
another reason. That they are one of the ways in which popular
values and views are formed, reinforced or influenced might for
our present purposes interest us less than that they are thought to
do so by way of *entertaining*. In the general economy of artistic
worlds, to be merely or primarily entertaining is not generally
thought to be much of a distinction. And one can see why. To entertain is, generically, to offer a stimulus which captures and holds
attention. Of course in the broadest sense everything which continues to engage our faculties is thus 'entertaining' and 'entertained,'
but the arts of entertainment presumably aim at and promise nothing more than to sustain an agreeable occupation of our faculties
of imaginative perception: to keep them, one might say, in play—
an appropriate word, distinguishing from work and pointing to
free, even frolicsome activity. What is entertaining in this sense is
immediately abandoned when the activity of entertaining it ceases
to be enjoyable in itself. When the exertion of our powers becomes
thus tiresome, or some finality other than mere continuing engagement in activity makes its demands felt, activity becomes laborious or empty. The object ceases to entertain; we seek other
occupation. To the indefatigably serious-minded, for whom every
exertion of ourselves is to be productively purposive, entertainment is likely to be always suspect and justified, if at all, as recu-
perative—a rearming, one might say, for the rigorous demands of
the battle of life. On the face of it, it seems unlikely that the unre-
mitting (and largely unpredictable) proliferation of forms of entertainment—among which we may number not only the popular arts
(the arts in their popular forms?) but 'spectator sports,' games (at
least those—such as "word games"—not built primarily on the en-

joyment of physical skills), and such curious entities as 'amusement parks'—actual 'lands' of fantasy and fiction.

Here, of course, the reader might well be reminded of Prince Pu-Ru's crab-apple orchard. With all due respect, surely one may ask what, after all, distinguishes 'Pu-Ru-land' from Disneyland? It is true that the effects of the one are provided in large part by machines (including mechanical animals) rather than by live bees, trees, and butterflies engaged in their own pursuits. This and other features of its design make it a 'year-round attraction' independent of the seasonal rhythms of blossom and pollen harvest, but were not both of them places crafted to "sustain an agreeable occupation of our faculties of imaginative perception"?

Again we may recognize this as a critical question which properly falls outside our present scope, but insofar as critical reflection would require consideration of 'fantasy,' it points to something relevant to our present purpose. In 'mere' entertainment, we have argued, it is sufficient that our imaginative faculties are kept 'in play.' In all aesthetic activity, as we have seen, there is a sense in which the mind, the psyche, enjoys its own activity—even in the sublime, where it can, so to speak, objectify its dominion over its objects. In entertainment, then, the mind is not only 'in play' but 'at play'—that is, it rejoices in that sort of engagement in which it is least constrained by the demands of objects and objectification, where, then, its objects are most clearly projections of its own 'undisciplined' powers. Almost at the beginning of this investigation we differentiated the imagination as, in the words of Bosanquet, "the mind at work, pursuing and exploring the possibilities suggested by the connections of its experience" from Bacon's emphasis on its independence of experience: "being not tied to the laws of matter, [the imagination] may at pleasure join that which nature hath severed and sever that which nature hath joined, and so make unlawful matches and divorces of things." As Bosanquet pointed out, emphasis on this feature of imaginative function has the effect of putting "a premium on the arbitrary and fantastic in beauty, rather than the logical and penetrative." [24]

---

24. For the quotations, cf. above, chap. 1, I (pp. 39, 40).

Here we need not quarrel about 'beauty,'[25] what is to our purpose is that one special privilege of the arts is to realize the possibilities of this feature of imaginative function. It may be most obvious in the fantasies and whimsicalities with which we amuse and entertain, but once we recognize the close kinship between that activity which enfranchises us to beauty and sublimity and the enjoyment and consequent interest the mind finds in the play of its own capacities, we may see a very wide range of what might be called 'quasi-aesthetic' satisfactions which profoundly enrich our lives. The possibilities realized in 'fantasy' hardly make a beginning of what we owe to the mind's capacity for 'arbitrary' arrangements and rearrangements of imagined materials. The manifold forms of wit, of verbal, visual, and aural play making "unlawful matches and divorces of things," the possibilities realized in farce, in satire, in the construction of systematically 'artificial' worlds—not only the alternative 'natures' of science fiction but the 'surreal,' the monstrous, the idyllic, the 'romantic'—all these in large measure celebrate the freedom of the imagination in that sense in which freedom is the absence of external constraint. No doubt there is bound to be much potential for triviality and moral (and aesthetic) corruption in such play. But it is also evident that it has its contribution to make to 'high art,' or, as we would prefer to say, to meeting the conditions of beauty and sublimity. How that comes about only experience (and genius) can reveal, though after the fact criticism may undertake to anatomize the result. But even short of such achievements the contribution of these 'quasi-aesthetic' activities and forms to the joy of living, to the enrichment of our perception of ourselves and others, to human intercourse and social coherence is, of course, incalculable.

VII

If in entertainment and 'fancy' our imaginative powers seem to aim at shaking off the trammels of the 'real world'—the world, that is,

25. Nevertheless, it may be significant that one might be tempted to use the word in connection with Prince Pu-Ru's trees and their attendant insects while refusing it to the creations of Disney. But this deprived observer, having experienced neither, withholds judgment.

as we conceive, perceive and imagine it in the orderings imposed
by the demands of knowing and doing—it is also obvious that aesthetic satisfactions and interests enter profoundly into our dealings
with it. We have already noted, in the most general terms, the possibilities of coincidences, coherences, and reinforcements inherent
in the common root of all these activities in the psyche. As it is,
however, it may be more often than not the case that the possibility
of such coincidence is confusing and misleading rather than properly reinforcing—as when what is found to be imaginatively coherent is taken *ipso facto* to be true and what is morally, practically, and
movingly right to be, without qualification, sublime.

But however this may be in general, art and the arts—and with
them some aesthetic impulsion—enter directly into the constitution of our concrete, artifactual worlds. And that world thus 'normally' shows the pervasive, though hardly predominant, influence
of aesthetic considerations. The instrumentalities of living so far as
they are not given but made, the forms of social life—political, religious, economic—as ordered in habitual expression, in ritual and
the shaping of places and buildings, all these—to say nothing of
the shaping, adornment, and regulated movement of human bod-
ies or the deployment of speech, of gesture, of voice—are, in fact,
generally taken to be the original home of the arts from which they
have gradually emerged and achieved an independent status, as we
just noted. It is frequently argued that much has been lost in this
process—the arts have become the special possession of the few
and been not only socially and economically but even physically
segregated in 'cultural' institutions. Of course it is bound to be the
case that insofar as there comes to be a more explicit differentiation
of art, the arts and of artistic traditions, communities and institutions the relation of the arts to other human shapings of our world
will change, but surely the change is more complex than such an
account might suggest. In contemporary Western democratic societies the arts seem almost to aspire to the condition of a "Fifth
Estate" in which the strands of aristocratic (plutocratic?) aestheticism, of social and political 'activism,' of art and the artist as
"prophet, seer and revelator"[26] promising the transformation of

26. This phrase ("prophet, seer and revelator") I borrow—with appropriate
apologies—from the Mormon tradition, in which, if I am not mistaken, it is applied

humankind and its world, mingle with the immemorial traditions in which the aesthetic impulsion functions unreflectively in all the forms of social and individual living.

To chart the resulting complexities is certainly not our task—they are the constant concern of critics as well as of the more sociologically, anthropologically, and 'philosophically' minded—but we should not forget that there is a sense in which they are the subject of this whole inquiry. For surely the idea of a reflectively mediated self-disciplining of taste and feeling as individual enterprise is itself part of that more explicit differentiation of cultural life in which the more or less institutionalized worlds of art and artists emerge. And that world provides in large part the milieu in which the individual enterprise with which we are concerned must be carried on. A moment's reflection on what we have discussed in the preceding chapters will confirm that the problems of developing an autonomous 'taste' largely, though not solely, take their present form in the terms of a cultural world in which there is assumed to be an approximation (if not identification) of aesthetic and artistic activity—an assumption emerging not only in sociological, political and critical discussion but concretely realized in the institutionalized professionalization we have noted, with all its ambiguities and tensions. And therefore inevitably aesthetic sensibility will, insofar as it must make use of the forms in which aesthetic activity is (if only broadly and confusingly) organized and identified, largely define itself in relation to the arts and their attendant functions and functionaries.

Of this fact this inquiry itself, as we have said, bears witness. Indeed, one way of reading it would be as a contribution to the growing literature devoted to patronage, connoisseurship, and perhaps even 'collectorship.'[27] Were we to think of it simply as a role in the social, the institutionalized system of art and the arts it might seem to be simply a plea for and assertion of the importance, the power and the rights of those who constitute the discriminating

---

to the president of the church. He is a claimant, in these terms, to powers never aspired to by any pope.

27. The literature is vast. Any selection would be arbitrary and misleading. Nevertheless, arbitrarily, I mention one curiously interesting work: Joseph Alsop, *The Rare Art Traditions: The History of Art Collecting and Its Linked Phenomena Wherever These Have Appeared* (New York, 1982).

constituency (the 'audience') of the arts as over against other claimants to authority in the making of taste. However, it seems unlikely
that even the most casual reader would conclude that the ultimate
moral of our tale is that 'in the long run' the art and music lovers
and the common readers not only will but ought 'to bury' composers, poets, novelists, critics and all other arbiters of taste. Nevertheless, it may well be that the "representative anecdote" which comes
to mind as encapsulating the stance we have taken does not come
from Pu-Ru's Peking, Coleridge's London or Hardscrabble Farm,
but from Florence where we began: from the Tribune of the Uffizi
where Emerson walked "coolly round and round the marble lady"
in his "continual effort not to be pleased except by that which
ought to please *me*," and ultimately found himself willing to ratify
the preference of "mankind," by his personal judgment: "gladly
[giving] one testimony more to the surpassing genius of the artist."

VIII

However, lest this anecdote *mis*represent what we have been doing,
we should remind ourselves that the autonomy of individual taste
is grounded in what is shared. As we said from the first, "the world
of art and artists, of scholarship, criticism and connoisseurship is
part of an organic aesthetic system through which the life-blood of
aesthetic capability circulates, flowing from deeper sources in the
human psyche."[28] We have treated the system as a pervasive human
enterprise, taking as our focus—and in that sense 'center'—the individual enterprise of the reflectively self-disciplining psyche, but
at every point we have found that norms of this individual development and the problems they generate implicate the systematic
enterprise as a whole. Nowhere should this relationship have been
clearer than in that very discussion of authority in which Emerson's
stubborn self-reliance[29] was useful to us. There we argued that the
"serious problems about 'authority' are questions about when I
have good ground for *docility* . . . what claimants to teach me must
I recognize and accept as legitimate?"[30] Those claimants we found

28. See above, Prologue, Part Two, IX (p. 33).
29. In Emerson's words, "But at the same time how useful, how indispensable
has been the ministry of our friends to us, our teachers,—the living and the dead."
30. Cf. above, chap. 4, I (p. 125).

in aesthetic objects, in discerning critics, in "the preference of mankind" and, perhaps most powerfully, in what we called 'absolute' artistic mastery, a mastery in and of the aesthetic enterprise so profound as to seem almost to constitute it, a direct manifestation of those vital impulses which are the "life-blood of aesthetic capability." In the felt cogency of manifest mastery, autonomously disciplined imaginative perception and autonomously ordered imaginative creativity meet in a shared activity of objectification—in the constitution of an aesthetic object.

Mastery of this absolute kind we may call 'genius,' not in that sense in which it is merely a hyperbolic attribution of skill (a 'genius' for or at this or that) but as the capacity to realize in the materials of experience objects radically artificial ('artifactual') yet having the organic formal coherence of 'natural' growths. This capacity—the most remarkable privilege of art—has grounds in common with the play of the mind manifested in the arbitrary and fantastic creations of we earlier called quasi-aesthetic, for both rest upon the recognition and use of potentialities inherent in empirical materials as such—that is, as materials for imaginative exploitation. But the difference between them is the difference between manipulation of what is given in the creation of a novel, an unexpected arrangement and the transformation of materials into formal elements of a unity realized in reciprocity of function, so that every part is both means and end, and the whole is a systematic unity of diverse functions. Such creations approximate to the conditions of a living organism in which 'structure' and 'function,' part and whole fully determine each other with a cogency to which Bosanquet was no doubt referring in contrasting the "arbitrary and fantastic in beauty" with "the logical and penetrative." But the 'logic' and the 'penetration' here are not those of formula or of form in isolation from material embodiment but rather, as in the creations of nature, of actual powers ordered to each other so as to constitute a self-contained, self-sustaining object. Whatever may have been meant by the 'Aristotelian' formula that 'art imitates nature,' it is in this sense profoundly true: not that art reproduces natural objects but that it emulates, in its own terms and under its own conditions, the objectivity of nature.

Those terms and conditions are those of imaginative perception with all the 'materiality' they entail. And thus it is that what

seems—at least initially—remarkable about art in its exemplary
works is that they seem to have realized radically novel potentialities of 'materials.' But putting the matter that way is misleading: it
is easy to say that music realizes the powers of sound and its concomitant attributes or literature those of words or language, but it
would be more accurate to say that only in the arts do we discover
what those powers may be. The matter is complex because 'materials' is a difficult notion: analysis of what actually is functional for
perception in the physical/sensuous 'materials' deployed in the arts
is one of the most worthy tasks of criticism, if the basic task of criticism is the (re)education of perception.[31] Yet if anything is revealed
by such analysis, it is the extent to which the materials of our experience are shaped for the purposes of art. In the case of music,
the transformation of 'sound' into the complex systems of 'tones'
and other regularities which begin to constitute a musical substrate
is often noted, but reflection will reveal that every art so orders its
material base. But again "so orders" is feebly after the fact: only
the achievements of art can show us what this ordering and shaping may be and how it is functional—that is, how it has dis-covered
aesthetic possibilities in empirical materials. Of course we tend to
take these complex achievements as given—as, indeed, relative to
us as cultural heirs they are. Yet in their way they constitute a set
of miracles—if not violations of natural law, certainly possibilities
naturally uncontemplated and unrealized.

IX

But such an emphasis runs the risk of suggesting that the miracle
is primarily 'technical'—that is, that it consists not in what is done
but in that it can be done, not in the quality of the created object
but in the virtuosity—the command of means—displayed in its creation. What is then remarkable in Beethoven or Michelangelo
would not be the sublimity of their work but that sublimity is there
realized musically or sculpturally. Of course such a distinction ignores the reciprocity of means and ends in organic aesthetic objects—what might be described as the thoroughgoing formality of
their materiality. Impressed by the individualization resulting from

31. Cf. above, Prologue, Part Two, I (p. 16) and chap. 3, IV ff.

this relationship critics have sometimes urged that there is a sense in which each work has its own 'language,' its unique vocabulary and syntax—whether that 'language' be literary, aural or visual—and with appropriate adjustments it may similarly be argued that each writer, each composer, each painter has a unique congeries of resources. (As Schumann is supposed to have said, "Beethoven's chromatic scales are not like other people's," a remark which seems to fly in the face of the commonest sense while at the same time merely stating the obvious.[32]) But individuality of resources entails an individuality of realized object: each work and the work of each artist has individual quality.

However, strictly it is only means identified as such that become re-sources—materials and devices repeatably deployable in shifting circumstances. The exemplary function of works of art depends upon the extent to which their materials and devices can be identified in the interest, not of mere repetition, but of comparable creation. The continuity (and discontinuity) of the arts—the existence of schools, traditions, influences and even of the possibility of revolutionary transformation—depends not only on the discovery of novel possibilities but on their artistic transmittability, that is, the discovery of possibilities not only as unique events but as controllable deployments of material and technique. In the broadest sense, this is a mere rehearsal of a generic, even a defining attribute of 'art': it is relevant here only insofar as it bears upon our present concern—the radical originality inherent in art, the arts, and artists.

It might seem that the existence of art as a learnable repertory of techniques, materials, conventions, forms and styles, each with its models and its inherent standards—in short the existence of art as formulable, as rule and canon—might seem the very antithesis of originality, and to the extent that any set of rules and canons is taken to exhaust the possibilities and is effectively frozen in place ('enforced'), that is, of course, true. The sources of such codifications and the motivations which transform them into instrumentalities for the control of art and artists are complex, but in con-

32. Donald Tovey, discussing Beethoven's *Emperor* concerto, attributes this remark to Schumann *a propos* a passage in the coda of the first movement. But he gives no source and I have not been able to find it elsewhere. (*Essays in Musical Analysis* [Oxford, 1936], vol. 3, p. 86—much reprinted in varying formats.)

frontation with a stifling orthodoxy it is easy to forget that in part, at least, the 'rules of art' at any time and place are themselves artistic inventions. Artists as such do not, of course, create rules and canons; they create the works which are taken to be exemplary of the practices which rules and canons attempt to capture in formula. Thus every artistic form or kind has, one might say, a double authorship and a double birth: in one sense 'the sonata' as we know it was invented by a series of composers; in another sense it was invented by analytically minded musicians and critics attempting to understand and formulate their compositional practice. It is only after the fact that inventors in the first sense are found to have exemplified a practice and observed its rules. It is almost inevitable that not infrequently it is found that they did not understand the practice and violated the rules.

Clearly this process, though essential to the cultivation, the 'traditionalizability' of the arts, is no simple process in which genius brings works into the world ultimately recognized as canonically influential—that is, as having a cogency requiring to be explored critically and artistically by artistic communities. But it is too easy to dismiss 'genius' because this version of the process is 'romanticized.' 'Genius' need not be a lonely figure in a garret facing a hostile world of orthodoxy while creating works destined to enjoy the "preference of mankind" and to be artistically and critically archetypal. In the broadest functional terms, 'genius' is that capacity for radical and shareable originality—however embodied and wherever manifested in the world of human culture—*constitutive* of *artificiality*, that is, of the world as anthropomorph, of what there is in the world uniquely attributable to human activity. This originality (origination) is thus constitutive of both the reigning orthodoxies in cultural traditions and the 'local' originalities which contend with them. 'Genius' as architect of the cultural *Lebenswelt* within which such conflicts occur is an attribute of humanity. Nevertheless, where we find this capacity specially manifested, giving new shape to the human world, where, so to speak, there occurs something like a mutation manifestly altering the cultural gene pool— the human heritage—there we give to human genius a local habitation and perhaps a name.

In aesthetic activity as manifested in the arts this architectonic capacity—what we earlier called 'absolute mastery'—is manifest, as we have argued, in the transforming revelation of possibilities inherent in materials and techniques, in the impact of works which seem to open up new realms of artistic endeavor and in the perceived individuality of works and, by extension, of artists. As distinguishable qualities, each of these enters into our appreciative enjoyment of art, for each is a different aspect of mastery. Where is mastery to be manifest if not in the complete command of material and device, in that cogency which sets standards for emulation and in the manifested capacity for self-controlled integrity? Yet as distinguishable, separable, and generally admirable qualities they are nonetheless slightly suspect, or perhaps it would be better to say that they easily become debased. Virtuosity and versatility are no doubt noble qualities, but 'mere' virtuosity and 'facility' are at best enjoyably insubstantial. Respect and admiration for what is classical, monumental, and epoch-making is uncomfortably akin to the worship of power; the sense of being in touch with a powerful artistic individuality is easily confused with more obvious manifestations of 'personality' or cultivated idiosyncrasy. The root of these perversities is found, of course, in a displacement which confuses admiration for and enjoyment of mastery with aesthetic satisfaction in the work(s) in which it is manifest, shifting the object of interest and satisfaction to master and mastery from masterpiece.

More subtly, however, emphasis on genius and mastery may have the effect of shifting attention not only to artists but to artists and artistry as shaping and directing functions in the arts as ongoing human enterprises. Inevitably this entails the risk of focusing discussion, as the preceding paragraphs witness, on what is transmittable, learnable, conceptualizable, and thus in some measure *reproducible* in the practice of art and its masters. But of course what is aesthetically valued in art—what constitutes the aesthetic value of art—is what is in its nature not thus universalizable: what is beautiful, what is sublimely moving is always *this* imaginatively perceived object, indeed the being of such an object is, as we said earlier, fulfillment of function in imaginative perception, the value inherent in the imaginative grasp, the perceiving activity of which the object is, so to speak, the shape. 'Art' as *aesthetic* impulsion has meant for us, throughout this discussion, "the attempt to secure some stability for satisfactions of imaginative perception by the control of their occasions," but control from the side of the occasion (the side of art) is limited to such disposition of the world within our power as seems to provide the materials of imaginative function and invite its engagement in a given way. But the actual constitution of the aesthetic object in an activity of imaginative perception is necessarily as much a matter of a disciplined and purposive engagement of a percipient imagination as of the disciplined provision of its empirical conditions. Ultimately, then, what art offers and what artistic genius may reveal are possibilities not of materials and devices, of forms and styles, of conventions, traditions, and associations but of imaginative functioning. Respect for creative genius is grounded in the beauty and sublimity actual in that activity of imaginative objectification; its power is the cogency of those fruits of beauty and sublimity in the orientation, the disciplining of our imaginative powers.

Above we said that "autonomously disciplined imaginative perception and autonomously ordered imaginative creativity meet in a shared activity of objectification." But these two 'autonomies' are of course the same—the autonomy of those human powers in that activity the normalities of which we have tried to articulate in this inquiry. In that sense what the arts and artistic genius reveal to us is ourselves and our powers—our independence of the empirical world as it is manifested in the very conditions of perceiving it, of constituting it in perception. The power of art is the capacity to produce objects adapted to such an exercise of our powers, but its end is not to show us how that may be accomplished but in the accomplishment itself, not, thus, in the adapting but in what is so adapted. Nature, in its 'artlessness,' its 'purposiveness without purpose,' admits of the same adaptation; art does not invent or discover beauty and sublimity. The radical originality of art lies rather in the unique actualities of beauty and sublimity it creates as an originating function in the enterprise in which the human imagination exercises its autonomy, the discipline of taste and feeling.

EPILOGUE

W hat, then, is finally to be said with respect to the second of the two tasks we set ourselves at the beginning of this inquiry? That is,

to determine, so far as is possible within the limits of this inquiry, what claim this kind of activity, with its internal claims, has upon us as human beings: why, in other words, we demand of everyone—and more especially of ourselves—a discipline of taste and feeling.[1]

We have discussed its "internal claims"—its norms—and in the process of that argument have emphasized again and again that they are the normalities of an autonomous activity and that this activity is a complex realization of human capabilities. In fact we might think we have made a good case for claiming that the discipline of our powers, which is the condition of that realization, is a human perfection, meaning by that no more (and no less) than that it is a deployment of capabilities which realizes a good available to us in the terms of and in virtue of our *human* capabilities. There are here, in effect, two claims: first, that the goods involved are realized only in this activity—that is, that they are not reducible to other goods—and second, that they *can* be demanded of everyone—namely, of all *human* beings in virtue of their humanity. But neither of these claims would amount to demanding them of everyone, unless we are to assume that all possible human perfections are demanded of all human beings. (It might be said that we came close to taking that position by adducing the 'distortion' of human

1. Above, Prologue, Part Two, IX (p. 35).

213

personality which would be constituted by exclusively aesthetic or even practical/moral orientations.)

We should note that we have imposed rather stringent requirements upon grounds to be offered: we are asking not for grounds of recommendation or persuasion but of obligation, of (to stay with the language we have been employing) not hypothetical but categorical demands. Were we to think in terms of recommending or persuading, we could hardly do better than to begin with Hume's formula: "a delicate taste of wit or beauty must always be a desirable quality; because it is the source of all the finest and most innocent enjoyments, of which human nature is susceptible,"[2] for, indeed, our whole analysis could be construed as giving meaning to what is meant by 'finest' (that is, most 'subtle,' or 'refined') and 'innocent.' Have we not argued that ultimately aesthetic satisfactions, even those in profound moral and emotional engagement are 'contemplative' and thus presumably *in themselves* incapable of harmful or injurious consequence? Of course, there would be much more to say about the quality of these "enjoyments," but have we not said it? Inevitably problems would arise were what is recommended to be a life *wholly, totally* dedicated to such satisfactions, but we need make no such recommendation, noting how modest or cautious Hume's claims in fact are. The 'finest and most innocent' (not the best or the only) enjoyments *among* others—such a status would support a recommendation for inclusion and some priority in one's world of satisfactions. Thus, as a human attribute, taste is "always a desirable quality. . . . In this decision the sentiments of all mankind are agreed." In this conclusion we might, emulating Emerson, be willing to concur, feeling that "mankind have had good reason for their preference." But, then, perhaps *we* hardly needed to be persuaded.[3]

---

2. See above, chap. 2, note 12.

3. So far as such claims offer support for priorities among satisfactions for 'aesthetic' pleasures, it could be said to rest upon their quality, their attributes as pleasures among pleasures. We may thus find ourselves—quite properly—where we began, with immediate satisfactions and their qualities and conditions. There we distinguished between "discriminations of ends or grounds of choice" based upon 'Benthamite' measurements ("*Intense, long, certain, speedy, pure*") and those grounded "upon discriminations of the activities of which pleasures and pains are at once the

But are we in a position to discuss, "within the limits of this inquiry," any 'claims' or 'demands' of a 'moral' or 'categorical' kind? Exploring the relation of 'art' to moral and aesthetic concerns, we argued that aesthetic discipline is an object of choice in two senses, choice either to deploy or to develop our powers aesthetically. (The distinction may of course be merely analytical—any given deployment probably serves both purposes and either or both may be in focus, so to speak.) But we also argued that aesthetic considerations in themselves offer no ground for either choice. 'Taste' as aesthetic discipline is not the function of making choices as determinations of priorities among ends and goods which invoke some systematic plurality of possible directions of our activity and agency. Such choices and their grounds are, we argued, inherently practical/moral and with respect to them the normalities of 'taste' as 'the discipline of taste and feeling' offer no guidance. Thus, short of embarking upon a full-dress inquiry into the normalities of 'choice' in the practical/moral sense, it would seem that we can have nothing to offer in the way of grounds for demanding of ourselves and everyone such a discipline as an obligation inherent in our humanity.

But as clear and cogent as these formal inhibitions may be, it is also clear that our inquiry into the normalities of aesthetic functioning has involved us again and again in discussions of cognitive and moral/practical matters, if only by way of differentiating these forms of human activity from aesthetic activity. In fact, that 'differentiation' has found us insisting as much upon the interrelation of cognitive, practical and aesthetic concerns, connections resting upon their common ground as deployments of the same human powers in diverse functional arrangement. If nothing else, this would suggest an intimate connection with our humanity—that is, aesthetic sensibility is as much a characteristically human kind of functioning as are knowing and doing.

Consideration of these interrelations led us so far as to argue

---

marks and the fruition" (chap. 1, I). In Hume's argument we may see something of the subtlety of these distinctions, for while 'innocence' might be thought almost equivalent to Benthamite 'purity' (that is, immediately unmixed with and not entailing pain by consequence), 'finest' in the sense of 'refined' and 'subtle' suggests a reference to sources and conditions not adapted to measurement.

that our whole inquiry is, in an important sense, an ethical one: "as being concerned with human perfection and human good in their reciprocity." But in that context that reciprocity was taken to be a *generic* feature of human activity, whether effectively oriented to 'the true, the good or the beautiful,' on the ground that the ability to carry on all human activities is acquired and stabilized in practice and mediated by reflection, so that, human goods are dependent upon the perfecting of human beings. Here we can only consider these assertions as presumptions to which our inquiry points and on which it might be said in part to rest as well as to confirm and exemplify, but under that caveat let us explore, in summary fashion, some implications for our present problem.

To say that human goods—not, of course, all the goods that accrue to human beings—are realized in activities consequent upon acquired and stabilized orderings of human powers in processes mediable by reflective intelligence is to say that humanity is a creation of human beings, that a concern with our humanity is a reflexive concern with what we have and can make of ourselves, with (to use an old-fashioned phrase) 'what man has made of man.'[4] We need hardly reiterate that while humanity is thus its own creator it creates neither *ex nihilo* nor *in vacuo*, that is, nature and circumstance are part and parcel of the conditions in which humanity shapes itself. But surely we have seen the sense in which an inquiry into the discipline of taste and feeling, 'the art of thinking beautifully,' is an exploration of human autonomy, as would be—no less and no more—inquiries into the arts of thinking truly and acting rightly.

In other words, here and in similar inquiries we are concerned with human freedom and its realization. But we must take note that we are not here concerned, save indirectly, with freedom as the ability to realize purposes, ends, goods. Freedom in that sense presumes that we have purposes we may or may not be able to pursue effectively, usually because of impediment to our activity. But the prior sense of freedom is the ability to prescribe purposes to our-

---

4. Current rhetorical fashion will no doubt find this phrase objectionable. I suppose that it might mean 'what male human organisms have made of male human organisms,' but in this context?

selves, to make our own functional orientation, to construct for ourselves a world of goods which then may or may not be actualizable. In this inquiry we have examined the conditions of engaging in one form of that kind of activity, always with the recognition not only that it is a form among others but also that our individual activity is mediated and sustained by the continuities of shared traditions which reciprocally it sustains, mediates, and (re)constructs.

In this sense freedom is constitutive of the human enterprise itself. It is appropriate to call it an enterprise since it is an endeavor toward an end—the realization of freedom. Freedom as an end is not an end among others or the realization of any end or ends but the constitution and pursuit of human good. It is, one might say, the architectonic end, the purpose of posing, realizing, and systematizing purposes, a finality of purposes and thus a purposiveness always present and never fully realized. Hence there is no choice and no obligation with respect to engagement in the enterprise itself. Choice and obligation accrue within it; they are not consequent upon freedom but freedom itself, as are the necessities and constraints to which choice is subject, not least in obligation. In the mythical language of Plato, it is the fate of human beings to find themselves thrust by cosmic events into the age of Zeus, wherein they must "undertake their own direction and provide for themselves," but within that cosmic fatality humanity works out its own destiny—until such time as divinity reassumes the guidance of the universe.[5]

If, then, there is obligation to engage in any form of human activity, it is because that form of activity is essential to or substantially inseparable from participation in humanity itself, because it peculiarly manifests the conditions of effective participation in the continuing human enterprise, in, that is, the creation, development, and realization of a systematic purposive order in the world. Preeminently, of course, we think 'morality' to manifest those conditions, but what *is* morality but the satisfaction of those conditions? If we can rightly demand taste and a feeling for sublimity from everyone and "presuppose them in anyone who has any culture at all," it must be because these are indices of individual ca-

5. Plato, *Statesman*, 259 ff.

pacity for and engagement in the effective realization of the enterprise which is freedom, and that is to say, in the terms at which we have arrived, that they are indicative of 'moral' capacity, that they signal a disposition for and an engagement with the human endeavor as such.

Our inquiry into the normalities of aesthetic activity has amply shown the powerful analogies between aesthetic and moral activity which led Kant to hold that "beauty is the symbol of morality."[6] Disinterested, objective, communicable, autonomous, authoritative, and yet affirmative or negative, accepting or rejecting, approving or blaming in the determination of individual occasions of experience, of actual situations in the world—aesthetic judgment is in these respects structurally similar to the requirements we impose, with different effect, upon practical determinations insofar as they meet the conditions of autonomous behavior. So much is true of the determining activity which issues in the apprehension of the beautiful. While, *mutatis mutandis,* much the same could be said of our experience of the sublime, it is in that activity that the ground of these proportionate similarities may emerge more clearly, for the sublime rests upon and indeed is the realization in imaginative activity of the proportion between the mind and the world, between the spontaneity of intelligently reflective activity and the experienced world. In the apprehension of beauty there is, as Santayana says, a "harmony between our nature and our experience," though that 'purposiveness without purpose' is entirely, so to speak, on our terms: "our senses and our imagination find what they crave . . . [and] the world so shapes itself or so moulds itself that the correspondence between them is perfect."[7] But in sublimity experience is found inadequate to the demands of the mind, so that our independence emerges not just as a bestowal of favor but as a rejection of empirical conditions.

We may thus see that aesthetic activity requires us to take up with respect to the experienced world what we may call the stance of freedom—an assertion of our autonomous independence on it. Such an assertion lies at the base of all our activity insofar as it is human; in aesthetic activity it has the quality of an assertion di-

6. *Critique of Judgment,* "Dialectic of Aesthetic Judgment" (sec. 59).
7. See above, chap. 1, IV (p. 50).

rectly in and with respect to experience, functionally actual here and now in the immediate perceptual grasp of things of this world. The capacity to take up such a functional attitude or stance toward the world is at once the condition and the fruit of human 'culture,' and therefore we may rightfully demand it of everyone and "presuppose [it] in anyone who has any culture at all."

INDEX

AUTHOR'S NOTE. This index does not attempt to construct an intellectual inventory or outline of the argument. A few terms crucial to the argument have been (unsystematically) included because I think they may be useful to a reader returning to the book and searching for remembered contexts. But the basic tool for that purpose is a reasonably complete listing of sources and references—authors, texts, persons, places, and things. Page numbers of direct quotations are set in boldface type.